# How We Became The American Zombies

## The Red Pill
by
Max Meeks

ISBN -**13:978-1502522214**

ISBN -**10:1502522217**

# Contents

# Introduction

If your life has become a mess that you're simply putting up with every day, then you've opened up this book for the right reason. Something has gone horribly wrong in our country. There are defeated and hopeless people all over the place. What you may not be aware of is that the same virus that made them the way that they are is likely the cause of your own bad set of circumstances.

You don't run an anti-virus program on your computer for ten seconds each day and then turn it off before it's finished doing its' job. Nor should anyone attempt to read a book like this for a few pages at a time if you actually want a life changing impact. Read this book from start to finish in a short period of time, and the results will be amazing.

In the 1940's, well known behavioral scientist B. F. Skinner was studying how to train animals. He found that through the process of conditioning that the behavior of animals was very easy to control. He quickly realized that the behaviors of human beings could easily be modified. The idea of training your dog to behave in a certain way isn't scary at all, but training human beings without their awareness is the direction that America has been taken.

What is the one creature that will hands down take the most abuse possible and continue giving out unconditional love? How many times have you come across situations in your own lifetime where you saw dogs being confined to a pen or even a small cage that they're locked in all day? These dogs only get to experience a few rare moments of real freedom. The owners of these neglected creatures don't think twice about how much time their own dogs are actually suffering. Even worse, the owners will often keep these same loving dogs locked away from the rest of the world from infancy until death. That is, unless the dog escapes.

The escaped dog must run far enough away so that the piece of shit owner can't reclaim their right to keep a loving dog locked down in oppressive circumstances for the rest of its life. We all know that some dogs have a much worse existence than dogs that have the run of the whole house, get a backyard to run in, and get walked daily by a loving owner. Caged and neglected dogs will still greet their owners with wagging tails.

At the very least, abused dogs cower in fear when an abusive owner shows up, instead of charging the owner in an effort to escape to a better home. The relationship is not between equals; there is clearly a master that dominates a subservient dog. All that a dog owner must provide in order to get loyalty is food, water, and shelter.

The reason why people love dogs so much is because dogs will accept almost any treatment that we give them, and reward us with loyalty and affection (even if, we treat them like crap). Dogs are by far the easiest living creatures on earth to keep in our daily lives to feel like we are receiving love and affection from. We may hate who we've become but our dogs help us to avoid this truth.

Abusive and dominating people are always looking for others that they can also treat like dogs. How many people do you know that are in bad relationships right now that are there due to quality food and shelter? Of these people that do put up with tons of unfair treatment for financial security, do you respect them more or less for staying in their relationships?

When it's somebody else (other than us) we seem to have no problem at all looking at their situation from an outside and logical perspective. We are able to see that the relationship that they are in is clearly degrading. However, when we attempt to view our own relationships, our brains contain an extremely distorting and deceptive lens.

We all have an ego and it is part of our primary operating system. However, most of us are completely unaware of just how badly our own ego has distorted the truth about our own doggish existence. Most people will justify their actions, no matter how abusive their own living situations have become. The human ego will automatically lie to an abused person and tell them that their life is going just fine (when it's not). The ego of an abuser will also deceive them and justify that they are treating the other person as deserved. Not all relationships are abusive. The intent of this book is to help adults form healthy relationships, and also help you to break out of bad ones.

It will become easier for you to be honest with yourself, so you'll be less likely to continue hurting others that your own ego has kept you unaware of. By taking actions to bring about positive changes in your own life you will begin making this world a better place to live in (starting with you).

Our country has become filled with disasters. Most of them have two arms two legs and a brain that's barely functioning. Our consciences as an entire country have been silenced. We stand together facing this opportunity to dive into the mother of all projects; to transform a country full of walking disasters into a country of loving, caring, and self-respecting people again. Only when we regain the ability to truly respect ourselves can we begin to stop taking abuse from others. Think of this book as a ballsiness installation kit.

Billionaires, politicians, and the very doctors that we have been trained to trust since birth have created an orange pill-bottle army of the walking dead. Just go out to any grocery store and you'll quickly see half-living people riddled with health problems all around you. These defeated people won't hesitate to attack anyone with working brains that actually challenges their TV trained belief systems. If politicians and billionaires could get the general population addicted to daily activities that produced a more dimwitted public, would they?

Picture a large brick wall that has been built around your heart. This wall is preventing you from seeing the world the way that you once used to as a young child. This wall has been intentionally constructed by billionaires to keep you trapped and feeling hopeless. Punching the wall 500 times appears to do nothing. Most of us have long ago given up. I assure you, the wall can be brought down.

Your cage can be unlocked and the restrictive collars around the necks of good men and woman can be taken off. The best people at keeping defeated people trapped in oppressed places are other defeated people. Consider this book a dog collar removal kit. When finished, there will be a key to unlock your own personal collar. There will be no way for your ex owner to return you to your old crappy existence. Once free, please share this key with other oppressed people. I dare oppressive and controlling people to try reading this book. Good people will gain freedom, and assholes will lose power.

# Chapter 1 – Getting honest with ourselves

People with high self-esteems and a healthy amount of self-respect don't stay in abusive relationships. People that like themselves tend to treat others with respect and dignity. It's always those whom hate themselves and suffer from low self-esteems that are the most abusive towards others. In many cases the bully has been abused by his or her own parents or family members, and is totally unaware of why they behave the way that they do. It's sad that most bullies don't even know why they bully. In fact, most bullies don't even perceive the fact that they are abusing others every day.

Individuals with low levels of self-control tend to be the worst offenders in their attempts to abuse and control others. Do you happen to know any people (other than yourself of course) that happen to have very little self-control left? I've met a few and I can admit that I'm a person that once had very low levels of self-control in my not-so-distant past.

Until my life became so unhappy that I had lost the people that I loved the most; I had been unwilling to admit that I had lost self-control with alcohol. Only at the admission of total defeat was I willing to drastically change my behaviors and rebuild my own self-esteem. Admitting that we have lost control in our lives is perhaps the hardest thing for an adult to do for one very simple reason, our ego.

Our egos lie to us at all costs as we slide down the scale of self-control. The more our addictions take over, the more our very own egos lie to us about everything. Reality becomes distorted, and lies become truth. There is a Grand Canyon sized gap between most addicts' perception of their daily treatment of others, and the truth.

Most of us cringe when we are faced with admitting that we have abused and controlled others for our own selfish gains. Yet, as a former alcoholic that has thoroughly worked a program of recovery, it's not so hard to believe. Once I got honest with myself, it became much easier to make the necessary changes to improve my life. More importantly, negative thoughts get replaced with positive thinking. Positive changes create a positive reality.

Once our ego finally allows us to admit that we had frequently harmed others; we then gain the ability to start making positive changes in our own daily behaviors. What human being has gone through life and has never hurt another person for selfish personal gain? This is where our minds play tricks on most of us. We all make lots of mistakes and that's ok, because it's part of being human.

Our egos lie proportionately to our remaining level of self-control. Over the course of years as a person gradually becomes more and more of an addict, (be it food, drugs, alcohol, or you name it) the lies that their ego tells them about their own actions become bigger and more frequent. The obvious addict (to the outside world) that often has a weight problem, drinking problem, and uses their addictions to drown out their pain, is completely blind to just how badly they have lost control. Popping 6 mind-numbing pills or beers a day is not the solution to our problems. The laws of cause and effect still apply to all of us. Quick easy fixes nearly always deliver long-term impairments. There are impaired Americans all over the place.

Most addicts are the last people in the room to discover and admit that they are addicted to anything. Somehow, the process of addiction truly blinds us no matter how terrible our personal health and quality of living has become. This is only made possible by the function of our ego. Corrupted or uncorrupted, we all have egos. A corrupted ego will wreck your body and prevent you from having good relationships with the people that you're most attracted to. This book is deleting those corrupted files so that you can live out your dreams and be happier more often. There will still be ups and downs, but you'll spend a lot less time feeling like a victim.

We are all taught that human beings are given the gift of free will. What the heck does that mean? It's the freedom to make your own choices and your own decisions whether they are good or bad, right or wrong. Does that sound about right? I often hear things like, "Don't tell me what to eat, don't tell me how much I can drink, I have a medical condition that requires three different mind numbing prescriptions three times per day". Does any of this sound familiar? Free will is our ability to make choices that affect our own destiny. On a different note, dogs have owners.

We all accept that a dog owner decides where the dog sleeps, when and what the dog eats, and pretty much trains the dog to obey his or her commands for the duration of the dog's life. We are all pretty comfortable accepting that dogs have owners. Some dog owners treat their dogs wonderfully while other dog owners are downright abusive.

At this point in history there are billions of unhealthy people that feel stuck in bad situations. The less healthy a person is, the more critical they tend to be of the people around them. Miserable people are really good at enforcing unreasonable working conditions on anyone fearful enough to listen to them (and keep taking the abuse). Worldwide, there are billions of people that act like dogs.

Millions of Americans have become addicts that are overly critical of their own friends, family, employees, and co-workers (all, in the name of survival). However, an addict doesn't see it that way at all. Their addictions have robbed them of their critical thinking abilities. It's all made possible with the corrupted logic contained in any addicts head.

The American pill and drink-addicted zombies have been tricked to value dogs more than people. Not so? How many of us look down upon the poor ignorant public as nothing more than millions of selfish, lazy, and stupid people? You know, those nasty Walmart shoppers that are all looking for a government handout.

Many of us have been conditioned to be ok with treating our house pets better than the people around us. This is the truth and we all know it. Millions of you spend all of your daily love, compassion, and forgiveness on a 10lb Shih Tzu-sized animal while the people around you suffer. An animal that's so evolved that it cannot remember to urinate in, or outside of your dwelling for the duration of its lifetime. When a down-and-out human being needs your love, compassion, and forgiveness it's too late, there's none left. This is a lie that has been sold to you by your very own ego.

Americans have lost so much self-control via their addictions to food, alcohol, prescription not-give-a-shit pills and TV; that we have been reduced to having little more free will than dogs that have owners. Somehow people seem to be ok with it all. How on earth have we allowed ourselves to get so lost in our addictions?  Where has our compassion for our neighbors gone?

Can you imagine meeting a married couple and having the husband say, "Hi, my name is Bob, and this is my owner Susan"?  Sounds absurd right?  What happened to that guy's balls?  Sadly, that is exactly what alcohol and prescription anti-anxiety (fear) medication has done to people.  It turns us into spineless apathetic pushovers that nobody respects and everyone abuses (because they can).

The incredible level of nationwide apathy is only achievable with the help of our Dr. approved medications, daily TV programming, and widespread alcoholism.  This stupendous level of not-give-a-shitness about the world around us has only been made possible by these performance-decreasing habits paired with TV.  There are also multiple studies indicating that testosterone levels in American men have been steadily declining since the 1970's.  Both our balls and our paychecks have gotten smaller while the politicians have all become multi-millionaires.

If a government intended to slowly decline the quality of living across an entire country without causing a revolution; do you get that they may have introduced foods and drugs into the population's diet that lower the men's testosterone levels?  Look it up, Google search "declining testosterone averages" and then Google "alcohol's effect on testosterone" and see what you find.  If I'm a long term government planner that lacks ethics then I'm going to work smart, not hard.  Why do you think all of the middle-aged men started needing Viagra?

America men have been duped into chemically neutering themselves.  We are all taught and conditioned to drink beer while watching sports on TV.  We've been trained to believe that this is the normal thing to do because everyone's doing it.  TV then shows wall to wall beer and liquor commercials during every sports game.  The commercials work and we all know it.

There are millions of Americans that now admit that they are totally dependent upon alcohol.  We call them rednecks.  They are probably the most honest social group in America when it comes to at least acknowledging their addictions.  They are functioning alcoholics with no intentions of quitting.  This is completely opposed to my rich intellectual uncle that stays "classy" while getting obliterated on wine each and every day. Both educated intellectuals and daily drinking Rednecks are owned by alcohol. Both parties have lost a bit of their sanity. I don't recommend the cult of AA for life, but I do recommend regaining self-control and then finding a happy medium.

How on earth with the number of hours a week that the average person spends watching sports is everyone not addicted to alcohol? We all watch sports so that we have a safe topic to discuss at work the next day. How do you expect millions of Americans not to become hooked on alcohol and pills? That's like sending a single straight man that hasn't been laid in a few months into a strip club, handing him $100 in singles, and expecting him not to get a lap dance. It's an unfair fight and most of us aren't winning.

We didn't have a snowball's chance in hell to avoid becoming a country of addicts. Until somebodies life becomes so completely terrible that they are ready to try anything, there is little chance of escape. Getting back your balls and becoming the strong proud person that most of us were at age 25 is well worth the effort. Most of us are feeling the pain of this horrible economy. If you don't want to be stuck working 50 hours a week while staying poor, then you're in luck. Actual solutions to your problems are being uploaded right now.

To the horrible economy since 2008, and banks foreclosing on millions of Americans I say, thank you! Billionaires have made life painful enough fast enough to actually inspire millions of Americans to try anything. The big banks actually created a fast and hard bottom for millions of good people. Good people with nothing left to lose are now becoming capable of making changes for the better.

Have I personally witnessed other people that transformed themselves in a matter of months by simply removing alcohol from their daily routines? Yes, but there's more than just drinking that's made so many Americans both apathetic and distracted. If you're still paralyzed for three hours a day in front of a TV, (while unconsciously eating) then a fat bloated zombie you will be.

It is now becoming possible to wake up the zombie masses. As a result, filthy rich bankers may finally get to have all of their actions held accountable. Americans that once would have done anything (while drinking and over-medicating daily) in order to pay for their mortgage, wife, and kids will no longer blindly obey the orders of billionaires. Why? In millions of cases, the house, the wife, and the kids are gone. Each time that this has happened one more American zombie has been freed from spineless corporate servitude. Many of these corporate jobs being offered are so miserable that they require daily sedation.

When everything that someone has worked for has been lost and the wages to regain the lost lifestyle are no longer available; then corporations are no longer holding metaphorical guns to our heads. This line of reasoning now applies to millions of Americans. We are now refusing to do the dirty work for A-hole bosses and corrupt corporations because there's nothing left to manipulate us with. We will no longer abandon our God-given consciences due to this fatal error in bargaining.

The smaller upper class seems to be drifting further and further away from reality. In the meantime, the majority of Americans are experiencing more and more pain. This pain is a good thing. The former middle class has been given a huge lesson in humility and something else that billionaires know nothing about, a huge spiritual awakening.

Rather than becoming broken messes after losing all of our stuff, there are some former homeowners have turned towards God (goodness, or just being a better person). The shrinking upper class that holds tons of worthless paper money is missing this massive spiritual awakening (due to their own blinding egos). Many of the new lower-class Americans have more daily fulfillment than those that are still clinging to money (while hurting people).

That's the big joke on the drunken and unsatisfied upper class Americans that are still left. Poorer people are now less enslaved to terrible jobs that are still necessary to cover huge car and mortgage payments. Upper class Americans have become slaves to their things. Only people that have already lost everything and made peace with it can understand what a huge joke it is to see miserable rich people that are now completely owned by their stuff. People that worship money (above all else) also frequently suffer from failing health.

America was not founded by spineless men and woman that accepted every abusive order given to them by their masters. When we start to get honest with ourselves, we can admit that the only reason that people continue on in abusive relationships is because they believe that they have no other choice. People that tell others that they are stuck in bad situations are for the most part full of shit.

In reality, people fail to escape the bad situation due to their own personal fear and lack of confidence (not bravery). There is no honor in allowing wealthier human beings to treat you like garbage in exchange for money. Self-serving rich people are welcome to keep their giant pile of money and all of the unhappiness and loneliness that goes along with it. The vampire class of America is about to start having a big damn problem, faster food that they cannot catch. The public can turn on brand names and products overnight.

We all make the daily decisions that create a happy or miserable life experience. We all choose to stay in or leave the situations that we find ourselves in. Assigning all blame to other party while chalking it all up to bad luck is a losing life strategy (that only losers believe in). Every day we are all faced with scores of small decisions that fall on the side of self-serving or considerate to your fellow man. Many people now belong to religious clubs, but the majority of their daily decisions are the opposite of what their idol would do. These people tend to have plenty of financial comfort, and little fulfillment.

Happy people tend to believe that they create their own luck (because we all do). We do this every day through our actions and with our attitude. Whether it's positive or negative, we are all creating our own luck as we go. We all know this deep down inside but many of us often drink, drug, over-eat, or medicate (guilt free, and Dr. approved drug abuse) in order to perpetuate these lies to ourselves.

If there is a God, I highly doubt that this God would prefer that we all cower down before corrupt men and woman that happen to have more money than us in a totally crooked system. Doctors that prescribe anti-anxiety and pain pills to everyone, and then drive home to a huge house in their brand new Mercedes are just about as prevalent and ethical as our politicians are. Both groups will do anything to keep driving that Mercedes. We all understand that people that have acquired lots of wealth will do all sorts of absurd things to maintain the lifestyle. Their egos perform incredible mental gymnastics to justify why they stay rich, and their neighbors begin to starve. If higher beings do exist, they won't be amused with any of this.

When we were all little kids none of us said, "When I grow up, I wanna be a spineless corporate employee that goes home to a loveless marriage that I'm financially trapped in" did we? Yet, how many people do you know that are only staying with lousy partners due to financial shelter? Do any of those people realize that they are stuck there due to their own perpetual drunkenness?

How many of these types of people are taking pain or "anxiety" (fear) medication every day? Do any of these people realize that their doctors have gotten them into an active drug habit? More likely these same grown adults that made it into their mid twenties with no diagnosed mental illnesses now tell the world that they have to take their meds just to function.

We're like a bunch of people that purposely poor sugar into our gas tank because we're about to drive on a retarded highway where the speed limit is 25 miles per hour. Driving around in a sober state of mind with a perfectly running vehicle is simply too frustrating. Slow yourself down, and fit-in with the zombies. That's the strategy that most Americans are going with right now. I would much prefer to be shot in the head than live a lifetime as someone else's drunken slave.

It's not an act of bravery to stay in situations that require daily sedation just to tolerate. How many really rich people have you met that seem to be completely miserable and also get drunk daily? The drunkenness kills their conscience so that they can screw people over all day (to keep that sweet dirty money without feeling guilty). Their money and their addictions now drive their behavior; Not, a healthy human's conscience. Our society is now being run by mentally ill people that would sooner let the whole country starve than do the right thing.

Politicians, corporations, and our doctors have proven over and over again for decades that money and profit are their primary motivating factors. How long will it take the population to figure out that our doctors have become legalized drug dealers? They do not care about us as much as they care about maintaining their wealthy lifestyle. Also, if the police in real life were as good at catching bad guys as the cops on TV are, then bad guys in real life would all be locked up, but they're not. On TV, the cops always get the drug dealers and the doctors are always making people healthier.

When it really comes down to it, for doctors, it's all about keeping the house, the car, and the benefits of being wealthy. Screw you, your elderly parents and all of the fat, pale, and bloated zombies that are the actual results of their best efforts while earning one hundred plus thousand dollars per year (in real life). It seems to me that it must be the most profitable for these prestigious people with rich parents to actually wreck the health of the rest of us. That's what the actual evidence that's hobbling through our grocery stores seems to be pointing towards. Doctors destroy health, lawyers protect criminals, and priests make sure that the citizens stay obedient to the criminals that run the government. The first 15 pages of "1984" explained it all.

Second and third generation doctors have sold us all out to large corporations just as badly as our politicians have. Many of them are just as likely to be "functioning" addicts as the rest of us are. The orange pill bottles in everyone's medicine cabinets across the country are all of the evidence that I need to make such a statement. Maybe it's time for the Great Pill Bottle Rebellion of 2014.

We might as well all be robots as far as the corporations and billionaires are concerned. They do not see us as equals. After all, they have a lot more stuff. They see us as a bunch of dumb suckers that keep falling for the same con over and over again, because that's exactly what we've all been doing for the last thirty years.

Our corrupt owners are worshipping a different God than the majority of us. They deserve to be fired because their actions speak louder than words. Clearly they value their possessions more than the people that they are supposed to be serving. Instead, they only serve themselves. Many of the richest people are also some of the most miserable souls, and rightfully so. Television fails to convey that message. Instead poor people continue clawing at each other in a vain attempt to escape their $8 per hour nightmare.

Doctors are supposed to be helping us to obtain better health right? Has that been happening for the majority of people that you see every day when you're out in public? Go to a Walmart in the not-so-good part of town and take a good look at the customers. Only shopping in the rich part of town and avoiding the majority of now suffering Americans doesn't impress God.

If you look at people walking around in the real world, you can see that our population has become less healthy while spending more and more money on orange pill bottles and alcohol. Unfortunately, the orange pill bottle army (limping through Walmarts across America) looks nothing like the models on TV that have sold us all on "too-good- to-be-true" in a bottle. When are those other miserable people with failing health going to abandon a failed strategy? I don't do what they do, and I feel a hell of a lot better.

Aren't the majority of politicians and corporate CEOs born into wealthy families? What about the rest of us? When on earth are we going to wake up to the fact that the majority of people can't afford to be part of the political process anymore? This includes the Upper middle class that is currently under heavy financial attack. By all means this book is not anti-millionaire. They too, are peasants as far as the 1% is concerned. If the political process won't let us participate in a meaningful way, let's deem it invalid and create a new system. As long as the majority of the population prefers the new system, it's a done deal. Unless you'd prefer to have a dictatorship-style of governance where the majority suffers so that a tiny political class can live in comfort, which is it?

Millionaires must realize that poor people that are fighting to avoid food stamps are on the same side. If this country falls apart and turns into a giant welfare state, then it's going to be a nightmare for all of us. Perhaps all of us do have the right to limit how much wealth (power) one person is allowed to have. I don't want a billionaire limiting the size of sodas, or telling anyone what we can or cannot eat for lunch. That definitely is happening in the U.S. now, and does violate free will.

We keep allowing billions of human beings to suffer, so that one human being can point to a number on a computer screen and tell his friends, "I've got more than you". If we are being honest, bragging rights and world domination are pretty much the only reasons to start competing against other billionaires. We are serving the few and their own minority agendas based on greed. Our rich aren't worried about harming the group or treating others as they would like to be treated. Hypocrites must be removed from power or the whole group will continue suffer accordingly.

If we were all monkeys in the jungle, it's as if a few monkeys have picked all the trees in the jungle completely bare (leaving no bananas for the rest of us). The result being, a few gluttonous monkeys with a giant stockpile of rotting bananas that is being guarded by idiots with machine guns; all taking place while the whole population of monkeys begins to starve worldwide. This is exactly what Billionaires on planet earth are doing to the rest of us right now.

At some point we all must realize that there are billions of us and only thousands of them. Until billions of us figure out how to regain control against a few thousand men, then we might as well be living on the planet of the apes. If I'm forced to choose a team, then I'm choosing team ape. We are not that smart as a group, but if there are a small handful of things that could vastly increase your own brain power and bravery, would you do them?

Only addicts and cowards keep taking degrading treatment from selfish people without standing up for themselves and walking away from their oppressors. If you are not a coward yet you still find that an honest look at your own personal situation reveals that things have become a lot worse, then perhaps it's about time to sober up and start making things better in your life. A lot of good people stay in horrible situations only for as long as they are on a set of chemical crutches.

It's about time that we drop the crutches, have our come-to-Jesus moment, and start walking across the stage. People sobering themselves up by the millions and refusing daily sedation (that has somehow become normal) would drive absolute terror into the cold hearts of our billionaire owners. Do they deserve to be terrified of us for the things that they have done?  Did any of the audience feel truly sorry for the warden that blew his brains out at the end of The Shawshank Redemption?  There are some bad people in this world. It's time that we bring their bad deeds out into the light.

# Chapter 2 – The root of the problem

People with low self-esteems don't like themselves (whether it's for good reason or not). A physically healthy and attractive person can be mistreated enough times by enough people around them to eventually believe that they are worth less. I've most definitely witnessed smart and talented people get treated like gold in one city and trash in another. The daily feedback from the people around us has a huge effect on how we feel about ourselves. Where do we see and hear nearly every piece of bad news that will affect our country's diminishing quality of living?

TV is the one common thread that "unites" (divides) the American people and "informs" (dictates) our ever worsening circumstances via a continuous drip feed of controlled information. We are told so in a very matter of fact manner every day of the week by a screen in our homes that strongly influences our buying behaviors. Do you really think that millions upon millions of people would be buying there $2^{nd}$, $3^{rd}$, and 4th I-phones for hundreds of dollars if it weren't for the power of advertising (hypnotizing)?

Any half way sane person that isn't 100% blinded by ego will admit that the TV ads do work. I want to buy some European hair remover called the "No No" after just 3 or 4 repetitions of their commercial. Do you not think that billionaires haven't already seen how effective the television is at selling the American public whatever they want to? Whoever can afford the most TV time can then sell us whatever they want to, if we keep participating in the con. Shoot the con-man dead by turning off your TV.

I don't like being sold something that I didn't need before the salesman <u>con</u>-vinced me to do so. Do you have a positive or negative feeling when you hear the word con-man? Yet somehow the world's slickest con-man ever to get past your front door and into your living room, family room, bedrooms, and bathrooms has successfully done so in billions of households worldwide. We all keep buying ideas that have failed to make our lives better. In fact, most peoples' lives are now getting worse, in direct proportion to hours in front their TV.

We keep on buying lies that we shouldn't believe in from our politicians and somehow, we keep the thing on that's been conning us all in our homes. Do you ever remember being convinced of WMDs? Did they ever exist in our minds before the TV told us that they were there in Iraq? **We Must be Dumb.**

We buy into all kinds of new products and ideas that our TV trained us to believe would improve or threaten our lives. Our TVs have conned us into trying tons of new products and services. Did anyone else out there get that exercise bike or that indoor snow skiing machine? How about that miracle golf putter that you bought at 1 am? Is any of this sounding familiar? We've all been tricked at one time or another by a too-good to-be-true product. Most of us never did get the six pack abs promised to us by the miracle sit-up machine.

The pills that promised walks on the beach with good looking sexual partners have failed us too. Unless both attractive partners worship in the same church of the holy pill bottle; that good looking date on the beach is long gone when they discover a medicine cabinet full of peace and spirituality. Replace that feeling of spirituality that drinks and pills have given you with something more accurate. Delusionality: a non-threatening state of existence to other delusional people. Cult members feeling comfortable while surrounded by other cult members or drunks in bars surrounded by other drunks are all comforted by similar people. Are both daily drunks and daily cult members at least a little bit delusional about their own level of morality?

Nobody wants to deal with the side effects that any drug addict or alcoholic cannot escape. There is no magic pill or drink. The only thing that those pills deliver is a greater likelihood of weight gain, selfishness, premature aging, and increased apathy to do anything about it. They are a trap. Cults that practice daily rituals and convince their members that they have gained the moral high-ground over the rest of society also produce delusional people. Our society has been carefully divided into different cults of Americans that are equally delusional about their own cult's level of morality. When you grow up attending a particular church, it all seems normal. The sheer repetition of just about anything can make an insane ritual seem normal.

In a true act of insanity, we continue to go out and buy the things that our TV teaches us all about that have resulted in a country that is now fatter, dumber, and poorer than we were just twenty years ago. It's as if half of the country has been completely hypnotized into a barely conscious condition. Most Americans are unable to refrain from the next (unnecessary) over-sized meal. It's nearly impossible to avoid scores of half-crippled and totally defeated people hobbling towards their next feeding in pain (like zombies).

The movies simply over-exaggerated the normal zombie symptoms: pale, bloated, not so bright, and constantly hungry. Is this not what we see every day? Why on earth would a person choose to become like this? Is it really a choice at all? Is it possible that we've indeed been conned into this weakened version of ourselves?

I don't know about you, but once I figure out that somebody is a con-man, I remove them from my life and refuse to let them talk to me anymore. I don't want to give that con-man one minute to open his mouth, bring down my defenses, and sell me something that I didn't need. Isn't that what con-men do?

They convince us of a deal that sounds too good to be true, and in the end we get ripped off by them every time. The conman is your TV. The belief that pills and alcohol will deliver peace and better relationships is the con. Unscrew the cable cord and the conman is neutralized. After doing so, you can get your health back and quit buying crap that you don't need.

Con-men say just about anything to gain our trust. Then, they take our money without a conscience. We never get the too-good-to-be-true deal and always end up with negative consequences after they have made off with our money. Don't we all know a group of people that will say anything to gain our trust and then take our money? Where exactly do we constantly see and hear from these people?

My God have I met a lot of hopeless adults with low self-esteems that have one thing in common, hours of television daily. Incredibly, they are totally unaware that the TV itself has programmed them to believe that, "It is…what it is". Many of those same TV watching people also identify with one of two possible cults, and will proudly tell you of their membership.

Television has conned them into believing that they are powerless over their own sad set of circumstances in life, (which is not true at all) and that the majority of their hardships have been caused by members of the opposite cult-like party. A few hundred million Americans have been convinced to believe along this line of logic. We believe that our cult has the moral authority and that most problems in America can be blamed on the other cult-party. Both cult-like parties have failed to deliver on their promises for decades. Whether you belong to the Democratic cult or the Republican one, you still continue believing that today's promises (lies) will deliver.

If you do everything that your idol on TV wants you too, and they break all of their promises after being elected, then why would you keep participating in that particular cult? If I have regular attendance at a church and pay my weekly offerings (taxes) over the course of ten years, and that church fails to deliver on any of its promises (while taking my time, attendance, and money) than I quit going. If enough other church members also decide to leave because all of the healthy looking church members vanished, then the church goes out of business.

The same preacher that failed to make good on his promises after taking other peoples' money for years might have to struggle financially like his sheep-like followers did while supporting him. Now that's some change that I can believe in. Our politicians deserve no less. The fact that individual Americans donate a penny while corporations are making all of the new laws is a joke. TV watching Americans from both political cults are sheep-like parishioners (foolishly looking to their cult-like leaders for salvation). Everyone that hasn't been hypnotized by assholes knows that salvation lies within. Small children could decipher such obvious scams, but grown adults can't.

The more television that a person is exposed to, the more powerless that person feels (because of the beliefs that their TV has sold to them). I began noticing these hopeless sad-sacks walking all over the city of Cleveland Ohio after relocating from Atlanta, GA. Anytime a person becomes accustomed to one culture and then relocates to a new area, the differences between two different cultures become painfully obvious.

I very specifically remember coming across a middle-aged fat man inside of a Sears store. I told the plump man how I had moved back to Cleveland Ohio after living in Atlanta, Georgia and stated that it felt like I had moved into an entirely different country. I was unapologetic about stating how much happier and more hopeful the Atlanta residents were compared to Clevelanders.

The plump man in a very matter of fact manner stated that Cleveland would beat the hope out of me in less than a year. He was wrong. I wrote most of this book while there in Cleveland and promptly relocated 1000 miles south to a beautiful city on the gulf coast. I am now surrounded by more hopeful and happier people.

I believe the term indoctrination is what the plump man was attempting to project onto my future. Luckily I have found a way to shield myself from these dog-conscious people and convert their apathy towards the fallen middle class into fuel for writing this book. In the fat man's defense, after twenty years of watching his home teams and local economy get demolished, he had been conditioned to be less hopeful. Many of us have become just like him without even being aware of it. Do you want to be like the fat man, supplying a voice of doubt to those that are younger and healthier than yourself?

Any human being that is conditioned to lose over and over again (during the course of years) eventually hopes less. After a while, supposedly "free" people start acting a lot more like prison guards and dog owners. Nearly all of the young working class of Cleveland Ohio (absent of wealthy parents) are assimilated into the lower-class culture. They can easily be identified by their tattoos, drunkenness, and anger. My persistent and vocal refusals to comply made me a very unpopular guy in the lunch room, and many meals were missed.

A vast majority of the lower class 18-45yr olds end up smoking cigarettes and getting covered in tattoos to let the world know what a tough life they have had. Cleveland sure did look like a giant open air prison to me. It has pained me to see an entire city of people divided into drunken, tattooed, smoking inmates while the clean-cut, non-tattooed, non-smoking upper-class views the rest of the population as trash. It was a whole city consisting of guards and inmates. What a sad and pathetic way to treat your neighbors.

We are all equals, but the Cleveland upper-class didn't see it that way at all. They somehow fancied themselves as some sort of royalty. They truly believed that they were just a little bit smarter and a little more deserving of a pleasant life than the rest of the inmates. This would be like being the wealthiest flies on a pile of manure. They may fancy their own positions, but nobody else does.

I have no tattoos, don't smoke, have a college degree, and also have parents of modest means. The result being that I wasn't accepted by the snobby upper class Cleveland elite because I couldn't afford to hang out with them. Likewise, the tattoo covered and frequently drunk working-class also avoided me. To them, I appeared to be one of the snobby rich kids due to my clean appearance and lack of tattoos.

My immense popularity in a dying rust-belt city provided me the time and energy to construct the body of this book in just a few months before seeking a better environment. Thank God I never gave up. Thank God that I never lost hope.

The old folks and retirees of Cleveland Ohio are severely delusional about the rapid decline of their once decent city. Sadly, they too have been blinded by the hypnotic trance that their TVs have put them in. This is no different amongst senior citizens nationwide. In manufacturing cities like Cleveland Ohio, many of the middle class college grads have fled. Or, they've been beaten into the drunken lower-class of half-conscious wage slaves.

Why do you think that the Cleveland Browns fans are referred to as "The Dawg Pound"? Only a bunch of dogs would put up with twenty years of constantly getting beaten and abused by their owners without walking away. I think it's a damn shame to walk around an entire city full of snotty rich folks and hopeless dogs.

It does piss me off to see an entire city of human beings that have been trained to act like slaves and slave owners. The city also looked and acted nothing at all like the vibrant suburbs that I had lived in down south in Atlanta. When a city or entire group of people acts shamefully, we shouldn't be afraid to speak the truth about it. Some places are hellholes. If that's where you choose to stay, then that's where you deserve to be.  Do hellholes exist?  Is North Korea a hellhole?

We have established that dogs do have owners and you are totally cool with that, right?  What if Billionaires devised a new strategy to have slaves but called them by a different name.  Something that sounds more respectful.  Something to make them feel like they have more control in their lives than they actually do, and something that gives an illusion of power.  Something like, voters.  Would politicians and billionaire tycoons devise such a strategy?

These "voters" will become part of a system that over the course of time becomes entirely controlled and owned by billionaires (from behind the scenes).  These "voters" will be divided into two opposing sides each of which is carefully trained via TV to blame all of their problems on the opposing side (instead of the billionaires that have hijacked the system).  The super wealthy will completely determine all political policy that the voters don't particularly care for but must obey.  Does any of this sound familiar?

Most Americans are totally unaware of how badly television has clouded their judgment and programmed their beliefs.  Imagine if the American zombies were all persuaded to watch the uninterrupted movie of George Orwell's, "1984" followed by wall to wall TV coverage the very next day announcing that TVs will now be called Big Brothers.  Also, all televisions must be kept on at all hours of the day (for our safety of course) by law and punishable by prison.  Everyone must also wear a tracking bracelet (Apple I-watch) at all times just so Big Brother can constantly know your location, and even listen in if you raise any red flags.

I can see the conversations between the stupidest people in America the following days saying, "Aw man, you've got a 60 inch Big Brother in your family room!  Damn!  I only got a 40 inch Big Brother in my family room!  I'll bet that 60-inch Big Brother trains the shit outta your thoughts!  In just a few months, I'll bet your ass will be gettin fat as shit, dumb as shit, and fearful and hopeless as shit!"  The removal of all free will and privacy is happening right before our eyes and no one seems to care.

Free minds would unplug the cable box and refuse to take orders from Big Brother. Nothing in the world would be funnier than giant piles of broken flat screen TVs deposited in the Billionaire slave owners' front yards to let them know that all of their dogs have finally realized how to take off their mind-controlling collars. Millions upon millions of Americans simultaneously cancelling their cable TV would surely give several of our loving politicians, heart attacks.

Think about it, if you are a king or a rich slave owner that wants as many slaves as possible to do the most work for the least amount of money, you use fear, right? What is the most effective way to control the largest possible audience of slaves with the same message at the same time? If television is the primary delivery tool for instilling fear-based beliefs and establishing a group consensus; this fear-based system of control must prevent voters (the peasant class) from standing up to the lying politicians (vampire class). Judging by our spineless actions, I'd say that it's working pretty well.

Tyrants and slave owners depend heavily on a general doubt of God and a strong fear of death to manipulate the most voters (suckers) possible. If there were events that proved beyond the shadow of a doubt that human beings have a soul, and that there are higher spiritual beings than us (100%, for sure) then people would lose their fear of tyrants. Why do you think that organized religion is so completely un-appealing to the average American? It was constructed that way by design.

The wealthiest human beings have corrupted our organized religions and used them to separate us from any real spirituality at all. For the record, I am for all religions that encourage love, forgiveness, and promote kindness towards all humans, regardless of what religion they were born into. Kings took good lessons from ancient texts and have corrupted religions to instead divide us all against one another.

How primitive do we all have to be to keep falling for the same con for thousands of years? God is good, so if you believe in God, then be good, the end. None of us need priests to tell us how to behave nor do we need the TV to tell us their visions. Our Politicians have used the TV to instill (install) terror into our imaginations. These "terrorists" were literally funded and armed by our own elites to destabilize their competition in foreign countries. Then, the same threat that our billionaires funded is used to put more surveillance on the American public.

Screw their visions. I have my own hopes, dreams, and imagination. Rich assholes are using television to tell me the way that things are, and the way that things should be (according to them). It is a total bullshit scam run by sociopathic people that don't care about the public. They want us to stay super poor and work 60 hours a week for them while they go golfing every day.

Picture a scale that is totally loving, forgiving, virtuous, and brave at one end, and totally selfish, heartless, and sociopathic on the other. Most of us fall somewhere in the middle just on the side towards goodness (but with plenty of room for improvement). We are supposed to be learning from our mistakes, and trying to work our way closer to the good side of this scale.

Unfortunately, television (tell-a-vision) has reinforced the belief that sociopathic behaviors result in greater personal wealth. TV also sells the illusion that wealthier people are enjoying their lives more than the rest of us are. They're not. Most rich people are miserable, and are always chasing after the next thing. They're like dogs chasing cars. People have become obsessed with gaining more money and are overly fearful of an early death (due to the constant violence on TV).

Slaves that gain true enlightenment would have no more fear of death, and therefore become damaged goods in the eyes of a slave owner. Do you get that if there was 100% recorded and provable evidence of life after death, that fear of death could no longer be used to control people? Kings and governments would go through tremendous trouble to destroy such evidence if it did exist, wouldn't they? Concrete evidence of life after death would completely undermine fear and guilt-based control systems.

There are books about near-death experiences where non-believers are suddenly and miraculously convinced of an afterlife and immediately lose all fear of death after their incident. Those with true spirituality cannot be forced to do horrible things by tyrants. All those other people that cover themselves with crosses but clearly are terrified of death, worship money, and live cowardly existences aren't tricking anyone but themselves.

Those with true faith and failing health wouldn't be throwing hundreds of dollars a month at prescription pills to painfully stay alive if they trusted that nothing scary was going to happen after death. These types of fearful people are lying not only to the group, but to themselves. We have been mind-controlled to fear death by our organized religions and by rich con-men that have infiltrated all religions worldwide.

Kings want the average man to intensely fear going to hell, or believe in nothing at all. The whole point is that the public loses faith in God and instead seeks protection from their government (lying politicians) that funded the overseas terrorists in the first place. This all takes place while the public is too drunk, too medicated, and too hypnotized by television to see how the scam works. Only our own stubborn pride and the weakened processing power of a TV addicted and alcoholic brain allows the con to continue. The Clintons and Obamas gain more control over your lives and you grovel to them for more food stamps.

Kings and billionaires wanting fear-based cheap labor would want the maximum percentage of citizens possible believing that there is nothing after this life. Or, that you're a horrible sinner that is going to hell, so you'd better stay alive as long as possible to postpone the punishment that is coming. If an entire army of voters suddenly lost their fear of death then the slave owners would have no one left to do their dirty work.

Organized religion has been filtered and controlled by governments for thousands of years. Are you aware that entire books have been removed from the Christian Bible? Such as: The Book of Enoch. The scientific recovery of the Dead Sea Scrolls proved this beyond the shadow of a doubt. Any smart king would be sure to remove ancient books that undermine his own authority. Have you ever heard of the King James Bible?

Even the History Channel has been leaking these little-known facts into the awareness of the American public. Can you think of any organized religions that make their followers feel guilty? Nearly all organized religions have impossible to follow rules when combined with our current political and financial systems. The logical computers in our American brains are totally crashed by these contradicting belief systems. Our church, the TV, and the declining economy that we have to survive in all completely contradict each other.

Two or more contradicting orders being given at the same time by different authorities make a brain freeze up and crash, don't they? When two bosses (that can both fire you on the spot) give you conflicting orders at the same time in front of each other, you freeze, don't you? This is what the combination of organized religion, television, and our current job market has done to the brains of the American public. Our hard drives have crashed, and this book is unfreezing them right now.

The processors in millions of our heads have slowed down badly, because we are damned no matter what we do. The only way that most of the working class people can keep functioning in an insane system, is to intentionally turn off our logic via alcohol or guilt-free prescription drugs (pill-form alcohol). Does that sound about right? To deal with insane logic, you must turn off the logic in your own head.

Through my own experiences, I now believe in an existence after this life and I attempt to treat others how I would like to be treated. This current belief system paired with sobriety has made working at most existing sales jobs nearly impossible. I do not see other human beings as sheep (to be fleeced and outsmarted). I don't want to get rich while worsening the financial plight of already stressed-out Americans.

In the absence of alcohol or pills my conscience is working as designed. I believe that the vast majority of people are born with one, but sadly, many of us have been conditioned and trained to ignore it. When we do ignore it, we later feel guilt or shame which then requires constant escapes from reality to keep functioning. Why do you think that most people spend so much time drinking, watching sports, and playing video games?

Aside from religion, kings came up with the most ingenious tool for manipulating human beings to behave against their natural consciences, money. Stop and think how many times in your adult life you have seen otherwise reasonable people commit shameful actions in the pursuit of obtaining or protecting their money. For a lot of people, money has become their God. After all, our televisions and life experiences have conditioned us to believe it. We see constant images of how people's lives are happier with more money.

Television is also one of the world's most devious (deviating from the truth) and effective propaganda delivery systems ever created by man. The Television tells you everything that you must want and buy, in order to be happier. The TV motivates people by showing us what to want next, and why we must sacrifice all of our time to obtain it. We all know that the next thing that we get is finally going to make us happy, right? Just put aside how you treat people and how you allow yourself to be treated in order to get it.

If you had told somebody 100 years ago that wealthy men would build a device that conned the masses out of nearly all of their time and energy (and turned them into mind-controlled slaves) the billionaires would probably ask this question...Why? Why would people allow such a device to stay in their homes? How could this device escape detection from the targeted audience?

We will be completely unaware that the device was always intended to train all of our thoughts. Imagine a villain giving a radio-active vase to his next target. The bad guy puts the expensive vase right in his unsuspecting target's family room. Unless they own a Geiger counter, the vase continues to do damage to the whole family (slowly ruining their health over the course of years). If something is gradual enough, it can evade detection from the smartest of people.

We've all been trained to worry about terrorists from thousands of miles away. Meanwhile, we're getting the message from a biological weapon that we've voluntarily paid for. We sit in front of it for hours a day while it slowly robs us of our free will and plants powerful ideas and beliefs into our minds.

Voters (peasants) will be trained to believe that the TV is strictly for entertainment and information only. People will also be trained (sub-consciously) to attack any person that proposes to them that television is mind control. They will attack those people that have broken free from the daily hypnotizing without even realizing it. With enough repetition, even a lie can become the truth. It wasn't that long ago that we all lived on a flat planet.

# Chapter 3 – Remain part of the king's flat earth crowd, or start using sound logic

Sky scrapers being demolished into a giant cloud of dust on September 11th 2001 by airplanes that were hijacked with box cutters, escaped NORAD's space age technology missile defense system, and were manually flown into tall thin buildings by crappy amateur Cessna pilots at 500 miles per hour, was, and is, one of the greatest lies ever sold to the American people on TV. To speak out against the official media accepted 911 story and attempt to reason with an average person using facts, logic, and evidence, is asking to make most Americans very angry at you. TV has badly brainwashed the public to attack their own fellow Americans for even attempting to ask questions about 911. These are questions that beg to be explained.

Not two but three buildings in New York City were obviously rigged up with explosives and demolished on the day of 911. Evidence of thermite (a high temperature explosive) used to cut steel beams was found at ground zero along with video evidence of cut beams. Yet, to point out the in-your-face evidence that contradicts the official (government official) version, is to get yelled at by the daily drunken zombies. Instead, we are told by government officials that it's anti-American and unpatriotic to humor such conspiracy theories. This line of logic was delivered on TV by George W Bush about 911.

When you stop getting drunk or sedating yourself with pills every day, then your perception of the world around you changes completely. Do you think that a completely sober person's perception of reality is more or less accurate than a daily drinker's? After all, what do architects, engineers, pilots, doctors, psychologists, and actual video evidence mirroring every other controlled demolition in recorded history matter, if our politicians have explained the whole thing to us (just as accurately, as they explain everything else)? I would rather be spiritually awake with a functioning conscience than too afraid to speak out against the (frequently drunk) American public. We know that we've lost respect for each other, so why should I worry about this particular groups' opinion of me for any longer? The group isn't that smart, is it?

Jet fuel from the planes that hit the twin towers (and not building #7 that collapsed at 5:30pm with no plane impact) burns at around 1700 degrees Fahrenheit. The steel framework of the buildings (woven together and still intact after each plane impact) melts at around 2700 degrees F. Other steel skyscrapers have had raging infernos that burned for hours and hours and did not collapse into a pile of fine dust. Also note that these buildings were filled with Asbestos, which would require an ultra expensive renovation.

Thermite (an explosive) was found at ground zero and burns at around 3000 degrees F. This is enough to cut through the steel beams as the video evidence in the days following the disaster suggests. Also note that days after the Towers collapsed that molten steel was found under the rubble at the bases of the two buildings. Many Fireman and rescue workers are on video testifying of the molten steel.

The owner of the twin Towers Larry Silverstein who had signed a 99 year lease (just 6 months earlier for 3.2 Billion dollars) profited greatly from the event. The insurance was only supposed to pay out 3.5 billion dollars, but, in 2007 Mr. Silverstein was awarded a settlement of 4.55 Billion dollars. He tried to collect more by claiming each building individually. In all, buildings that had required a massive Asbestos removal costing roughly 200 million dollars, and had been banned from demolition by the NY Port Authority, (due to their Asbestos content) had been successfully removed. When it was all said and done the building lease holder had turned a 1+ billion dollar profit in just 6 years (and never had to pay 200 million dollars for Asbestos removal).

A young film maker made a movie called "Loose Change" that completely contradicts the official (government official) 911 story. Millions of Americans have now seen the documentary. Those whom haven't are behind the learning curve. Had the movie been proven to be slanderous against the super wealthy people that are implicated, then the film maker would have been legally ruined, but wasn't. If the average person even thinks about going to battle against a billionaire, then the average Joe will get legally decimated. Unless, their claims and evidence are so damning in the public eye that the billionaire is best to stay quiet.

Those whom even humor the possibility that billionaires would lie to the public should try Google searching "911 Truth" and see what you find. Just because the mainstream media sets up one Straw Man celebrity (Charlie Sheen) that questions the validity of 911, does not mean that Dick Cheney's version of the story is the truth. Do you remember both Dick Cheney and George W Bush getting to testify together to the 911 commission, not under oath, and off the record? There are tons of brilliant people worldwide that completely disagree with the official 911 story. We all agree that the public is full of idiots, so why wouldn't government psychologists use proven tactics like the Straw Man argument to squash public curiosity?

Burying our heads in the sand and uncontrollably yelling at strangers attempting to present new information to us (while calling them conspiracy theorists) ought to be disturbing to you. Stop and ask yourself, "why did I get so angry"? Do you realize that television has trained us to become the thought police whenever one of our fellow Americans (someone whom you greatly respect in all other areas of life) proposes anything contradicting the government's version of the story?

Do you understand that billions of dollars were made by multiple individuals after the events took place? I see people lie for hundreds of dollars. Plenty of people have murdered and been put in jail over thousands of dollars, right? Why is it that the public finds it so hard to believe that a few evil people wouldn't be capable of murder when billions of dollars could be made? War profits, government coups, and oil rights are easily worth billions of dollars.

Have we not caught our politicians lying to us over and over again for decades? We all know the honest answer. Why wouldn't our politicians be capable of carrying out just one more momentous lie amongst a lifetimes worth? To accept that such a thing could happen in America is very upsetting. However, people living in other countries from around the world don't have such a hard time accepting that possibility.

How was the American public not outraged when our 10% approval rating congress formed the 911 commission and found that no government officials had messed up? Their report never even mentioned building number 7 (the 3rd New York sky scraper that was demolished on the afternoon of 911) and has eluded the zombies' awareness entirely. Having our politicians investigate an attack on our country would be like having a bunch of mobsters investigate an attack on a competitor's casino in Vegas. Also, when questioning two different Mob bosses from the same family; I'm sure that the public would be just fine if we allowed them to be cross-examined in private, and together in the same room, at the same time, and not under oath. It makes no sense, but that's what happened.

How long is it going to take for the American public to accept that our politicians are not our protectors? They keep piling up their own wealth while we all get poorer. Even hardcore democrats like Nancy Pelosi are now worth tens of millions of dollars, you know, fighting shoulder to shoulder with us poor people. It's all a huge sham. This is obvious to anyone that's not constantly sedated. At the very least, they are the farmers and we are the sheep and cow-people. We are being sheered and milked more frequently, and kept in smaller pens with worsening food.

We have been trained to hear the words "conspiracy theorist" attached to any news item at all and then we immediately accept the politician approved version of the story. Why are we still buying the politicians' consensus of reality? Both parties seem to always get caught lying to us. Only flawed logic and a delusional ego would allow a person to keep plowing through life without addressing this immense problem.

There are intelligent people that outperformed their classmates in school and are excellent problem solvers in many other areas of their life. However, when these same bright people attempt to shed light on the truth about a phony sounding news story, we've all been conditioned to call them a conspiracy theorist (thought criminal). These same smart people have a much better track record of truth than the billionaires that own all of the major news networks.

If one thing is for sure, it's that all billionaires must be the most honest and the most ethical of all human beings while acquiring 999 times one million dollars in assets. Several hundred million dollars is simply not enough to feel successful. When will we realize that these people are off on a crazy power trip?  The rest of us must regulate them because they see us as ants, not equals.  At some point, when will 6 or 7 billion people ever get together and renegotiate exactly how much power 1 human being is allowed to exert over the rest of us?

We are allowed to limit how much power one person has.  These are flawed human beings just like the rest of us, not gods.  Humanity is totally entitled to remind any billionaire of this, and if we so choose, we can strip them of all of their power in an instant.  There are billions of us and not a whole lot of them.  They have no cape, are not bullet proof, and cannot shoot laser beams out of their eyes.

Billionaires are fallible, just like the rest of us mindless zombies.  We had better get things back to where reasonable and good people are running the show before billionaires build robot armies.  It sounds ridiculous I know, but there are already robot planes (drones) that blow their enemies up now.  Ask civilians living in Pakistan if this is a joke?  Training moronic kids from the ghetto to carry out remotely controlled murder, has already been done.

Six or seven billion of us can choose any type of money that we want and render one sociopathic billionaire's money invalid.  There are more of us, a lot more of us.  We are only stuck in this worldwide servitude system for as long as we remain a collective group of morons.  If we so choose, we could require that all current billionaires be stripped of their assets due to crimes against humanity.  In the light of concrete evidence (which is likely out there) most people reading this would argue on the side of justice.  We do want billionaires with no conscience to be removed from power, don't we?

We could offer them all jobs at McDonalds, life in prison, or allow them to graciously blow their own brains out.  Once again, this is only when their close business partners, friends, and family provide evidence of crimes against humanity.  These people have not been very nice to the rest of us and I do propose the McDonalds plan.  I think working at McDonalds is a pretty fair deal when our current billionaires have allowed hundreds of millions of people to spend lifetimes in poverty (in spite of their near infinite financial power).

Tell-a-vision has successfully trained the majority of us to call critical thinkers, conspiracy theorists.  For God sakes, does anyone not see the similarity between George Orwell's 1984 and the present world that we now live in? It has become impossible for intelligent Americans to reason (using logic) with their neighbors about any information that has not already been broadcast on television to the entire herd. How any person could miss the exact correlation between thought criminal, and conspiracy theorist is beyond me.

We've become an entire country of battered wives, smacking away any hand that tries to pull us out of our abusive relationship. We keep telling people that the politicians love us, but guess what, they don't. The rich kids wearing expensive suits that investigated 911 don't care about you and they never will. They have no respect at all for the American public and they shouldn't.

As a group, we're acting like a bunch of cowardly lions that have accepted more and more abuse over the course of decades. We've become fatter, dumber, and more apathetic with each generation. The only way for any of us to get any real relief is by ending the relationships with things, substances, and people that no longer serve us. We must first sober ourselves up in order to regain the balls and brains necessary to create something that works for all of us.

We are supposed to be the people in charge in the first place, not a minority of morally bankrupt assholes. Over the course of time, we have allowed and consented to whatever our government is and has become. All of us are partly responsible for what our country has become. For years of my adult life I was guilty of letting somebody else deal with it. Not anymore, I am making noise and becoming an inconvenient trouble maker in the American lower-class.

The good news is, we are allowed to drastically change things on the fly if the majority of people are suffering (which they are). Sorry rich people, but if more than half of all Americans are suffering badly then we must overhaul the current system that is no longer working for the majority of people. There are fifty million Americans on food stamps. I have news for old racist white people; they are not all poor minorities looking for handouts.

Millions of former middle class people of all races (including college educated white people) are now working at the best jobs available (minimum wage jobs) and still cannot afford rent and food.

In spite of my strong work ethic, near-constant sobriety, and a positive attitude, this system is <u>not</u> working for me. Please refer to the movie "Cinderella Man" starring Russel Crowe, and understand that millions of decent Americans are feeling that kind of financial stress right now.

Retired old people have no clue what is truly going on. Please stop yelling about Obama, one man didn't do this to us. We all did this to ourselves, including grumpy old white people (that take fifty pills per day just to stay alive). Even though, many of them appear to be miserable. To all miserable old people out there, for God sakes, if you feel that awful then stop praying to the God of the orange pill bottles.

All of the best pills and all the best doctors have resulted in millions of miserable old people. Please stop your own suffering and stop taking the pills. We all have free will and do not have to suffer for ten more years just because pills exist that can keep us in a crippled and dying state. Watching grumpy old white people live a slow pill-popping and alcoholic death is certainly <u>not</u> watching a graceful (God's grace) experience. None of us like watching our loved ones leave us. If they are living in misery, then we need to let them move on to something better if they so choose. Free will has been replaced with free pill.

We ought to steer the zombie Walmart shoppers back towards the politicians that have been controlling them via their TVs. You've heard of the movie I-robot. How about I-zombie? It's where the massive heard of American zombies gets reprogrammed by those of us that still have free will and self-control. All of those dirty conspiracy theorists can reprogram American Idol fans without them even knowing it (not you of course).

Any reader that hears the words conspiracy theorist (that condemnation towards any actual intellectual curiosity) regarding subjects <u>not</u> government approved and drip-fed to the zombies via television gets an extremely negative emotional reaction. Ask yourself why you hate these theorists for thinking? Why is questioning the honesty of our politician's televised version of the truth a bad thing? Is it possible that we've become an entire nation suffering from Stockholm syndrome?

Do battered wives get angry and start defending their abusive husbands when friends and family try to reason with them to leave? Only after a severe beating will a battered wife even consider walking away. If you're still an alcoholic or a prescription pill addict then I have to ask, have you had enough yet? Has the beating you've taken in this economy been sufficient for you to try something new?

Do you really like rich men in suits on TV dictating a rapidly declining quality of living to an army of three hundred million bottle worshipping Americans? Are you one of them? How many pills or drinks to you actually take per day?

Just like the people in the book 1984, we've been trained to attack those seeking truth and those asking questions. We all know damn well that our "elected" representatives keep lying to us all. We yell at our friend, neighbor, or co-worker that has always been good to us if they so much as mention a non-government approved thought. We then defend the "official" congressionally approved version of the story that billionaires and politicians have investigated themselves. Maybe you should actually try unplugging your cable box for a month and see what happens to your belief systems. See what happens to your own level of anxiety and see how often you think about terrorists.

The processors between most American's ears have been infected with a virus that somehow makes them keep trusting a bunch of con-men in suits. See if you side with a millionaire in an expensive suit, or your next door neighbor that has never been caught lying to you, after, you've unplugged your TV for an entire month. I assure you that the battered wife analogy will make much better sense to you if you try the experiment.

TV does paint an entire picture of reality. We have been lied to by rich men's PR agents on television for decades. We call them politicians and news casters (script readers). Every time that we throw one crook out he is immediately replaced by another agent in a suit coming from a seemingly endless line of con-men. How the public could miss the point of an endless supply of the agent Smith character in "The Matrix" movies is again, beyond me. Journalists have failed the public and would also more appropriately be called billionaire PR agents because that's what they are. Our news reporters read scripts like robots, and if they ever do try to question the validity of a news story on air, they get fired.

News reporters do damage control for billionaires, and the American public always foots the bill like a bunch of obedient dogs. How many politicians have been removed on the spot, stripped of their wealth, and forced to work alongside the rest of us for $8 an hour? Why on earth should any of these guys fear doing harm to the group when none of us ever holds them accountable?

We have been trained to attack and ridicule anyone proposing a theory about a possible truth that has been concealed by wealthy people that now own all of the TV networks. Nothing would unite the American people more than coming together and overturning the momentous lie of 911. It has been used to lead us into a war under false pretenses. The truth can unite, while lies tend to untie our common bonds.

We are supposed to stand for truth, justice, and the American way. The truth is that the American public all got manipulated and deceived by our TV sets on the morning of September 11th 2001. Only a very small percentage of the psyches (in a country full of stupid people) have allowed our officials' version of the truth to be challenged at all. In light of the damning evidence that does exist, it's now time for this to change. Public opinion about 911 is beginning to change.

Do you want to be one of the zombies that is last to finally discover the truth? I don't, and I'm willing to be ridiculed for proposing alternative theories that are far more logical than George W Bush's and President Obama's consensus version of 911. Half the country thinks that everything coming out of one guy's mouth is a total lie, yet both Presidents back the same story.

The thing about truly demoralized victims is, even in the light of overwhelming evidence, they will continue to side with their master (just like an abused wife does). This is what has happened to the same American public that we see featured on "Jay Walking". Somehow, we are allowing them (the idiotic public) to police us. The idiot masses have become so well-trained to defend the politicians' lies that honest people dare not speak the truth in public. Now you know why

Orwell created Winston in 1984. The dead (brain dead) always attack the living (functioning brain) just like in every zombie movie ever made.

This point was very smugly made by former KGB agent Yuri Bezmenov when explaining how Russia had demoralized its people. Stalin took full control of a super power sized country. The citizens were trained to police each other while criminals ran the economy into the ground (while millions of people starved). You can bet that most of the ignorant masses in Russia had shit-eating grins on their faces during that fiasco. The majority likely mocked the intellectuals (critical thinkers) for trying to reason with them at the time. My Indian name is walks-amongst-zombies, and I'm break dancing in your brain.

The intellectuals in pre-communist Russia failed to break through Stalin's mind control. They later got shipped out of the country after the takeover was complete. After all, you can't have brave, reasonable, and logical people hanging around a bunch of defeated human beings (undoing years of careful programming). If you don't realize that the American public has been systematically and scientifically conditioned to act as the government's watch dogs, (thought police) than you're most likely one of them. That spell is being broken right now so you won't continue being such a dick to your neighbors.

Why do you think abusive husbands won't let their wives have self-respecting friends? We've become a country full of drunks that must conform to the televised version of the truth. Otherwise, we get attacked by our abused and indoctrinated neighbors that aren't ready to end the abusive relationship yet. They don't have the balls to confront the real issues that keep them from escaping their own abusive lives. Instead, they drink, pop pills, and get high daily.

Once you take the chemical escape, the result is always the same. Let somebody else deal with it. As a result, the whole group suffers due to abundant sources of cheap slave-like labor that doesn't demand respect. Reasonable people that won't replace God with worship of the Government become less accepted by their indoctrinated neighbors.

It is now time for all of us to take our thumbs out of our mouths, put on our big-boy pants, and face the truth that we were conned on 911 in order for us to support billionaires' oil rights. There was a pre-existing long-term military strategy as in, "The Project for the New American Century". Please Google it, and see what you find. Understand that in 1997 this think tank was formed in Washington D.C. to lay out future plans to ensure world dominance for the next one hundred years. The plan involved overthrowing multiple middle-eastern governments and also installing increased controls on the American people. This was all drawn up before 911 took place.

We aren't just going to send our children off to war to line the pockets of billionaires for no reason. An enemy attack on our soil makes sending our kids off to war a lot easier for all of us to feel good about. I'm sure you're aware that Dick Cheney and his former employer Halliburton made Billions of dollars in profits after the events of 911.

We were all lied to about the true perpetrators of 911. Just like in Hitler's Germany and in Stalin's Russia, it's all fun and games until your neighbor's eyes become filled with rage when you attempt to explain the truth to them. Did both Stalin and Hitler rely on the Idiot mob to keep the brightest and most loving citizens silent? The same has been done regarding 911 in America. At this point, getting Americans to realize that 911 was a false flag attack is like being a third grader in the special ED class breaking the news that Santa isn't real. You're going to take a beating, but you've got to get the class up to speed.

Before 911, the American people did not allow our phones to be tapped or ourselves to be treated as suspects every time we wanted to get on a plane. There's a very interesting film online called, "Invisible Empire" relating to this topic. Youtube it. We all understand the concept that super wealthy men may become hell bent on controlling the course of history. There are control freaks in this world that pursue positions of power and disregard the groups' best interests.

Is it possible that they would rig the game in order to make themselves wealthier, even if it meant blaming the 911 attacks on a proposed target? To propose that men with no conscience do not exist, is to deny first hand life experience with such people. We all know that these types of people do exist and often seek positions of power. It is possible that a group of crooks would allow an attack, and then blame it on their enemy.

We've all crossed paths with liars and cheats during the course of our lives. We either choose to continue being their victims, or stand up to them and confront their lies. The reason that we don't do this very often is that we're afraid of the confrontation. We would rather lie to ourselves, than be in a necessary confrontation with the unethical people that are bullying us. We do anything to avoid discomfort, even when the uncomfortable action is the honorable one. If we want to regain some freedoms in America then we're going to have to force some uncomfortable confrontations with the shady people that have taken over our country.

Have I ever shown up and knocked on the front door of a person that ripped me off? Yes, they respond as any little kid does, with fear and anger. Have I survived the confrontations? Yes. I've also maintained something that most Americans have lost; my dignity and self-respect.

I've forced those who have boldly ripped me off throughout the years to face me eye to eye. As a result, they fear me, not the opposite. Criminals are cowards and the public has been hypnotized by TV to believe the exact opposite. Let's force scummy shady people to lash out at us for confronting them with the truth. This is much more honorable than silently sliding into the tyranny of Orwell's nightmares.

If we want to live in a free country where good people are in charge using love, logic, and reason, (rather than fear) then some unpopular conversations have to take place in all of our lives. We need to knock on our oppressors front doors, stare them in the faces, and confront them with the truth. Posting things on Facebook is a masterbatory effort. It fails to address bad behaviors face to face.

Stare evil in the face and speak the truth. Evil will most often run out of the room, or dismiss you from their lives. After the confrontation is over, you cease to have an ongoing relationship with a bad person. The universe rewards true bravery and personal courage

44

with both immediate and future freedoms. I haven't lived a mundane and pathetic life and don't believe in groveling to unethical bosses. Staying surrounded by hopeless co-workers will only be rewarded with a lifetime of miserable servitude. Not to God, but to rich assholes that only pretend to believe in God. People's actions show whether or not they believe in God.

When I have found myself employed by completely dishonest and self-serving bosses, I call their asses out on their own shameful behaviors. For those whom have crossed paths with me, they know this to be true. I refuse to be a long-term victim that's stuck in an unfair arrangement with a wealthier asshole. Instead, I have taken risks and negotiated reasonable deals with reasonable employers that choose me because of my strengths not my weaknesses.

## – The exact tools used by a wealthy minority to dominate us

Have you ever seen something on television that you were so sure was going to be great, and then in real life it turned out to be totally different? I've seen thousands upon thousands of beer commercials that show guys drinking beer and having fun. I was trained to believe that buying their beer would make my life better. It didn't. As I drank more of their beer to improve my life, things somehow got worse. I ended up becoming addicted to the alcohol that made me temporarily dumber, more delusional, more apathetic, and lowered my standards.

Sedating myself (into a more zombie-like mental state) in order to blend in with the rest of the zombies was a terrible strategy. Thank you TV for selling me the zombie-in-a-can solution. Luckily, after a decade of using the weekly alcohol fueled escapes from reality, things finally got bad enough for me that I decided to quit drinking for a while. With the help of AA and a belief in something better than getting drunk daily my outlook on life quickly improved. If you have a dependency on alcohol, then I highly recommend quitting for long enough to break the chemical dependency and address any issues that made daily escapes from reality seem necessary.

I asked God for help and started following the advice of other people that had successfully stopped drinking as well. I did what they were doing because they not only appeared to be intelligent, but they were also extremely kind people. Now that I have escaped from the quicksand of alcohol addiction, I intend to break as many other people that are reaching out for help as possible. I'm not proposing zero alcohol for life (as many AA people insist) but I do propose quitting for long enough to regain your full brain power and address your reasons for drinking.

I understand that if somebody doesn't want help or isn't aware that their addiction has become a problem that there is no helping them, yet. First a person has to become aware of their problem and then must become willing to ask for help. Mailing out fifty million electronic food cards each month (without addressing the obvious

46

substance abuse issues of the recipients) is a big damn waste of energy.

I'm pretty sure that Stalin had a bunch of drunken Russian people receiving welfare too. Guess what, millions of Russians starved while the majority of citizens passively waited for positive socialist promises to come true. All fascist dictators promise socialist equality and abundance, and then rob the country blind during the process. That didn't work out so well for their country, did it?

It starts with getting honest that things have gotten bad in our own lives and then seeking help from others that have changed for the better. If you distrust the government and hate the idea of being dependent upon an electronic food card, then maybe you should stop copying the daily behaviors of everyone else with food cards. Does that make sense? If your life has become miserable then what do you have to lose? If your answer is nothing, then that is the greatest gift that our greedy politicians have given to the American people. They took away so much so fast from so many of us, that we are finally seeking solutions to our problems.

Billionaires can take their zombie-in-a-can and zombie-in-a-pill-bottle solutions back because I'm not buying them anymore. Are you? Dumbing ourselves down daily just to blend in is a terrible life strategy. Over the course of years you end up becoming one of the walking dead, without even knowing it. That's changing now.

Those of us that have lost everything since 2008 have finally become open to new ideas not involving snake oil that's been sold to us for years on our TVs. That is not what rich criminals running this country want. Turn off the TV programming and start ignoring the bullshit excuses that politicians and billionaires are trying to sell us (scare us all with). It's time that the masses start to get smarter, abandon the daily sedation, and get back some God-given self-respect.

Those of us that have brains, a positive attitude, and once had middle-class incomes to afford a home should not lay down while corporations attempt to treat us all like slaves for $8 an hour. That's what's happening all over America. No thank you. I'd much rather be a noisy wage slave that spreads discontent to all of the other $8 per hour suckers that were taking their beatings like dogs. I have tasted enough freedom to know better than this, and I will continue to un-program other wage slaves until reasonable wages are offered for those of us with working brains. Give me liberty, or give me death. I certainly won't be an $8 per hour wage slave for the next thirty years. Death by tyrannical government for speaking truth sounds much less painful to me.

Unfortunately, the zombie army that's limping in every grocery store is going to have to be dealt with. We have to rehabilitate these people that are clearly zonked-out. What do you call fifty million people that are only concerned about their next meal, can barely think, and attack anyone with more brains than them?

The Billionaires that own everything should never have taken away millions of mid-level jobs and shoved smart people into the same dead-end jobs alongside drug-addicted and alcoholic zombies. I am now planting seeds of logic and reason into the minds of as many wage slaves as possible, as fast as I can. Suddenly, people that would have been perfect cheap labor for another decade are now organizing, rebelling, and demanding livable wages. The fast-food workers have started to do this.

Demanding $15/hr is near retarded to start at, but the fact that fast-food workers are organizing at all is an encouraging start. Given the actual food inflation costs, I think that $10-$12 per hour would be a much more reasonable demand. Planting the idea that we deserve more rights makes once hopeless people begin to bargain for themselves. Thanks to the elites' greed, millions of once hopeless people are now working alongside smarter and braver ones. This will not stop until the whole group has obtained livable wages.

The former middle class is now advocating for people that were once below them. Thanks 1% for locking Andy Dufresne-like people inside of prison-like institutions all over the country. Will lots of warden-like business owners get backed into corners by displaced former middle-class-ers? Yep, the biggest cheats in our society are now playing chess against some very tactful under-employed employees that have no money for entertainment, and a lot more time.

These Dufresne-like people do exist and previously had no bone to pick with the greedy upper class in America. The highly

48

intelligent middle-class could plainly see that most rich people are miserable anyways, and didn't want what they had. The majority of the former middle-class just wanted a nice house in a quiet neighborhood and to be left alone. For a small percentage of those quiet God-fearing people, the sub-par treatment of our working poor neighbors in America can't be ignored, because we've experienced their nightmare. So, I will now focus my energy on empowering the lower-class. The thing about me is, when I obsess about something, I will hammer, and hammer, and hammer away at it, until it's done.

This starts with educating the lower-class about the primary tools of manipulation that have been used against us. It used to be them, but now it's us. I intend to break as many poor people as possible free from the privileged class that's been dominating us with sneaky tactics and double standards. Much of our history has been manipulated and filtered by the rich in order to control the maximum number of working-class people possible. Are you a working-class person? If you're like me then you thirst to see justice for those who only pretend to serve God.

How could such a massive event like 911 get pulled off by a small group of people and then blamed on another? This is where the history buffs and engineers get together to provide a more logical explanation. Engineers tend to be very logical and analytical people. They like to build things and figure out exactly how things work, right?

We all put our faith in the problem solving abilities of our engineers and architects every day, don't we? We have also been taught throughout our lives that history repeats itself. We are told to learn from humanities past mistakes if we don't want to repeat them. Yet, in regards to 911, we seem to be ignoring the logical conclusions of the same engineers that we otherwise trust with our lives daily.

No one goes around saying, "ignorance is strength". That ridiculous phrase came directly from the pages of the novel "1984", and was a prophetic warning to future generations. Has the American public in general become pretty ignorant? I would argue that we have indeed (but not you reading this of course). Nor your friends and family, just all of those other dirty people from the other political cult.

Your team of fat cats in suits on TV would never do you harm. What an insane line of logic that only TV watching marks would buy into.

If you haven't already read the book 1984, at the very least, take an hour and a half to watch the movie remake. There's also a more modern version of the exact same premise called "Equilibrium" that is relevant to the prescription drug epidemic that has tranquilized half of the American public. We all have friends, family, and co-workers that got sucked into the daily anti-depressant trap. Have any of these people (that we know) that are taking these heavy duty anti-depressants become healthier and more physically fit? Most don't. They probably never will while remaining (prescription) drug addicts.

The indoctrinated public in the book 1984 had been trained to act like moronic and heartless children that constantly tattle on each other, rather than question the authority figures that they served. The book perfectly illustrated how grown adults can be made to act like children. A government can successfully train its very own citizens to accept horribly oppressive living conditions without rebelling or pushing back at all. We all know this, because we see it in other countries around the world today.

The people in "1984" had been conditioned via screens on the wall that constantly gave them orders and told them how to behave. In that book the people feared their government and were terrified to speak out against it. The people were also monitored constantly by video surveillance nearly everywhere they went. Does any of this sound familiar? Anyone that dared to question the televised version of reality was immediately called a thought criminal by other "normal" people around them. Being an average person meant that you believed in Big Brother completely and had the mentality of a child.

Strangely enough, that book is no longer part of the high school reading curriculum in our public schools, weird. Only when we become conscious of a possible future can we reject it. Big Brother doesn't want well trained morons getting sound logic from classic movies or from new books. Maybe that's why there are no more movie stores and very few young people reading books.

The powers that be can't imagine that their dimwitted worker-class would even be capable of reading a full length novel. I happen to know differently. When I was well-paid, well-housed, well-fed, and well-sexed by the larger middle-class job market of 2004, books meant very little to me. Only after hard times did I develop a huge hunger for knowledge. This is now true for millions of Americans. We want out of our shitty financial situations and are open to new ideas. Knowledge is sexy, and it's increasingly obvious to everybody that our politicians are a bunch of crooks.

At the same time, Redbox has successfully closed down libraries of information from coast to coast with no replacement. The Nazis burned books and Redbox has burned down our movie stores. If you stop and think about it, movie stores were libraries of thought provoking information (in easy to digest video form). They're gone.

Sadly, Walmartians aren't getting any exposure to movies over ten years old unless they buy them. There's a reason that some movies are called classics. It makes very little sense to have a smaller and smaller video library that's easily accessible to the public as our technology increases.

There ought to be huge libraries of one dollar rentals available, because the actual DVDs are so cheap to produce, but there aren't. Why not? People under more oppressive living conditions always have less access to knowledge as their freedoms are slowly stripped away. Billionaires know that they must slowly phase-out unwanted sources of knowledge, so that the zombies won't notice.

Borders Book's stores have also been closed across the country. Those stores always seemed to be busy when I was in there. Why are they all gone? I guess that having two major competing book chains was simply too much for us all.

I'm betting that the Walmart zombies aren't returning home to libraries full of classical movies, books, or music. Even if they do have rare libraries of information, the ideas do little good for people that cannot overpower a 12oz aluminum can. If you can't function without pills coming out of a guilt-free orange bottle, then you are just as dependent upon mind altering drugs as any other drug addict that has to alter their brain chemistry daily to function. We live in a country of addicts and because of this we're getting our asses kicked.

I think that crack, heroine, and crystal meth ought to be carried around in neat little orange pill bottles with nice labels on them that are printed out and sold to you by a nicely dressed lady inside Walgreens, or CVS. If it hasn't occurred to you that we now live in a nation of heavily medicated drug addicts, then you're missing the drug distribution centers in every big grocery store in the country. So long as a doctor's name is on the orange bottle, and it says to take 3 times per day, you can pretend that you don't have a drug habit that's slowly wrecking your health.

Please stop pretending that a guy that drinks two beers a day (but takes no prescriptions) is somehow worse than somebody that pops 2 anti-anxiety pills per day. It's the same thing. Both people are ingesting a mind altering substance that is addictive. Both things make the user stop giving-a-shit about their problems. Both things tend to make your memory worsen over the course of time.

Once the pill or the drink is in the person, giving a shit about your problems, is damn near impossible. Our country is in a big God-damned mess. More than half of us appear to have those pills or that drink in our systems each and every day. We are alcoholics and drug addicts that are in denial about our own daily dependence on magic cure-all pills and drinks. While we've been on this escape from reality, things that were once normal have been disappearing without us giving a shit.

The beauty of the movie store was that people walked into a store seeking movies both new and old. Redbox has effectively erased a library of old movies that were produced in a pre-911 existence that was much less restrictive to all of us. More restrictions on good people, means less freedom. Kings used to burn the books of conquered cultures, didn't they? After 911, our modern day ruling elites have decided that us Walmart shoppers (that can't remember jack shit) ought not be looking at them there old movies. If we did, we might remember the way that things used to be. For the most part, we don't.

You don't want to evoke memories in minds of zombies of the personal freedoms that once existed in a pre-911 America. Otherwise the citizens may demand that old rights be restored. So, close nearly all of the video stores containing 90% of pre-911 movies, and the zombie public will be removed from old movies that might trigger old memories of a better way of doing things. This can happen. We did have more freedom, and it has been taken away without us voting for any of the negative changes. Did we vote for the TSA, Homeland Security, Cameras everywhere, and surveillance of everything that we do on our phones and computers?

All of us at the bottom of the pyramid can demand that certain freedoms be returned. If we do so in numbers, it will be done. Wouldn't it be nice to show your kids old movies that you didn't have to spend $10 on? This is what we used to do before Redbox killed movie stores.

Let Walmart zombies keep drooling in front of Redbox while we start shopping at real movie stores with more than one hundred choices. Redbox as our only real rental choice is equally as ridiculous as shutting down all public libraries and then placing automated machines across the country that only contain our government's favorite 100 books. Being limited to only 100 movie choices from coast to coast is a huge loss of freedom.

Psychologically, it's much harder to go online and commit to buying an old movie that you know nothing about, rather than renting it for just a day for a dollar or two. Does that make sense? Take away the public's ability to rent old movies and you've separated millions of average non-reading people from a pre-911 library. Do most of the dumbest people prefer reading books or watching movies? I tend to do what's easier.

If you were the ruling elites that brought in vastly more control after a staged terror attack; would you eliminate video libraries, or actual public libraries? Even stupid people that see old movies of a world without constant video surveillance just might demand the same level of personal freedoms as-seen in old movies. If you're an elite, and if you don't want an army of brain-dead morons to even consider what pre-911 America was once like, then you cut-off easy access to movies and TV shows showing people that had more rights than we now do.

Hey Walmart zombies, Redbox is all you're allowed to watch! Please don't watch old movies showing Americans with more rights than you have because you may get ideas from them. American people fear and obey our government just as doggedly as the citizens in 1984 did. There is actually a government funded advertising campaign that says, "If you see something, say something". Each and every government official took an oath to serve the will of the people. Have politicians kept their end of the bargain?

Our political system has been corrupted with a virus of greed and the actions (not words) of three hundred million Americans seem to say, we don't give a crap. So long as we can eat and get drunk or high each day, then someone else will handle it for us. Always counting on somebody else to be the more responsible moral authority is a bad idea. If we aren't careful, someone might take us up on our offer.

When this is done, it will be the stupidest of our neighbors that are used to police us (while the country continues to go downhill). Everyone else that disagrees with the next set of restrictions for our safety will be outnumbered by a mob of idiots that blindly obeys the man on TV. This is what happened in Nazi Germany, Communist Russia, and can be seen at your local airport today.

From personal experience, after just a few beers each day, it's very hard to give a crap about anything. Also, a family member of mine admitted to me that a prescribed anti-depressant made her feel nothing when someone that she had greatly cared about had died. She quit taking it because she recognized her complete absence of humanity (while pacified by pills). Emotions are a gift. It's hard to experience the electricity of love if you numb yourself daily.

The TV advertised solutions to our problems have robbed us of our humanity. The somewhat crappy B-movie "Equilibrium" does show the nightmarish existence that we're headed towards as our sell-out doctors throw Prozac at all of our problems. It is ok to feel all of the human emotions. We are supposed to experience both ups and downs in life because the lows make the highs so much higher.

How are the majority of citizens supposed to make our democracy better if half of us have been robbed of caring about anything? Our medical doctors have really let down the American people by writing a prescription for every TV hypnotized zombie that walks through their door. When someone says, "I'm feeling really down" what about telling them the truth? Maybe you feel like crap because you weigh 300 pounds.

If the doctors weren't selling us out, then they would confront people's real problems (and probably lose them as patients) for telling the truth. Doctors that lose patients for telling the truth in a society full of delusional fat people, lose money. Then, they may default on massive student loans. We can't have that or they may start to have a destroyed credit report like the rest of the working class zombies do. Our doctors have become high-class drug dealers that will prescribe away your health to maintain their pampered existences.

Our doctors give their addicted patients whatever they ask for, rather than telling them what is really wrong. What a crazy idea for a doctor to improve their patients' health. Instead, they pay-off massive student loans, maintain perfect credit, and drive a BMW; that's what our doctors are mostly concerned about, credit, car, and lifestyle. Our doctors have sold out the zombie public to save their own sorry asses.

The people that are currently America's upper class don't just have a problem with not respecting the public, they don't even respect themselves. Hundreds of millions of us are allowing a small handful of con-men suffering a spiritual void to steer the ship towards disaster. Clearly the ruling elites' actions have illustrated that money and power are their greatest pursuits in life. These vain attempts of people with a spiritual void are leading to our societal meltdown. The founding fathers of America weren't 100 times wealthier than the average citizens.

We are all so fast to blame republicans, or democrats, or poor people, instead of the elites that have grabbed after everything. While doing so, we are leaving out one very important party, ourselves. We are largely to blame for counting on these other people to improve our lives. We must first restore our own health before anyone will start respecting us, or listening to a word that we say.

People buy stuff from the people that they want to become. People all nod their heads and pretend to listen to the fat delusional person in front of them, while thinking that they are totally full of crap. Like all of the other fat Walmart shoppers that long ago lost self-control; if you're a TV addicted overweight American attempting to help other people via verbal advice, then you might as well be a zombie that's groaning at other zombies. They don't hear shit, and you're not helping anyone.

The people that are programming your poor stupid neighbors via television are the ones that you need to go after. How? Show your neighbors something that they want and inform them that removing themselves from the TV programming, prescription pills, and constant alcohol, is how to get it. Poor people do whatever they are trained to do. So, change who it is that's doing the programming. Pawns fighting pawns is a big damn waste of time. Only when you become so healthy and so attractive that zombies are drawn to you, can you begin to unplug them from their current controllers.

You can't attack an army of programmed zombies because they are simply operating as programmed. They are going to keep running their programs, and there are too damn many of them. You must attack the programmer that programs them all. In the year 2014, anyone that believes in the republican vs. democrat paradigm, is currently part of the billionaires' zombie army. If you truly want out of the matrix, then you'll have to fully unplug yourself as described in this book. The results will be shocking. You won't be disappointed with the changes that happen to your body, your brain, and within your heart.

Surely you can agree that millions of Russian citizens walked around believing that Stalin was the good guy, right? The same went for Adolf Hitler in the eyes of the German beer-drinking people. If those guys hadn't successfully programmed the public to follow their programs, then the people wouldn't have participated in a superpower of the dictators' making, but they did. We are no less at risk of being programmed ourselves. The good news is, you are being un-programmed right now.

The Germans were not stupid, but they sure did drink often. What about the Russians? If you became aware that someone has hacked into your head and has been controlling your actions, would you want to cut the connection? I am proposing a possible way to unplug the line between you and the master programmers of our entire society.

Zombie Americans that simply repeat the republican or democrat talking points, are still buying the magicians trick. Believing that democrat or republican makes any difference at all, pretty much confirms that you're running on TV programming. Democrats blame republicans, and vice versa, leaving the Billionaire programmers of all public policy, untouched. More than half of the public is completely dissatisfied with our government, all of the time.

Zbigniew Brzezinski is the brains behind Obama's TV character. Men like Mr. Brzezinski and Henry Kissenger are the ones that have steered our society in the direction that we are now going. In fact, they are so cocky and believe that the public is so stupid, that they've written books announcing their exact plans. This is fact, and you can read their books. They do exist.

If you really don't get that they look down upon the public as a bunch of programmable zombies, then you're mistaken. The guys in office actually get-off on how badly they can lie to us without us even noticing. I was a salesman for years of my life and I definitely witnessed other salesman that only seemed happy while ripping the customers off. Haven't you met people like that before?

The way that politicians speak to the public on TV is exactly how the con-men salesmen I've personally known spoke to their victims. These are the type of people that are only happy if they are getting away with something. Haven't you ever met someone that's always attempting to better their position, no matter how good they have it? These architects of our society will continue asserting more control over the public for as long as we allow them to. Nothing shy of complete global control and world domination will satisfy them.

We cannot allow people like this to continue selling us on the idea that we need more and more police and surveillance everywhere. Otherwise, we will be living in a completely controlled society with no freedoms at all. The next big goal is to have troops on our streets, and have the public <u>welcome</u> it.

How?  The same assholes that want troops on our streets would allow ISIS to attack on American soil, and then insist that martial law is needed.  Why?  They don't want you getting lippy when they dissolve your 401k account and cut Social Security benefits in half, in the near future.  Detroit cut its people's retirement benefits recently due to bankruptcy, and nothing happened.  Do you not get that the federal government is also going bankrupt right now?  Have you heard about Homeland Security purchasing 1.6 Billion rounds of hollow point bullets?  Sounds like zombie ammo to me.  Seven Billion people cannot allow a few thousand people to hoard all of the world's resources for themselves while holding guns to the rest of our heads.

Millions of Americans should have been out in the streets the day that our supreme court ruled that a corporation was equal to a person, but we weren't.  Those corporations can now contribute unlimited funds to any candidate without public disclosure.  In January of 2010, our government officially told us all that corporations can now legally buy any election.  Only a country full of zombies on pills would accept a policy change that huge without rejecting it.

Until January 2010, there were limits that protected the American people from being outspent in political campaigns by mega-powerful corporations.  This is one of the most ludicrous rule changes imposed on the drunken public after the post 911 apocalypse.  We once had a framework of freedom and protections against tyranny known as the Constitution.  It only works in country that has citizens with working brains, hearts, and some courage.  Do you presently see a smart, honest, and courageous public?

Clearly the constitution states that our elected officials must obey the will of the people.  Are they?  Be honest, are our "elected" officials acting in the best interests of the American people?  Or, have corporations and the elites completely taken over our government?  We all know the answer, but we're all too afraid to confront the con-men that keep ripping us all off.

We are controlled by profit making machines, rather than by rational people that care about the groups' well being.  I'm not comforted when the Walgreen's workers tell me to, "Be well" just like the disarmed and spineless future Americans featured in sly Stallone's "Demolition Man". Try going to Redbox for that movie, it's not there.

We all know that America is up shit creek, but have no idea what to do about it. We have been programmed and intentionally sedated to do nothing while this happens. If you want to help America, then start by changing yourself in a way that boosts your own level of confidence first. The directions on how to unplug from the control system are very straight forward. You have the free will to choose whether to unplug yourself or not. The controllers think that you are too damn dumb and too damn hypnotized to walk over to your cable box and unplug it. Prove them wrong and take back control of your own mind.

I'm not telling people to do things my way, but I am proposing that there is a solution for people that are unhappy with the direction that our country has gone. People that have successfully unplugged from the programming end up with less fear, less anger, more energy, and a greater spiritual connection. Not church people spirituality, and not pill-bottle spirituality, but something that strangers will see and will want. Once your own consciousness has been boosted, others will begin to want what you have and become willing to change their behaviors to get it. This is how we save America. This is how you can change the world.

We must empower ourselves first. If we continue refusing to change ourselves for the better first, then a minority of super greedy people will continue dictating a lower quality of life to a bunch of hypnotized zombies. That zombie army will be ordered to eliminate people with brains and resources one day. So you'd better get busy un-programming them if you don't want them pounding on your door in the middle of the night in the not-so-distant future. It has happened before.

Stupid people can be trained to do anything. Because of this, stupid Americans are an important issue that you, I, and everybody else should be concerned about. These are valuable people that can be unplugged from their TV programming, weaned off of their drinking and drug habits, and brought back to full consciousness again. It can be done. We need them on our team, not the dictator's. It's time for a nationwide intervention. It starts with you becoming an attractive person that they'll listen to. If they want what you have, they'll listen.

What do you think Nazi Germany was like for the wealthy Jewish people right before things got really bad? Are you really telling me that all fifty million Americans on food stamps are fully conscious, physically fit, healthy, and enlightened people? How about we all demand drug testing for food stamps? This kind of logical change is something that the majority of hard working Americans would likely support.

We must face the underlying issues that have created a country full of self-pity filled victims. Those were exactly the drunken Germans that were handed sharp looking uniforms and used to carry out anything that their government told them to. What do you think the TSA is becoming?

Do you know how many employees that the TSA now has, along with the department of Homeland Security? There is literally an army of TSA and Homeland Security agents that are heavily armed (tanks included). There are videos of trains shipping tanks across the U.S. during the last two years. What do you think the average IQ is for all of these new homeland security agents? How many of them are on power trips and will do anything that they are ordered to do?

Do you know how many of them are uneducated and have drinking and drug habits? How many of Hitler's Nazis do you think had drinking and drug habits too? The German economy had been crap for ten years before moronic citizens would do anything for a high wage and a sharp uniform. What will drug addicts and alcoholics do in order to continue funding their habits and feeding their families?

What percentage of Americans would now qualify as prescription drug addicts, or alcoholics? Do you really understand exactly how far along our country has been taken in a similar direction? Do you even think that the majority of TSA agents are capable of reading this entire book from start to finish? Do you think that the Nazi soldiers that were used to conquer Germany were well-read and had high IQ's?

Clearly the politicians and billionaires have been outmaneuvering the public. If you want vampire speed then you've got to stop following the slow zombie diet. Stop getting outrun by faster people with more brains and speed. If you like the idea of a much faster processer in your own head (and a better body) then I am telling you exactly how to get it. If we weren't being outsmarted by these people, then only a few of them wouldn't be in charge of all of us, but they are.

If we had more intelligence, then rich politicians on TV would no longer be dictating directions to us. The same could be said for the police that are just as TV-programmed to protect rich assholes while pepper-spraying average citizens for speaking the truth. Police are good people with good intentions. If all police completely stopped watching TV and refused the slow zombie diet, then they too would realize that they are being used to protect evil men (and are completely expendable). Nobody protesting scumbag bankers would get pepper-sprayed by TV-free police officers, because they would be conscious of their actions rather than blindly following brutal orders.

When picturing food stamp people, do you picture someone that is physically fit, quick-witted, and spreading joy wherever they go? Do you think most of these people believe that they create their own destiny, or are victims of circumstance? We all know the truthful answers to these questions.

What percentage of food stamp recipients do you think are alcoholics and drug addicts? How many hours a day of TV do you think food-stamp zombies are watching? If you don't like this happening, then unplug them for God sakes. What do you think that this book is doing to you right now?

I'm sure being an alcoholic or drug addict has no effect on your level of hopefulness, or on your ability to solve problems, does it? At some point, an insane person is faced with the premise that they have lost their sanity. If you have completely lost control of your drinking or use constant prescribed pills to feel "normal", then at some level, you have lost control of your mind. If this wasn't the truth, then you would not need the daily drinks, or the daily pill sedation to deal with your perception of reality.

Unemployed Americans don't realize that it's your TV that has created the present belief system in your head. If your present belief system has you sitting at home unemployed and feeling sorry for yourself, than it's time to unplug from the current system by simply unplugging the cable box. By doing this, you can begin to install new beliefs into your new operating system. This change will produce a healthier you with a more powerful brain. This new operating system will actually begin to solve your problems and your life will start to get better.

The new brain power will allow you to out-compete the other TV hypnotized zombies. Your brain and body will operate like a virus free computer system, fast. Consider watching television like visiting virus infected porno sites that already wrecked your old computer. If you want a fast processor in your head that allows you to create a better body, then refuse to tune into virus-infested television programming. The politicians on TV cannot lie to you, if you aren't watching them. Does that make sense? This is how you begin to regain control of your life.

Whether we vote Republican or Democrat, the minority of super wealthy will continue to simply tell the President what to tell the zombies. As long as we're all tuned in to our TVs, we the zombies will slowly move in the desired direction. To pretend that half brain-dead people aren't littered all over the place is to deny the slow-moving and bloated people that you see every day. How on earth could the whole scam be ended by something so simple as everyone unplugging our TVs for a whole month? Could it really be that simple?

George Carlin has a stand-up routine that clearly points out the obvious sham of the current political system. Mr. Carlin was not afraid to speak truth regarding the true ownership of not only the current American political system, but billionaires' common belief that they own you. I think a quick YouTube search of George Carlin and the words, "they own you" ought to prove my point.

How dumb do we have to be to keep falling for the same trick year after year and decade after decade? We must face the truth, come to accept the truth, and only then can we actually do something about it. How many times have the American people voted one Presidential party out of office, only to have things get worse when the new leadership takes charge?

It's like we all have a big bully that asks us if we would like to be punched in the face, or punched in the stomach. Either way, we're all getting punched and having our lunch money stolen by a group of frat boys in nice suits. No matter who wins half of the country is totally pissed-off by it. The other half that did win gets totally double-crossed, by their very own team. Of course the winning team (losing public) is too proud to admit that their candidate completely abandoned all values after being elected.

We're all like married people that have an openly cheating spouse and we all stay silent because we're still in a decent house in a good neighborhood. Fear of ending up in worse place to live, or worse, can't find a job and end up homeless is what keeps us all quiet. Really, we have lost respect for ourselves, and our cheating politicians know it (and love it). Cheating has never been so easy for them.

For how long does this obvious scam have to continue? I now live in a country where a bunch of mentally impaired adults keep on going along with a con-game that only less-than average people would buy. We are all equally valuable human beings that share a common planet and common interests. Please YouTube the following video that explains how we have let things get so bad without even noticing: KGB Bezmenov 1985 - Four Steps to Subversion of a Nation. Listen to the smugness of the man explaining how it works (because he knows that it will work again).

The children of tyrants and known criminals do not deserve to control the rest of us with stolen wealth. As a group we must come to grips that these same royal bloodlines have used television to perpetuate the very belief that they are more special than the rest of us. They're not. They are just people and are equally as fallible, flawed, and unimportant to the universe as the rest of us.

If the actual TV programming didn't paint the picture of just how powerful they are and how powerless we are, then maybe we would figure out that it's all an illusion. Millions and billions of us have vastly more power than only a few thousand of them worldwide.

63

This is a fact. They only rule over the masses with perceived power. When 7 billion people decide that a new way of life is needed, it will happen.

If Aliens were to show up here on earth today and we attempted to tell them that we were a vastly intelligent and highly evolved species of which billions suffered (while a few thousand of equal intelligence and strength ruled over the rest of us) they would laugh in our faces! Most Americans have an ego that will defend their slave masters at the previous statement. After all, we've been subjected to a lifetime of conditioning (like dogs) to defend our masters (no matter how poor we're getting). Did this not already happen to millions of people in Stalin's Russia?

If there is a God and some sort of higher existence above and beyond the world that we can see, isn't it possible that higher intelligences would attempt to reveal the control system that is oppressing billions of us? Our discovery of new ideas and acceptance of new concepts has improved our quality of life throughout recorded history. Do you really think that the current owners holding control of the masses would be eager to let go? Do abusive spouses easily let go? The good news is that humanity far outnumbers the few bad eggs that have been abusing our group.

The public has been carefully trained to ridicule new ideas that could teach us how to turn off the wizard's movie projector. A few really greedy billionaires have created an army of idiots (not you of course) to do their bidding. The elites don't care if they destroy the middle class and the millionaires that helped make America great. In return for offering me a lifetime of poverty for refusing to hurt people for money, I am now happy to teach all of the most heavily indoctrinated wage slaves exactly how to unplug themselves from the current control system. Humanity is good, and I intend to help.

History channel has purposefully been showing lengthy documentaries about Hitler's rise to power and the poor economic conditions prior to Germany's great change. Hitler and the other Nazi leaders were extremely interested in the use of propaganda. The Nazi's proved beyond the shadow of a doubt that huge groups of previously normal human beings could be manipulated to do just about anything by a tiny number of clever (evil) people. Millionaires need to start identifying and unplugging poor people from the main source of propaganda (TV) before history repeats itself. We are much closer to full blown tyranny with troops on our streets than the public realizes.

German people that became Nazis didn't go on to do all of those terrible things because it was their childhood dream; they were skillfully manipulated by others to act out terrible behaviors. Hitler proved beyond the shadow of a doubt that the human mind can easily be programmed to do anything. Regardless of how selfish and destructive the master is, when a human being is fed the right formula of beliefs then he will act accordingly. Do you think that TSA agents patting down little kids with clean cut middle class parents is a normal behavior? It's pathetic. We're being conditioned to feel like inmates while the additional cameras, guards, and rules are being constructed right in front of us.

There are quotes from Hitler and his high ranking SS officers speaking about the use of propaganda. They boldly said things like, "Even if we tell a lie, if we say it enough times, it becomes the truth". How many times have we caught our own politicians doing the same thing? When exactly are we going to sober ourselves up for long enough to face the truth that we have been in an abusive relationship with assholes in suits?

How many married people do you know that only stay in their relationships due to low self-respect or more appropriately, fear? It's never comfortable or easy to end serious relationships. However, the benefits and self-respect that go along with doing the right thing are well worth the short-term pain and discomfort. It's much better to be in pain for a week, than remain a slave for a lifetime. We all know people that are suffering long term pain with miserable people or jobs. We only have ourselves to blame when "stuck" in these situations due to our own lack of personal courage.

I remember seeing a bumper sticker on a beat up late model Oldsmobile that said, "Stuck in Cleveland" just before I left town. I told everyone around me in that hopeless city that I was going on a 1000 mile journey to a better job market. All of the oppressed Clevelanders (low-income majority) quickly justified to me why they couldn't do the same. Over and over again people said that I was lucky, and then immediately hurled an excuse that cemented them in their bad situations for life. It was like the land of a thousand excuses. My God did I hear constant self-pity during my one year stay in 2012.

Millions of Americans keep running back to the comfort of the bottle because they are too afraid to face the truth regarding their own lousy job, spouse, or self. It is now time that this changes. It's time for us to stand up for ourselves as a united people with common interests at stake. There are universal laws of cause and effect that apply to all of us. How we treat others and our own level of bravery or cowardliness is directly reflected back at us, over the course of a lifetime. Short term events both good and bad do take place, but our reaction to these events and our choices thereafter are what determine our destiny. We must accept that we are building our reality, one decision at a time.

However, those living in corrupt areas where the majority of people act completely selfish will not get positive feedback for positive behaviors. The positive action in that scenario is to walk away when you're badly outnumbered. Not all battles on all fronts can be won. If you find yourself surrounded by miserable people that all seem to be experiencing hellish situations, then you may be living in a hell hole. If you come to believe that you don't deserve to be in hell, then leave.

Once we can finally admit that we have been lied to by our leaders for years, then, we can actually start formulating a solution. We must shrink our ego in order to admit that someone has successfully manipulated us. It's not fun to admit that someone else got one over on us, but it's better than living in denial. No one likes admitting that they've been duped, but I know for sure that I was.

When the best and brightest architects and engineers start speaking out against the official (government official) 911 story, we need to start hearing them out. At this point we're all like the third grade special education class arguing with fourth graders over the existence of Santa. We are all so God-damned sure of ourselves. At the same time, pro wrestling is totally real to us and we completely depend on somebody else to pack our lunches and tie our shoes daily.

I worked for six months at a special needs facility, and the staff members were barely more intelligent than the patients, by design. Maximum patient escalations equal maximum state funding per patient (to upper management's bank accounts). Oh how humanity has evolved.

Breaking through years of brilliantly orchestrated mind control via television is not an easy task, but it's happening right now. Walls constructed by assholes are being demolished at a rapid pace. Once somebody becomes willing to listen, then we can shine a light on when, where, and why our country was lied to.

We may have been tricked on 911 by a handful of politicians to behave in a way that they desired. Have we ever caught our politicians in a big fat lie before? What is so different about this particular subject? False Flag attacks have been used by governments and kings throughout history in order to sway public opinion and control the masses. These attacks directly benefit the perpetrator of the staged event while blaming the attack on a proposed target. This is perhaps one of the darkest sides of human history that we must face in order to empower ourselves now (and ruin a billionaires day). Evil men should fear us, not fleece us.

Pretending that no monsters have infiltrated our own government is just as ridiculous as pretending that no monsters infiltrated our most sacred and holy of places (churches). If evil sick men were able to hide in the Catholic Church and dress up as holy men, then they could certainly hide in the shady world of politics. Clearly man has demonstrated that a small percentage of sick people will pursue honorable positions (showing no fear of God). God-fearing people need to stop projecting their own consciences onto a small group of men that have none left. Humanity is greatly guilty of this mistake. We keep on projecting our sense of right and wrong onto the criminal politicians and bankers that are dominating us. It's time that this comes to an end. We all deserve better than this.

If Hitler and the Nazis successfully pulled-off such a stunt against the German people, then, it is very plausible that it could be done in any country now. Just a handful of corrupt Politicians are all that it would take to pull-off a False Flag attack. Don't we sometimes refer to German engineering when speaking of the best and the brightest?

Surely you would have a hard time arguing that German scientists were not considered to be smart. We now know that Nazi scientists were brought to the US after World War II had ended. They were brought here to help us compete against the Russians. This is a fact.

NASA and the United States space program was headed by an ex-Nazi scientist named Wernher von Braun. This is a fact, and the American public should be fully aware of Project Paperclip. The German people that got tricked by Hitler's False Flag attack (using the Reichstag Fire which swayed public opinion toward Hitler's secret agenda) weren't dummies (but they were tricked none the less). The American people are not all dummies either, but it is entirely possible that we too were tricked on 911.

A famous speaker named David Icke has recently coined the phrase "Problem, Reaction, Solution" to describe exactly how corrupt politicians can use staged terror events to sway public opinion in any direction that they want to. No, none of us would ever do such a thing, but most of us also wouldn't run for office, would we? We all seem to acknowledge that the political world is full of liars and crooks. None of us normal people would do any of this, but we have witnessed bad people in good positions throughout our lifetime. It does happen and the rest of us that do have consciences must force dishonest men's lies into the light.

It is so painfully simple to understand how False Flags are used. If you YouTube it and then try to approach the subject with an open mind then you'll likely find credibility in what I'm talking about. There are strong implications that the Gulf of Tonkin incident was also a False Flag operation used by the US government to justify Vietnam. That is a huge deal but is completely missing from the data files in most American brains. Do you get that the American people need a good reason to be willing to send their own kids off to war?

Barring an attack, selling the American public on the idea that a few wealthy men will get a lot wealthier would not be enough to justify war. We won't risk the lives of our own lower and middle class kids if our emotions haven't been stirred up sufficiently. That is where the False Flag operation comes in handy for our loving slave masters, I mean politicians to use on us all. War has been used to grab cheap resources from foreign countries (for the benefit of the super wealthy only) for thousands of years. Things have not changed very much, because the common morons fail to see the manipulation, but you're likely seeing a little more already aren't you?

If we are all told that we were attacked by terrorists from a foreign country (that just so happens to have something our owners want) then we're all for it! Boy have we been a bunch of rubes. I don't want to be a rube, but I certainly can <u>admit</u> that I have been duped into supporting wars as seen on TV.

I remember watching Desert Storm on TV and cheering against Saddam Hussein. What most people don't know is that our U.S. government had funded and backed Mr. Hussein, and only later, double-crossed him. Look this up, and find out if I'm telling the truth.

In the name of money, a few bad billionaires may be capable of lying to the rest of us. The public acts as if there are no politicians capable of this when dismissing 911 claims. As far as my lifetime has taught me, rich men wearing suits are capable of anything. There are both good and bad people that exist across all walks of life. Evil is a strong closer, no matter how far-fetched the to-good-to-be-true deal offered to the marks (public) may be. The bigger the lie is, the greater the line of sheeple forming to accept it becomes. You are being removed from the sheep shearing assembly line right now.

When a person gains a greater understanding of how something works, they become enlightened on that particular subject. When we come across extremely intelligent individuals that happen to understand how many things work, we often refer to them as bright. Bright people can learn many new things, retain information, and then solve a huge variety of problems with ease (compared to slow-moving Walmart zombies accepting welfare checks). As with every deal with the devil, the welfare recipients will be forced to support full-blown tyranny, or lose their checks. Too good to be true, does not exist. We must work hard if we expect to be rewarded accordingly.

Do you think that a slow moving and bloated Walmart zombie (sadly rolling past you in their scooter chair) has laid out this set of revelations? Do you believe that they are pro-government handout for the rest of their lifetime or not? Do you want to work 40+ hours a week for the rest of your life to support "disabled" fat people?

Those same people receiving monthly get-out-of-work free checks are about to start voting away all of our freedoms at a rapid pace. They wouldn't hesitate to vote Constitutionalists and any non-party members to be sent straight off to the FEMA camps, in order to keep that magic disability check. What would the angels say about welfare cheats?

Do these half-conscious addicts have a vested interest to keep on supporting the government approved 911 story, or not? You do see that if a corrupt government gets taken apart by honest people, than all of those that are cheating the system will lose their free meal tickets, right? So, the least healthy and the least honest will be the strongest resistance to the truth. If someone is slow moving and annoying you in public, then start talking to them about 911. Hand them a copy of this book. If you're disgusted with their laziness and gluttony, then please attempt to help them.

If there were very easy to follow instructions on how to become much brighter, then most people would want the instructions. Well, not exactly if you look at the actions of many Americans that seem to be hopeless and lost these days. How did this happen to us? How did America become a place where people seem proud, to be stupid? Weird Al Yankovic hit it right on the head with his Devo (de-evolution) tribute song, "Dare To Be Stupid".

Is it possible that the elites have successfully placed walls between average Americans and increased intelligence? What if the people at the very tippy top of the financial pyramid, referred to the people at the bottom as "the walking dead"? Would that bother you?

I believe that the content of this book has the power to bring down the walls that have been carefully constructed by the very few to control and oppress the many. Greedy assholes have purposefully separated the public from their God-given potentials. They deserve to lose their power because they've been cheating against the rest of us.

In a universe of cause and effect, when you cheat using mass hypnosis, then eventually the zombies will turn on you.

Human beings all over the world have been oppressed very heavily with a steady diet of fear, stress, drugs, and alcohol. All sold to us in large by what we have been told is entertainment on our TVs. Through the zombie diet the elites have successfully knocked down our levels of consciousness to the bottom of our true human potentials. Those of us operating at this spiritual minimum are indeed referred to as, "the walking dead" by upper-level Free Masons.

Do you get the tremendously ironic Joke about one of America's most popular TV series? We're actually watching a show about ourselves in the eyes of the "enlightened" ones that own everything. We're like a big herd of cattle that loves watching a TV show about only slightly less healthy cattle getting shot in the head for an hour each week. Moooooooh!

Why do zombie Americans also seem to love watching other weak people get ripped off on History Channel all day long? Seriously, why are fat tattooed assholes that rip people off all day (and wear sun glasses indoors) on our History Channel? Maybe it's to document the historical account of how decent honest Americans stood by (like cattle) while fat tattooed pieces of crap (that completely lack a conscience) have stepped into the new management class of America. This is the televised liquidation of fallen American assets.

Whenever there's a bunch of drunks and drug addicts living in a particular part of a city, what types of stores start popping up on every street corner? Did it ever occur to you that your favorite TV show may really just be a training video for defeated Americans? It's to prepare you not to be afraid of the fat tattooed man in all black at the sheering station. These shows are humanizing the parasitic people that are about to sheer your poor drunk and drug addicted ass. These TV shows are zombie training videos. You can turn off the training whenever you want. Just unplug your TV and stop doing what the other weak people are doing. You are no longer a victim, the programs are being broken.

Masonic Lodges appear in cities and suburbs throughout the country. They are associated with the free masons and illuminati that anyone attempting to talk about is ridiculed for until recently. In the Masonic lodges individuals that work their way up the scale of enlightenment also refer to spiritually unaware people as dogs.

Checkerboard floors are also a symbol that pokes fun at the ignorant public. The checker board pattern infers that we are pawns being controlled on somebody else's chess board. Do you want to be somebody else's pawn? The Internet and even the History Channel has opened the flood gates regarding the existence of secret societies controlling vast wealth in the US. Also note that our troops that are on the front lines in wars for the elites wear dog tags.

There are plenty of God-fearing and well intentioned human beings that belong to these secret organizations. The majority of their members are at lower ranks much like people at the bottom of a corporation. Most Masons have no idea what the people at the top are actually up to. Low-level Masons are misinformed of what the people at the top of the organization are ritualistically worshipping, Lucifer. Yup, you read that right. The top level Masons worship Lucifer, an angel of light according to them and Scottish Right Free Mason founder, Albert Pike.

A very infamous character named Aleister Crowley happened to be a 33$^{rd}$ degree Free Mason and had heavy occult ties. History Channel has a show called Brad Meltzer's Decoded that actually proved that the Statue of Liberty is actually a Masonic symbol that portrays Lucifer, the angel of light. Do you get why the masonic lodges all over the United States don't talk about what it is that they are worshipping?

The Free Masons and the illuminati have kept their societies secret from public awareness for hundreds of years. George W. Bush and John Kerry are recent high-level officials that belong to the Skull and Bones Society (Illuminati) at Yale University. It turns out that many Presidents and politicians are members of this secret good-ole-boy network that just so happens to practice occult rituals (just like Hitler and the Nazis did). Once again, twenty years ago nobody would have accepted that tons of priests around the world were molesting altar boys, but molest they did.

This sounds outrageous right? Google it. Please check for yourself to discover the non-televised version of reality. Very powerful scumbags have been sneaking around for way too long and it's time that the truth is revealed to everybody. We are grown adults and we can handle this. These guys aren't having bake sales to raise money for new bowling shirts. They worship a different God than the rest of us do and it's not a God that allows for a strong conscience.

We are talking about wealthy men practicing dark rituals and requesting help from negative entities (not God) to aid them in dominating the rest of us. They really believe in this stuff, and we keep allowing them to make decisions for our group. This is the exact same belief system that Hitler and the Nazis were extremely interested in and practiced as well.

Good people that believe in God need to remove these men from power. When we started finding out that priests were molesting boys we investigated, found the hidden truth, and booted their asses out. I think it's now time that the same is done for devil-worshipping rich dudes that incredibly, do exist.

Super wealthy men in these secret societies have kept this stuff secret for a reason. Generally, when people are doing something really good for their group, their ego wants to receive praise right? We all want to gain acceptance from the group that we belong to. Throughout our entire lifetime what type of deeds do we normally keep secret from the rest of the world?

If the Free Masons are up to good deeds that benefit all of mankind, then why don't they come out and show us all? I'm guessing because selfish and self-serving behaviors are taking place. Which option sounds more logical to you? It's about time that you turn off the 3 hour football game (excuse to get drunk) and start addressing the evil men that are threatening the futures of your children.

It all sounds so completely unbelievable. However, if you actually research Bohemian Grove then you'll quickly find that some of our elites have some very dark secrets. Ignorance is not bliss. If there happens to be some rich dudes that are worshipping some dark idol that encourages them to behave without a conscience, then the

American public ought to know about it. We need to do something about this now. Watching TV for three hours a night and getting drunk is not going to change anything for the better.

I like knowing the truth, even if it turns out to be very ugly. We cannot improve things until we know what's actually going on. If you research this subject at all then you will find a mountain of information giving credence to these claims. Cows that never investigate what's on the other side of the fence deserve to be slaughtered (according to our leaders).

We are not supposed to be behaving like livestock (docile, dumb, and unaware that someone else sees us as nothing other than a source of energy). We have been pacified with booze, drugs, and a television that dominates 85% of the population's ability to reason. The top 15% of the brightest individuals are still able to critically think while watching TV and movies. The other 85% is toast after just a few minutes. Most of those Walmart zombies are toast and you know it.

Your ego jumps up and says, "Oh, that's me, I'm the 15% that is immune to TV's hypnotic effect". Really? Have you always scored in the top 15% of your class? Have you ever met a really stupid person that was completely unaware of how truly stupid they were?

This is supposed to be the "ah hah" moment where if you didn't always score at the top of your class with ease, and you watch hours of TV per day, then you're likely one of the zombies that's currently hypnotized. If you want to be free, this is an excellent time to walk over to your TV and unplug it. I was once a beer-merican zombie myself. One day, something beyond my understanding gave me the impulse to unplug my TV. From that point on, the world was transformed from certain disaster into a brighter world that's going to make it! My mental chains were broken just as yours are being now.

# Chapter 5 – Consciousness, how to increase it, and things that kill it

Clearly our world has some individuals that worship money and power. Changing others violates their free will and is usually a big damn waste of energy that always backfires. It makes more sense to focus on small things in our own life. If there are super wealthy people that have become drunk with power, then their corrupted egos have justified to them that they are entitled to control the rest of us (for as long as they're alive). We are going to have to save our own asses by acquiring knowledge and raising our own level of consciousness beyond the normal 85% of TV-hypnotized zombies.

What is consciousness? It's your level of awareness, perception, self-control, and the ability to assess a situation using your heart-based conscience (not fear). People at very high levels of consciousness are governed by a very large conscience making it nearly impossible to lie. These people tend to be at peace with mankind, lack fear, and use love as their primary reaction to life. They will not screw over their fellow man in order to benefit them self, because their conscience won't allow it. We do know people like this. We all know some people that are simply more honest than what's normal. They do exist.

To develop a truly high level of consciousness is to become a truly unselfish person, but not a doormat. Surely you can think of some human beings throughout history that were willing to sacrifice their own lives for a cause that gave more rights to the masses like Abraham Lincoln, Gandhi, Martin Luther King Jr., and Jesus to name a few. These were real people that fought on behalf of the best interests of Humanity and honest Abe was no pussy.

How many of us feel completely overwhelmed and choose to hide in our homes and avoid the public as much as possible, unless buzzed or all pilled-up into confidence? For really smart people, alcohol is the magic elixir that allows you to blend in with the 85%ers without them attacking the crime of too much thought. If you were completely sober and attempted to start reasoning with the sedated 85% ers then you're likely going to get yelled at.

Your psychologically defeated neighbors are simply following their training (just like the German and Russian citizens once did). It did happen back then, and has happened in America since 911.

We are not supposed to be sedating ourselves to accommodate hypnotized idiots that will attack anyone who violates their politician approved TV programming. Not-give-a-shit in a can is not proving to be a good nationwide solution to the American zombie epidemic. Our country has grown dumber, and fast.

In oppressive places and in stressful situations we naturally revert backwards to our primal instincts. That's exactly what has happened in America following 911. When people get badly stressed out they tend to act like primates that are mostly concerned with food, sex, and shelter. Corrupt government leaders know this and have used TV to inject a constant stream of <u>fear</u> into the public's heads. Most elderly Americans watch tons of TV and are extremely fearful citizens as a result. This is explained by Maslow's Hierarchy of Needs pictured on the next page:

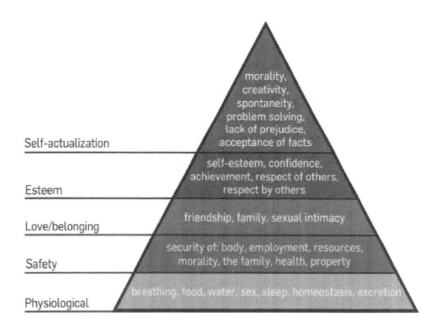

Self-actualization
— morality, creativity, spontaneity, problem solving, lack of prejudice, acceptance of facts

Esteem
— self-esteem, confidence, achievement, respect of others, respect by others

Love/belonging
— friendship, family, sexual intimacy

Safety
— security of: body, employment, resources, morality, the family, health, property

Physiological
— breathing, food, water, sex, sleep, homeostasis, excretion

Out of 7 billion people on earth, how many do you think have achieved security of their own property, health, family, morality, and employment? Does our planet deserve a passing or a failing grade?

We do have people that we call our world leaders right? If a super intelligent and spiritually gifted group of ETs landed on earth today, do you think that they would find humanity to be more like highly intelligent beings of logic, love, and creativity; Or hairless monkeys that just learned how to speak?

The actual numbers of people on the bottom of the pyramid would more likely tip the scale towards monkeys that can talk. Isn't it about time that all of us "walking dead" at the bottom of the pyramid started raising our consciousness in order to bust through the walls that have been separating us from safety, security, love, esteem, and self-actualization? Those walls are being broken now.

The act of maintaining frequent sobriety from alcohol and pills is now a rejection of the control system that we now live in. Staying sober forever is not the goal, just for today, and each day after until we force scumbags in suits on television out of power. It can happen and we can do this. Their worst nightmare is waking up one day to find a world of citizens that has quit believing their lies. It's happening now and the world elites are panicking. Each next stunt to scare us all, is failing.

Once they are no longer in charge of us, we can celebrate. However, at the present moment, we are never going to win a battle against billionaires when we are constantly intoxicated as a group (which we are). The first few weeks are scary when you unplug from everything that is familiar. Do you have the bravery to go two weeks without TV and without liquid courage? If your answer is no (but you don't want to die a drunk) then find somebody else that has quit and ask them how they did it. Healthy former drinkers may be scarce, but they do exist.

In the present moment, we have become surrounded by beer-bottle, pill-bottle, and wine-bottle zombies. In case you were unaware of the intent of most zombie movies ever made then please watch the 2013 release of "Warm Bodies". It will explain why every zombie movie ever made, was made.

Clearly we can all accept that the American public is being outsmarted by those that have billions of dollars. Otherwise, the rest of us that do work all the time would not be so damn broke, but we are. Now that I am sober and work 40+ hours per week, I deserve access to the same food, shelter, and feelings of safety and security as screw-up rich kids that are constantly drunk and are working less. They are not superior beings with more brains nor do they have superior strength than me. I will not allow them to dominate me because they don't deserve to do so. I didn't get born on earth to be dominated by shameful human beings for a lifetime.

If you're one of the working poor that allows richer assholes to treat you like a second class citizen rather than demanding respect, then it's your own damn fault. The working poor across this earth need to figure this out. There are way more of us of equal intelligence and strength that have the power to renegotiate wages, rents, and exactly who is making the rules.

A good exercise to change your perspective on the people all around you is to look at them as little more than monkeys that can talk. I'm not talking about you of course, but look at those Walmart shoppers and sports stadiums full of drunken screaming idiots as little more than hairless monkeys that just learned how to speak. Think about how extremely comfortable nearly everyone is about saying how stupid our fellow Americans are. We all seem to agree that our country is chuck full of idiots isn't it?

We actually had a TV show called "Are You Smarter Than A Fifth Grader". We also see "Jay Walking" on Jay Leno which showcases the absolute ignorance of the people in the United States. Our psyche chooses to laugh rather than feel shame at the sad truth that surrounds us all every day. All around America we see people wandering through life that aren't much smarter than well trained chimpanzees. These are valuable human beings that have been badly separated from their God-given potentials. Their brains and hearts can be turned back on again to reasonable levels. Then, these same people can be reasoned with using sound logic and facts. This can be done, and it's happening now.

If most people were given the opportunity to bring down the walls between them and consciousness, they would. I'm talking about the 85%ers that we've all been conforming to. Political correctness in a criminally run society (given that most politicians are liars and cheats) is a losing strategy. The more that my words seem to offend the Bushes, the Clintons, and the Obamas the better! We often have to be drunk or on pills just to tolerate the group that we now belong to. I choose to rebel by simply not dumbing-down like the rest of a group (that most of us have lost respect for anyways). It's time to leave behind old beliefs that only serve the political elites.

We can unplug ourselves from a system that only seeks to serve itself and is leaving average people in ruins. If this wasn't the truth then 50 million people wouldn't be on food stamps in America. Who wants to be dependent on the same government that they have nothing but contempt for? If you're on food stamps and you don't like rich old white guys in expensive suits, (that belong to secret societies) then please find a different owner to supply you with your daily meals.

Obama may be the spokesperson, but he's no different than the front desk worker at a hotel. The customers never get to see the real owner face to face. We all know that a bunch of billionaire old white guys own most of the world. The Presidents do what the billionaires tell them to. Our "leaders" seem to be acting out of fear, not respect for the public's best interests.

If it were possible for a relative handful of super wealthy people to intentionally dumb-down the masses into little more than obedient monkeys that can talk, would they? Just stop and think about how grown adults act when they get drunk. Are they not missing words, have lost any sense of shame, and are seeking sex and food?

When drunk, your brain power goes down and the other dumb people all around you become more tolerable. Getting drunk makes our ability to give-a-shit temporary disappear. We've all been duped into self-administering this easy to obtain bio-logical weapon. Billionaires have sold us daily brain damage via TV programming in order for us to tolerate an otherwise intolerable world that they have engineered.

Two totally sober adults in a public library would rarely ever approach one another, no matter how lonely and attracted to each other they are. However, throw consciousness killing alcohol into the equation (and as soon as normal brain activity has been lowered) and inhibitions brought on by societal control and belief systems quickly melt away. Our base primal urges take over and we then do what's on the lowest level of our needs chart. When we kill our consciousness, our top priorities are still on the lowest of levels. So, if you drink often enough, eventually you become a low-life. I once was, and that's ok because we did come here to learn. The point is that we can learn from what doesn't work, and then change strategy.

This is not an attempt to sell the benefits of alcohol, because as many former addicts know all too well, as time passes, the benefits that it once brought about quickly get replaced with drawbacks and problems. Over time, while using drinks and pills our problem solving ability gets worse. A lot more people end up treating us like crap and we accept it, along with our near constant dependency on alcohol or pills. There are no magic drinks or pills. It's all been a con and we've been the marks.

None of us can rely upon a miracle in a bottle without having it eventually backfire on us. Just like every other too-good-to-be true solution that we have come across, eventually there's a downside. Normally the good things that make us truly happy require some hard work, discipline, and some courage. Facing life with no liquid or pill-bottle bravery takes true guts.

Continuing to be a drug addict or alcoholic is not on the path of hard work and true bravery. How many of us refer to the politicians of the other party on TV as lowlifes? I'm betting that most of those rich kids in suits on TV are drunk pretty often; perhaps just as often as those lowlifes in Walmart that none of us respect either. Why do we keep allowing these people to lead us?

Do politicians have a bigger or smaller conscience than those of us that do work 40-60 hrs per week and aren't addicts? Maybe this is why they are doing such a terrible job, because they are just as unconscious as the rest of us. When you stop drinking and unplug your cable box for a month, then you'll start to see that our leaders are just following orders from their higher-ups (not from the public).

Our politicians are following orders in a corporate structure just like any other half-conscious guy or gal in a suit at your local bank. We've become a country of puppets, and very few people are sober enough to even see the strings. Sober people that don't run to their doctors for mind-numbing drugs actually become harder to control in an increasingly brutal job market. In Cinderella Man, working a tougher job for less money created a powerful left hook. 1%, you've toughened up Americans and made us less fearful. Good job.

The few people that are pulling most of our strings know we're waking-up, and are doing everything that they can to encourage constant public self-sedation. Do you sedate yourself (drink) daily? If so, then chances are that somebody else is treating the sedated version of you worse than a completely sober you would put-up with. Does that make sense?

Boosting your own consciousness through the few changes outlined in this book will give you more guts than when drinking daily. If you don't believe this, then try it for two weeks to prove me wrong. Many single American adults have been conditioned to associate alcohol with happiness right? What if the popularity of alcohol has all been a huge con on the public, just to keep us trapped in servitude?

For drinkers, it's very often when we are out getting drunk that most new sexual encounters occur. In a world full of monkeys that can talk, associating alcohol with new sexual encounters, and then showing constant TV ads selling it, nearly guarantees a country full of drunks and addicts. This is what we've become, a country full of weakened citizens. Only drunken and delusional people look the way that most of us now do. When you're completely awake and sober, please take a long look into the mirror at your own naked body. What do you see? Is this the person that you always wanted to become?

Our flawed religious, economic, and educational control systems have corralled us into alcoholism and drug addiction (myself formerly included). There is a way out. We have all been intentionally conditioned into killing our own consciences to make us easier targets for billionaires to fleece. None of this is an accident. Not church, school, television programming or the beers that we drink after work while watching sports. This diet has made the public easily manageable by our loving elites. This way, we'll do what they want.

It's all been set up this way on purpose by those few people that now own everything. The average American has gone from successful homeowner, to a piss-poor wage slave that's living in shitty apartments. The majority of citizens can stop this ridiculous slave class and ruling class absurdity at any time that we choose. If one human being is abusing 1000 human beings, then the group of 1000 God-fearing people is allowed to renegotiate the living conditions of the group.

There is also the constant television induced hypnosis reinforcing the idea that alcohol improves anyone's otherwise mundane existence. There are constant beer and liquor commercials saying that alcohol will make things better. This is a lie. It's like pouring hard liquor into an already burning fire of delusional thoughts. With enough repetition, it's hard for any TV watching adult not to want to at least try alcohol. We do buy what our television sells us don't we?

For any of us with an even slightly stressful existence, (and god help us if we have an addictive personality) once we try the proposed stress reliever of alcohol sold by TV, we're hooked. It's not even a fair fight! If you show me infomercials, then I will want to buy it. How many people reading this have friends that are also addicted to coffee? They have to have their coffee every single day right? It's no longer a matter of choice is it?

Most of the non-coffee drinkers (health nuts) in this world tend to be the people that naturally have high levels of self-motivation. In return, because they are more motivated and disciplined than us, we call them nuts. It sure is nuts to put health before wealth.

Surely none of us have ever seen extremely wealthy human beings that died in vain suffering from fear, anger, and resentments that dominated their thoughts and actions. How many of them also loved to have a few drinks? Perhaps a short viewing of the movie "There will be Blood" outta do it to prove my point. All of our "leaders" should have to piss in a cup daily just to prove that they're not drunks and drug addicts just like the idiots that blindly obey them.

This world has become chuck-full of rich assholes that also just so happen to be drunks and drug addicts. The Wolf Of Wall Street at least drove that point home. Rich assholes certainly don't care about the public, and never will. More likely, the super wealthy are worried about their next drunk or high just like your trailer park neighbors are. Thank God for the rich assholes that the zombie public hasn't figured this out yet.

I think Steve Jobs may also qualify as a good example of a person that let health slip away while pursuing the black hole of material wealth. The movie about Mr. Jobs wasn't exactly complimentary. The unquenchable thirst for more power and prestige is a tricky trap to escape when a corrupt world begins throwing more money at a human ego. My God have I gotten sucked in and thoroughly chewed up by the same cyclone of insanity that "successfulness" in America offers.

Would you like to outlive the ripe old age of 56? Mr. Steve Jobs died still carrying resentment towards Bill Gates for stealing and mass marketing Windows even after the creation of the I-pod, the I-phone, and the I-pad. Any recovered addict knows that addictive personalities suffer from what is referred to as "The disease of not enough" (AA jargon).

Being happy and healthy now, is the best revenge against someone that harmed you in your past. Holding grudges against other people only hurts the grudge holder. Ironically, the biggest grudge that most of us have to forgive is with ourselves. This happens due to a lifetime of impossible to follow and conflicting rules. The wealthiest people don't follow these same impossible-to-follow rules that are being imposed on the rest of us. Thank God that the zombies haven't figured this out.

Remember, it's over, gone, and done. Start enjoying what's in your life today. We can be better people today by the way we treat other people and by the way that we treat ourselves. I have met several business owners during my own employment career that chased financial power to spiritual emptiness and early graves. Many of them tried to buy respect from others through material success, but didn't seem to like themselves. Can you think of any miserable rich people in your own life that also seem to be addicts?

The tremendous irony is that the very children that stand to inherit the financial fortunes (never enjoyed by their now dead parents) often resent the parent that died young pursuing material fulfillment. Many rich people are cursed with always planning for tomorrow, while sacrificing today's happiness and kindness towards others. It's always about the pursuit of future benefits. If you try to live for the future, it's easy to miss the joy in today.

We all know how crazy it is to place personal health and healthy relationships as a top priority in the present. Why spend each day making an effort to be thankful and doing things that make you happy today when you can be miserable for ten more years piling up money that you never get to spend? It's sad seeing so many people that have lots of money but failing health. A lot of these financially strong and spiritually disconnected people can't figure out why healthy optimistic people won't stick around in their lives.

The answer is that you must embrace health, and become healthy yourself. Otherwise you're inadvertently sucking the life out of the people around you. The term emotional vampire is worth looking into. Once you do the work to be healthy now, then healthy people will begin to appear in your life and spend time with you. We must do the work to get healthy ourselves first, and then healthy people will spend plenty of time with us.

Many unhappy people spend most of their time hoarding away a huge stash of money to be spent at a distant future date. What is the opposite of confidence? Anxiety, right? Or, if we really want to be honest with ourselves, fear. That four letter word that your ego likes to pretend does not affect your daily behaviors (but it does). Rather than face fear, many Americans now drink daily or pop pills. We know this is true.

If you suffer from anxiety and also drink often, smoke, or constantly pop pills to relieve said anxiety, then you're living in fear. Lying to yourself daily changes none of this. Fear of future availability is what makes people hoard money and resources today.

If you want to pick out the most fearful people in the room, look no further than those people that are carrying around a ton of weight, and a ton of money. This fear is often the product of a spiritual void brought about by the 85%er zombie diet. It's hardly our fault due to the system that we've been born into. There is a way to escape from a life demanding daily drunkenness, over-eating, or pills. The method of escape is being delivered now. You will choose whether or not to free yourself.

Admitting this to ourselves is the first step to getting rid of a pitiful fear-based existence. One of the most stupid simple realizations that I made during my first year of sobriety was that coffee actually caused me to feel more anxiety than without it. I was shocked at what a huge effect one little cup of coffee had on me, but it did. I couldn't believe that something most people drink every day gave me such a definite feeling of fear. When you're in fear, are you better or worse at solving problems? Then, later on in the day, what do people often reach for while on edge?

Simple activities are no longer easy for fearful people. We have been tricked by television to throw pills at our fear; pills, food, or alcohol. Does that sound about right? As a non-coffee drinker for the first 32 years of my life, I then decided to give coffee a try in the rooms of AA. AA is a great place to quit drinking but just like rehab, at some point you need to rejoin the real world. Many AAers are guilty of turning a practical solution that can be done in a year, into a lifelong cult that separates them from society. Tackle your addictions and move on with life. We are not life-long victims.

Tackle your addiction, and then find a happy medium. Drunk in a bar every day or spending years of your life in a seven day per week cult of sobriety are both over-doing it. The human ego definitely provides plenty of room for assholes that quit drinking, attend AA constantly, and are still sociopaths. The point is to tackle your addiction and then rejoin society.

I strongly advocate finding a happy medium and avoiding organized religions that demand all of your time and energy. Seven days a week drinking or talking about not drinking are both extreme. Coffee is nearly always on hand in AA rooms because of a four-letter word (in my book) called tradition. Incredibly with extreme consistency, when I introduce coffee into my own system, I then experienced anxiety (fear) which has never been a problem for me before. If this is the case for me, then could it possibly be the case for anyone else that drinks coffee daily? Try substituting a health store energy supplement for a month, and see if your own anxiety drops.

I will also attest that chewing nicotine gum caused me to experience heavy anxiety. A terrible and generally unfamiliar feeling of fear sweeps over me when using coffee or cigarettes. Would billionaires want the working class to be physically addicted to fear-inducing substances? Cigarettes and alcohol aren't the go-to staples of "relief" for working class wage slaves by accident. Greedy business owners prefer having fearful employees.

If there's one thing that the absolute poorest people in America (homeless people) have in common, it's coffee, cigarettes, and alcohol. Does that sound about right? Getting millions of people hooked on anxiety-causing products that then get treated with daily sedation (all for profit) is brilliant. Make even more money while keeping the moronic slave class as fearful and sedated as possible. Be a good zombie and keep eating your slow zombie diet.

If you think that these are wild claims of an unreasonable person, just observe real people in the real world, and make a T-chart. Our slave masters that trick voters every four years, have most of us hooked on liquid fear in the morning, and vapor fear all day (cigarettes). To top it all off, many of us use liquid not-give-a-shit (alcohol) at night just to fall asleep. We are super predictable and have totally taken the bait that's keeping us conquered.

We're the only creature on earth that must chemically knock ourselves out at night after ingesting fear-inducing stimulants all day (that are sold to us by our trustworthy overlords). We sure are smart. If you're a really classy addict, then you pop Dr. approved pill-bottle not-give-a-shit every single night just in order to achieve the most basic function of every single creature on God's green earth.

If you T-chart real people in your own life, then you'll likely find that the heaviest people with failing health share coffee, pills, and alcohol in common. Oh yes, and diet soda. If there's one thing that seems to wreck human bodies faster than anything, it's diet soda (with brain numbing aspartame). The health nuts that you observe are more likely to be drinking water, no coffee, no cigarettes, and no guilt-free and doctor approved drugs. Did you know that Aspartame breaks down into wood alcohol in the human body? Google it.

If the stuff knocks you out, (turning your brain off) has it ever occurred to you that doing that to yourself over and over again every night for years might be why you can't remember shit? We are not all permanently dumber. The effects of the zombie diet are very much reversible. We are temporarily weakened and these weapons of mass sedation can be quickly flushed from your system.

The miraculous reversal from poor health and daily suffering to feeling and looking good can happen in months, not years. You just have to stop copying the diet of the least healthy people that you know. If you make these changes then your brain will come back to life along with the rest of your body! Simply abandoning diet soda and then drinking a gallon of distilled water daily can work miracles. I have seen it.

# Chapter 6 – Letting go of traditions shared with Walmart zombies

Traditions exist only until the majority decides that there is a better way of doing things. Are some Americans ready to admit that the way that we have been doing things is not working out so well for us? I think that we are finally ready to start trying new things because many of us have nothing left to lose. Even our pride can be set aside in the face of personal disaster.

Even gay pride may be a bit under thought out. You're proud to have the right to be married? Now you can get contractually stuck in a relationship where the other person stops trying as hard to keep you with them. If you do decide to leave a partner that has become totally unfair, then you will lose half of your stuff if not everything. Divorce attorneys (pampered rich kids) can't wait to get their hands on divorced gay people's hard earned life savings. We do all agree that a chunk of both parties' life savings gets consumed by legal fees in every divorce right?

Good luck enjoying millions of relationships where the more selfish partner is about to start acting a lot more selfish. I'm willing to bet that lawyers supply substantial funding for gay marriage legislation in every state. It's like a council of vampires trying to pass legislation that will start construction of new blood banks in every town across America. Greedy rich kids need some way to keep that half million dollar house and the Mercedes in the driveway.

There is a huge market share to be tapped into. Gay people ought not be prevented from all of the logic and reason that entering into a legal marriage contract has delivered to straight people. About half of the married men that I see look like they want to be shot in the head.

The only thing keeping many disgruntled people married, is the intense fear of breaking the contract and loosing half of their stuff; That, and alcoholism. To all future gay people that are marrying for money: Alcohol and anti-depressants are the best way to financially drain your next victim while keeping them too unaware to see the true nature of the relationship. Shitty spouses that are only in relationships for the money, heavily depend on the regular sedation of their partners. These types of people should be ashamed of themselves, and ought to feel like total pieces of shit after finishing this book. It's called a conscience.

I find that the absolute best way that I like to learn from other people is to look at an entire institution that has failed more than half of its participants (resulting in intense pain, and financial ruin) and then, I copy those people. Rather than trying a slightly different approach, I just copy all of my friends, family, and co-workers that have crashed and burned right in front of me. I do the exact same activity that they did, and expect different results.

How many of us know wonderful and thoughtful people that have suffered great destruction from a bad divorce? Human beings have proven over and over again that they can behave well enough for just long enough to get married. Only on a planet of talking monkeys would such an obviously flawed contract continue to exist without being modified.

If your marriage is out of love, then you don't need a piece of paper to enforce rules. The belief that legal marriages will provide you a better behaving life-long romantic partner is crazy. This is just as insane as believing that politicians whom swear an oath, will better serve the people.

The least honest people in society seem to be the most eager to get into contracts promising decent people future services. Our wives, husbands, and politicians don't deserve contractually obligated terms lasting years let alone months or even days. These contracts only set up the more honest partner for a lengthier period of abuse. Look out if your poorer partner sends you to the doctor to start taking anti-depressants or brings you home alcohol during the week and encourages you to constantly be drunk. If so, you're likely being used for your financial resources like a drunken cow being kept in a stall for milking. Moooooh!

Marriage has always seemed like a horrifically thought-out line of reasoning to me. Perhaps that's why a mirage and a marriage are so closely related to one another in spelling. It's a fantastic illusion that looks very promising from a distance, but once you get there, you get less sex and less effort in all other areas from the more selfish partner. I am pro love, pro loyalty, and pro affection with one monogamous partner for as long as the relationship is loving and honest for both partners. Getting married is an honorable action that is ideal for raising families. All we need to do is completely remove the chance for financial gain from lawyers and dishonest spouses. Take a crooked legal system out of the equation, and leave in the love and commitment.

With the infinite number of examples where a seemingly good partner turns terrible after the contract has been signed, why doesn't the standard marriage contract eliminate any chance for financial gain? There sure would be a lot less wrinkly old men with hot young wives. Plus, those delusional old men (many of which are drunks) would stop getting secretly cheated on by their gold digging wives.

Old men with strikingly beautiful wives that are clearly there for the money must stop kidding themselves that a money worshipping woman wouldn't also be sleeping with younger studs on the side. True loyalty can't be purchased. People without consciences don't want just anything, they want everything. When they get that, it still won't be enough. Drunken husbands and wives may not see this happening, but sober ones do and they cease to remain victims of assholes that are only using them.

Over and over again, life has shown us that the people that we become financially and contractually obligated to, treat us a lot better than those people that aren't gaining money from us, right? Like our cell phone companies, congress, senate, and the cable company. We all know lots of people with miserable husbands and wives that they stay with. Fear is what keeps them there. People become comfortably miserable.

These are the types of deals that we allow ourselves to become contractually obligated to (often for a set number of years). What an insane premise this is in a country full of not-so-bright people. The moment that there is no longer a line of unintelligent customers willing to hand over their money for an unfair deal, then a particular business will cease to exist.

After no less than hundreds of examples of seeing the exact same types of contracts re-negotiated in the real world, we just keep signing up for them. Drunkeness and television have a lot to do with buying lies that nearly always fail to deliver on what was originally promised to us. These long term contracts with flawed humans that aren't spiritually awake rob us of our health and energy.

Inviting a spiritually asleep person into your own life is like inviting a vampire to come sleep on your couch for a few years. Not putting two and two together while your health slowly fails (and you wake up feeling like crap every morning) is pretty fricken dumb. Emotional vampires do exist. To escape detection, they depend heavily on partners that have drinking and pill habits. If you're clearly an alcoholic that drinks daily, (and your poorer partner doesn't) who do you think has the upper hand in manipulating the other?

Emotional vampires are simply parasitic people that seem to feed off of others money and anger. They are always creating situations that upset their partners to obtain that next meal of anger. Drunks and drug addicts make the easiest long-term victims for emotional vampires to spend years feeding off of. If you're the person with the larger income and a larger drinking habit, then your partner who drinks less is more easily able to manipulate you.

People often assume that I'm a young college student in my early twenties when meeting for the first time face-to-face. Strangers assume this based on the health of the person standing in front of them. After discovering that I'm 35 people are amazed and nearly always say, "Wow, you look so young!" and then quickly return to whatever they are busy trying to accomplish.

However, a small percentage of people do stop and ask, "You look so young, what's your secret?" and I answer them honestly. I tell them that I've never been married. Most laugh, and then convince themselves quickly to ignore my answer and move on to a less threatening subject. Who wants to admit that they are part of a largely flawed institution that a healthier person refuses to participate in. For most American adults, heading into marriage is a lot like heading into the Presidency. Almost immediately your hair begins to turn grey, you get serious wrinkles and look ten years older after four. Sign me up.

Nobody that is smack dab in the middle of a horrible contract (with their own health slowly failing them) and has no exit strategy in sight (other than death) wants to hear from somebody else that never signed up in the first place. A very small percentage of people laugh, then think for a moment (accept my answer as truthful) and then quickly move on to a less traumatic subject. In places where most people are totally oppressed and are very unhappy, the truth is a very unpopular subject. A large proportion of Cleveland Ohio residents seemed to prefer that I vanish. I did. It truly was the land of the dead.

Relying on a legal system owned and operated by the rich people's network is a joke. Rich people will only begin to fear poor people if just a handful of the super rich were actually held accountable and stripped of power by the public. A few years in country club prison while the rest of us spend a lifetime in poverty isn't cutting it. Maybe that was the point of making the movie, "The Wolf of Wall Street" to completely piss off the public at the men that have no respect for us anyways (and never will).

If 150,000 years of human evolution has taught us anything, it's that other humans that we enter into legal contracts with for a set number of years tend to treat us the best. That is, if we like being treated like crap. If you hire a prostitute for a 4 year contract, is that prostitute going to line up as many side customers as they can during the 4 years? What's the difference between that logic and our current political system? Do rings around married people's fingers stop them from violating the contract if, they so happen to come across a better deal? We all know that our politicians have been offered millions of dollars to do whatever billionaires and corporations tell them to. Stop giving these people so much credit.

We should trust our politicians about as much as we trust our strippers, for a few minutes at a time while they are physically on our laps. Sure enough, that person that charmed you and made a soul connection with you thirty minutes earlier will be on the highest bidder's lap before you can drive home. Our Politicians are more like money robot prostitutes than defenders of the Constitution. Corporations have driven up the price of these whores so drastically that the public can't afford five minutes. We know this is true.

When are we finally going to leave the strip club and seek out other people that aren't drug addicts that had loveless relationships with their fathers? Prime example: George W. Bush. The crazy thing is, several of our recent U.S. Presidents lacked good relationships with their fathers and likely have some additional skeletons in their closets. Bill Clinton: Daddy issues. George W. Bush: Daddy issues. Barack Obama: Daddy issues.

How many of us have tried to have healthy and loving relationships with known addicts suffering from daddy issues? The chances of receiving a fair deal when bargaining with these types of people is somewhere between not going to f-n happen, and what the f did you expect? People with these traumatic issues should not be groomed to be the future leaders of the free world, but they are.

Horrifically, that is exactly why the true powers that be have selected them to be the front men of America. The CIA is known to have developed a trauma-based mind control program called MK Ultra a long time ago. Read a book about it and you'll begin to understand the relevance of this paragraph. Have you ever met people with daddy issues that are only happy when they're getting away with something?

Have any of you reading this ever dated anybody? Was the first six months when the other person put forth the most effort to treat you the best, or not? What happens to the more selfish partners actions the second that a couple decides to move in together or gets married? Some scarred and damaged people simply aren't satisfied unless they feel like they are getting away with something.

Our politicians are no different at all. Selfish and self-centered people are most definitely reliant upon the steady energy supply that the traditions of marriage and political office supply to them. It's a parasitic relationship and guess who's part of the cattle-class of people? I'm tired of being the energy supply for parasitic people that are emotionally damaged and totally abusive towards the rest of us. They have no right to feed off of me, and I'm showing all of their victims how the scammers operate. Do you want to continue being somebody else's drunken meal ticket until they've slowly bled you to death?

The only thing that politicians sell us, are future promises that never deliver. Just like the Wolf of Wall Street, our politicians continue to live like drunken kings now, while we don't. We know that this is the truth, and only a country of hopeless drunks and pill heads would fail to do anything about it. We are their marks and they have no conscience left to care about us. No one is coming to save us. We must unplug our own TV set, and go find other people that escaped from the same problems that we currently have.

Maybe this is why Leonardo DiCaprio went out of his way to make a movie that most likely annoys the public. Sometimes if an actor truly cares about the best interests of the people that worship him, he may purposefully make a movie that he knows will consciously disappoint his audience. It doesn't matter whether you like or hate a particular movie if it delivers a powerful blow to your sub-conscious beliefs. Once you've seen certain truths, you cannot un-see them.

Being married and raising a family is a wonderful tradition, but perhaps the lawyers and contracts that seem to have empowered the more vampiristic types of people in our society, need to be heavily rethought and re-written. The vampires have been writing the rules of our society for the last 5000 years. I vote that people with consciences re-write the rules that govern our lives in a way that lets all of the vampires starve out. Stop being their food supply.

Another common part of our lives that relates to being easy prey is our daily coffee. For the first 32 years of my life, I remained a non-coffee drinker. After only a few days of drinking a single cup of coffee per day, I began to feel anxiety and nervousness that had not existed in the 32 years prior.

People that have known me for a lifetime know that I'm not a fearful person. Despite me figuring out that the coffee was what made me feel new anxiety, I continued drinking it for another week. I was hooked, that quick; as are millions of people reading this that are also part of America's rapidly growing victim class. If nearly everyone in the 50 million strong food stamp army drinks coffee, than I'm not. If there's one thing that all of the fattest and most fearful people in most rooms share in common, it's coffee.

My short-lived addiction to coffee had kept me coming back to the very same thing that had made me feel fearful each day prior, just as it possibly does for millions of other Americans that drink it daily. Do you have anxiety and then drink alcohol or prescription pill-pop for relief? We all need to smash the word anxiety from our vocabularies, it's <u>fear</u>.

I now live in a country that's filled with fearful people. The only time these same people feel confident is when they've popped their prescription anti-anxiety (fear) pills, or have deluded their self image with alcohol. I'm sick and tired of catering to the delusional egos of fearful Americans that badly need rehab and a hug. Somebody needs to be honest with these people so that they can begin to get help. Why are healthy people allowing a bunch of physically and mentally ill people to become the new American norm? Come get me zombies.

Just because the average working class Joe hasn't put 2 and 2 together, doesn't mean that something isn't easily solved. How many farm animals spend a lifetime in one small field that is guarded by a few small electrical wires and a paper-thin fence? What's keeping those animals in that field? I would argue that fear, stupidity, and apathy are the answers. Do many of those animals die of natural causes, or get slaughtered for food?

Dressing things up with prettier words doesn't change who and what we've become. I could walk around saying that I was an excitable and passionate person before I stopped drinking too much, but the truth is that I was an angry guy that lacked patience and forgiveness (when drinking was my daily coping method for life). When I finally tackled my own addictions, my anger was incredibly reduced and I regained something wonderful: self-control, peace, and forgiveness towards humanity.

We're all flawed and are constantly making mistakes while living this human experience. The point is, we're supposed to be learning and not intentionally hurting other people all day long to benefit our self. Treat others how you would like to be treated, it's that simple.

It was years ago that I made the big change and finally decided to tackle my own addictions. I've found no reason to go back to the old way of doing things, because I enjoy more peace and freedom now. After linking coffee consumption to my own anxiety, I decided to post this epiphany on my Facebook page.

The non-brand specific post connecting coffee to anxiety (daily fear) was deleted by Facebook immediately. It hardly seems logical to me that an opinion that coffee could be the root cause of people's general anxiety would deserve censorship. The posting simply stated that many people are addicted to coffee that likely makes them anxious during the day. They then drink alcohol or take prescription pills at night (which they are also addicted to) to relieve their anxiety.

In a true act of insanity, most Americans drink more anxiety causing coffee to relieve the hangover brought about by the fear relieving alcohol or pills used the night before. This repetitive cycle between stimulant and depressant is an insane tradition for millions of people. Would Billionaires want a fearful workforce with low levels of self-respect due to excessive weight, anxiety, and alcoholism? Would they then drop these hamsters that they owned into this wheel of insanity?

The description of that very cycle of addiction was censored by Facebook. Ask yourself why the opinion of a working class person making a non-brand specific statement about an addictive cycle would be deleted from existence by Facebook? Is morning coffee an American tradition? Would billionaires distribute an addictive substance to the masses if they knew that coffee kept us all just a little more fearful every time that we drank it?

Might this theory be totally ridiculous? Probably so, but it may also have some validity to it. The only way to find out would be by removing the variable of coffee entirely for an entire month, and see if you suffer from less anxiety and feel more daily peace. Who wants more peace in their life? Perhaps taking a leap of faith and humoring a ridiculous sounding theory wouldn't be a bad experiment to try for a few weeks.

One of the best ways to manipulate masses of people into lower levels of consciousness is to do it without their knowledge. Once we become addicted to something, we've lost all control in choosing to consume it or not. It becomes part of our daily routine, and rather than admit addiction our egos conveniently lie to us about having any real choice in the matter or not.

David Icke beautifully explains how problem, reaction, solution is used by the few to control the many. Our ego is the part of our psyche that will lie to us and tell us that we are in control, when we're not. Nobody wants to admit they've become addicted to anything do they? Admitting to yourself that you have totally lost control over a particular substance makes you feel less powerful, so most people remain in denial (due to their own blinding egos).

Nobody likes to feel powerless over their own behaviors. Our dogs are powerless over lots of behaviors aren't they? As human beings we want to exercise as much free will as humanly possible. We call it freedom, when really we've become the free dumb. Our wealthy slave owners have successfully trained a couple hundred million people to follow orders that keep making our lives harder and less free while they become wealthier. Everything is now watched and under surveillance, all, in the name of safety (fear).

This all took place after our leaders used television to scare the shit out of all of us on 911. Even if they didn't plan or allow the attacks to happen, they certainly repeated the image of the planes hitting the buildings and the buildings imploding, no less than hundreds of times. It was like watching a loved one get run down by a car and being forced to re-watch the accident hundreds of times. It was mass mind control and it worked perfectly.

We were all suspects in the interrogation room on some cop show being forced to watch a traumatic video over and over again. Eventually we cannot handle the image anymore, and will do anything that the person playing the video asks of us. Did we go along with a huge increase in airport security, internet spying, and phone tapping? It was all in the name of not showing us that horrible video anymore.

Eventually, all that our beloved politicians had to do was simply mention the word 911, and we all jump before they play the video again. We all got psychologically scarred that day. We were all fearful enough and therefore dumb enough to go along with the con. This is how mind control works. Freak somebody out really bad with a traumatic event, and then take control of the situation while the person's brain is still in panic mode. We don't think well while in panic mode.

We all know that the logic in our heads gets shut-off during traumatic events. We then go into fight or flight mode and end up thinking more like primates than people. As a country, we've acted like a bunch of children that took a severe beating from our parent with a belt and every time that our politicians want to get us back into a state of fear, they only have to show us the belt and say the magic word, 911. Trauma based mind control was used on us all. That damage is being repaired right now. Our heads were hacked by assholes. All of their shitty programs are being deleted, and their future plans will fail. We are not a fear-based Republic.

Breaking millions of Americans free from trauma-based mind control would be my pleasure. Do you want to continue being manipulated by rich assholes in suits on TV? I don't like bullies. If a bully takes off his belt off to scare a room full of kids, then I'm going after him!

We used to have movies that showed these kind of images like "Indiana Jones and the Temple of Doom" where Harrison Ford takes on the scary man whipping little kids down in the mines. Only after the slaves see someone else stand-up to the slave master, do they begin to overrun the badly outnumbered guards. Our politicians deserve the same treatment after their shameless abuse of the word 911 on our TV sets. All of it was a program, and that program is crumbling.

There is video evidence of this claim, showing them repeating that number over and over again. I choose to turn that cursed number around (that has been used as a weapon of enslavement) and am turning it back into a weapon of liberation. We don't attack the politicians that have betrayed us; we ignore them and leave them with empty venues. They can give their deceptive speeches in empty rooms that nobody is paying attention to anymore.

If you want the politicians to stop whipping you with words, then turn off your TV. It's like taking the whip out of the whip masters hand. I'm no longer afraid of the greedy old white men that are no longer holding a mental whip over me. I'm not even paying attention to them. Refuse to watch TV and their whip is gone. Does that make sense?

Of all the 18-55 year-olds making up the U.S. workforce, how many of us use alcohol or mood enhancing pills just to cope with life? We all know that this is true but we are pretending that half of the population isn't all drugged up and half drunk all of the time. How often do average Americans get buzzed? If I'm trying to pick the losing horses in the human race, then I'm betting on the ones that can't stop from getting drunk every day. That too can change right now.

Are you just another one of the cowardly slaves that dare not challenge the whip master? If you truly refuse to watch TV and stop drinking liquid fear (coffee) every day then you'll soon have new balls to look over at the man that once had the whip and see, that it's no longer there! The terror in a bully's eyes when you're coming at them is something that a loving God would approve of.

No loving God would want us to live lifetimes of fear while bowing down to evil men without consciences. Good parents that raise respectable people are proud when they see their little kid stand up to a big bully. Bullies often pick on the weak and the unhealthy, not the strong and the brave. It has only been through TV, pills, and drinks that our criminal politicians have gotten away with bullying us for this long.

The average physical health of Americans has gotten significantly worse in the last 30 years. If you're not sure about this statement, just watch any movie from the 1970's like Caddie Shack, and observe how skinny all of the extras are. That's what most of us used to look like. If we're being honest, average has gotten a whole lot fatter hasn't it? Whatever activities are the most common of the dumbest, fattest, and most fearful people need to be abandoned. When you do so, you will find strength.

An extremely easy way to regain a huge amount of self-respect is to break the addictive upper and downer relationship between coffee and sedatives. Getting help is much less shameful than living a lifelong lie that nobody is really buying but you. Most people around addicts know that they are full of crap but never say anything.

100

Just let someone else deal with it; that has become the new national anthem. Is my suggested brand of sobriety totally different than the coffee drinking, smoking old men of AA? Yes, it's 2014. The brand of sobriety from 1940 is no longer effective during the internet age. Also, all or nothing cannot be expected to be followed forever, that's ridiculous. What I am proposing is quitting for long enough to regain self-control and to address personal problems that daily drunkenness and prescription pills have failed to address. Once you have regained self-control, try to find a happy medium that allows you to rejoin society. Hiding in AA rooms for years of your life is hardly recovery. Tackle your demons and then rejoin society.

It's completely doable to quit drinking without non-stop coffee and cigarettes. In fact, most of the healthiest and happiest people in AA rooms are the young ones with bottles of water in front of them, not coffee. Just because something was the best way of doing things 70 years ago does not mean that it's the best way now.

There is a proven strategy for eliminating addictions to all mind altering substances without expensive psycho-therapy, and it's anonymous. If our doctors have been failing to make us healthier (which they have) and have really become legalized drug dealers then shouldn't we stop seeing them? If the rest of us have become poor while our doctors have remained wealthy then don't we owe it to them to reward their lack of results with empty doctor's offices?

What self-respecting person keeps going back to somebody that always lets them down and has failed to improve their quality of life (after thousands of dollars spent, and years of failed treatments)? Millions of Americans and people from around the world have successfully escaped the insanity of all types of addictions using AA. I don't propose staying there forever, but I do propose using AA to break free from serious addictions. Once you've regained health and balance then wean yourself off of the rehab group. Otherwise, it can become just as isolating as Scientology or any other 7 day per week cult. In general our society avoids 7 day per week fanatics. Find balance and long-term moderation. Let old AA-Nazis throw a fit.

Unless millions of recovered ex-drinkers are all smarter than you, (and I assure you they're not) you can do the same thing if you want to (using the same directions from the same instruction manual). Just look for the healthiest people in the rooms, and ask them how they did it. You may have to visit several locations until you see some people that have what you're looking for. Remember, the rooms are good, but it's 2014. Turning off your flat screen TV showing constant beer ads is the actual way that I was able to succeed.

Are there still people in the AA rooms that ignore this logic and run to the doctor to confirm their chronic depression (that their television sold to them)? Yes, you can enjoy all of the pill-bottle sobriety that you want rather than changing the true underlying issues that made you constantly drink or pill-pop to escape from reality in the first place. Of course, the pill bottle God will eventually deliver you all of the same benefits (drawbacks) that king alcohol once did.

Pill bottle zombies are still welcome in AA rooms too. Just don't make statements to the rest of the room claiming to be drug and alcohol free, if you pop pills daily. Prescription drugs...are still drugs. Much of this is blasphemy to hardcore AAers. How dare I propose to people to quit drinking and then lose dependency on a religious-like group with an all or nothing philosophy? Well, AA has something like a 3% lifetime success rate. Meaning, that 97% of society eventually decides to walk away from the meetings.

If you stay on a pair of emotional crutches indefinitely, then your legs will never heal and become as strong as the people that put all of their crutches down. We all end up becoming as strong or as weak, as the best excuses that we can say to God. We all have the right to be as healthy or sick, as we choose. Are tons of AA meetings totally corrupt and full of hypocrites? Yes, absolutely, but unlike church there's an instruction manual that has sobered up a lot more alcoholics than going to church on Sunday has.

If you've grown tired of the hangovers and are annoyed that you have to keep drinking in order to function, then AA is a good place to start. We all get to choose how long we stay somewhere. The first few months of sobering up are the hardest, and that's where AA rooms can help the most.

Where do you think the people that can't stop drinking, that had kept trying church end up? Even if you happen across a room of

AA A-holes, the book itself that it's all based on is extremely effective at tackling addictions. Take what's good from it and what works for you. Getting help from a group of people that did the same thing is much easier than quitting on your own. The general instructions of AA definitely helped pull me off the ground, along with a belief in God. That was years ago, and the relief has lasted. The amount of peace and overall brain power that I got back has been well worth the effort.

Like anything, even AA can be overdone and isolate a working person from their peers. My advice is to tackle your addiction, and then find a happy medium that works for you. Drunks in a bar will crucify you for going to AA, and cult-like AAers will crucify a recovered person for leaving the AA rooms healthy.

We can't make everyone happy. So far as I understand, about 20% of ex-problem drinkers remain sober in the absence of AA. Only 3% of AA people maintain continual sobriety until they die. The point is, a lot of ex-drinkers use AA to quit, and then leave the rooms after gaining some long-term sobriety. Southpark did an AA episode, and I can hardly argue with it. The benefits of not drinking often are why I continue to avoid frequent alcohol use. My memory works so much better without it.

Throughout our lives we've all been told that human beings only use 10% of our brains, right? I don't know about you, but if 10% is all that we are using, I don't want to get addicted or continue being addicted to anything that shuts down any more of that 10%. If we actually start getting honest with ourselves we can probably admit that a drunk's intelligence is barely beyond that of a monkey that can talk.

If you're saying no, then perhaps an enlightening exercise can better help to illustrate my point. Simply visit a few local bars at closing time in a completely sober state of mind, and observe how the drunken people talk, walk, and behave. To pass out is to become un-conscious, right? As you consume more alcohol, little by little, you become less conscious.

Over the course of years these frequent escapes from reality slowly rob us of our consciences even when we aren't drunk. The processors in our heads end up running slower on a full-time basis.

We end up becoming less intelligent, and more, full of crap. Only the daily drinker believes their own bullshit.

Daily alcohol consumption will allow a person to get abused all day long at a life draining job and somehow takes away our will (willingness) to walk away from the relationship. By simply having a few alcoholic drinks (often accompanied by soul numbing anti-depressants) the daily abuse is reprieved until the next morning when the insane cycle resumes. The logical part of the brain that should be utilized to effectively solve problems has been bypassed by a poisonous cocktail of TV, alcohol, and pills. Rich assholes love this. They've supplied us with the perfect daily solution that always keeps us coming back for more abuse the next day.

The daily drinker that wakes up the next morning feeling kind of crappy and then mindlessly makes coffee to sober up is doing exactly what our masters want. The coffee that we drink keeps us just anxious (fearful) enough to make it back to the same crappy job that had abused us the day before. All for not enough money to afford a decent spouse that might actually give us enough confidence to ask for a raise.

So, we drink after work, in order to tolerate the annoying person that we are now stuck with. Many of you know that this is true but will never do a thing about it. Not for as long as you keep running back to your magic cure all bottles. Crappy employers and spouses are dependent upon your daily drinks.

I can just picture my old cell phone boss doing an impression of his game plan. He'd say, "I'll drink ya pretty" in a slurring fashion referring to the woman in his life at the time. How true is that for millions of us? We then stay just fearful enough of the man in a suit (our boss) not to tell him off or ask for a raise that we deserve. Instead, we drink some more after another frustrating day at a job we don't want to be at anymore. Spiritual beings having a human experience, how brave we've been.

As the economy of America has slowly been shipped overseas by our fearless job creators, prescription drugs and alcohol have been bombarding the psyches of the American public. Our TVs have prevented us all from doing anything about the rapidly declining situation accept for drinking more and taking more pills that make us numb. Millions of us run to Starbucks every day just to revive ourselves after the previous night of self-administered sedation.

You can walk away from this hellish cycle. Unplug the TV, quit drinking coffee, and stop knocking yourself out each night. That is the zombie diet; that, and your self-administered fluoride doses each day that you've been tricked into taking since childhood. Your fluoride toothpaste does decrease your problem solving abilities because fluoride is a known neurotoxin.

The corporations selling us this diet via television commercials do not care if they are perpetuating bad relationships and horrible jobs. They don't care about your true quality of life. They want the most work for as little money as possible and they're getting it. You're simply a target and they're aiming straight for your brain.

Do you get that really rich men may get their buddies to sell drugs on TV that create the perfect worker zombies for their benefits, not yours? Do you want to behave exactly how the billionaires are expecting you to? I don't. So, I don't follow the same diet as everyone else.

My diet is far from normal, because I don't want to become an American zombie. There is light in my eyes, a spring in my step, and love in my heart for people not money. I don't want to have my free will hijacked by unethical corporate machines.

Think about it, aren't there only a relative handful of billionaires that own the largest U.S. corporations and Banks? Haven't those same billionaires bought off our politicians and government leaders during the last 100 years? The billionaires decide the policies of the FDA. Perhaps the FDA has rigged the system to get the most work from the American sleep walkers as possible. Would rich peoples' consciences allow such a thing?

Have you ever come across a rich person that didn't play fair? You know, a real win-lose negotiator that rips off everyone that they deal with? Isn't it possible that some of the richest of the rich would be willing to manipulate the public using sneaky tactics? I think you know it's already being done. We haven't been honest with ourselves about exactly how much free will has actually been stolen from us.

Nobody wants to admit that they've been outsmarted, but I know for sure that I was. If you don't want to be part of the ignorant crowd, then stop ignoring the truth. If Scientists come up with drugs that make a human being feel less depressed about their shitty job, then you can bet your asses that billionaires will support their sale and distribution to the public.

How many orange pill bottles are in your own medicine cabinet? What part of prescription drugs prevents you from realizing that you're dependent upon drugs? We have been conned on a massive scale by the very people claiming to provide us with solutions. Instead, half of the country has become drug-addicts and alcoholics. The U.S. represents 5% of the world's population and consumes 80% of the prescription drugs. We've been hypnotized by our televisions, conned into drug addiction, and are having all of our assets liquidated by global bankers right now. We're being robbed blind.

Perhaps pills and drinks that numb us to the worst situations in life may also be numbing us to the greatest gifts that this human lifetime can offer. We can't have it both ways. If the majority of people are bloated and limping through the streets, then perhaps we should start avoiding the doctors that those same people go to.

What do you think prescription Anti-depressants are? Just because a Dr. (drug distribution expert) has had expensive schooling, doesn't mean that he or she won't push aside morals in the name of money. The pills aren't addressing your life's true problems. Many doctors, lawyers, and politicians are functioning alcoholics and prescription drug-addicts at this very moment.

Life experience should have taught us by now that morals are not guaranteed by the wealthy or even the highly educated. Look at our politicians for God sakes. Our doctors at this stage of the game deserve no more trust or respect than one of two awful choices that you're forced to choose from every 4 years. Abandon these wealthy well-dressed criminals that deal only in empty promises that never deliver. They have stayed wealthy, while we've all become poorer. The game has been rigged. Walk off of their chess board, and let them panic.

Do you not know people in your own life that are definitely alcoholics, yet they have no trouble at all keeping their jobs? We just trust the alcoholic doctors, lawyers, and politicians because they happen to be dressed in expensive suits while they are giving us shitty advice. These quick-fixes (pills) lower our self-respect, all in the name of profit (not health). The question is, are you going to keep participating in their scam? Once you've been shown how a particular scam works, you then become one less person that falls for the trick.

I spent a few years attending AA meetings and I've got news for you, there are doctors and lawyers that I have seen in those rooms of AA, but strangely enough, no politicians. I've never seen one, and I have been to a lot of meetings in multiple states. Therefore, there must be zero alcoholic politicians out there. That's probably why our politicians are so good at telling us all the truth; they must all be drug and alcohol free.

No moral lapses of judgment from that crowd, huh? They must be superior compared to us working class simpletons. That's why they should continue to make the decisions for the rest of us, because their consciences are so much bigger, right? Do you feel a weird tingling sensation in your brain? It's called logic.

Would a tiny minority of power hungry billionaires use TV commercials to get an entire country addicted to not-give-a-shit pills and alcohol to keep us all under constant sedation? Am I at all concerned about being knocked-off by corrupt billionaires because I am shining light on their primary bio-logical (affecting our logic) weapons? No.

I believe in life after death and cannot continue watching people get abused without speaking up in an effort to help them. My conscience won't allow it any more. When I was drinking on a weekly basis and then daily basis (during my final 6 months) it became easier and easier for me to ignore the truth. We all have God-given rights and ought to have lives that don't require pills and snake oil to keep us moving forward. I believe "moving forward" was a recent campaign slogan after 300 million people witnessed 4 more years of broken promises from 2008 until 2012. We are such an intelligent group of highly informed voters aren't we?

We have been kept just numb enough to keep ignoring all of the lies of a corrupt few.  Bill O'Reilly and the millionaires on Fox News aren't going to save you either.  They will most likely be on private jets to South America if things in this country get any worse.  There won't be any room on their jet for you so please shatter that delusion right now.

We will only stop the backwards slide of middle class America when enough of us stop following the walking dead diet.  The solutions to gaining greater awareness and personal power are in this book.  It starts with the very water that you drink every day and what is in it.

Once you're aware of the exact brain-numbing and soul crushing activities that all of those other (not you of course) stupid Americans share in common, then you can stop repeating them.  If you eat like the idiots, drink like the idiots, and take pills like the other idiots, then how do you think that you're not subject to the same brain handicapping effects?  Three years after originally quitting, I now choose to barely drink at all, because I hate what it does to my memory.  Before actually quitting, it wasn't a choice at all.  A social beer or two once per week is the happy medium that I've adopted after two plus years of complete sobriety.

That's a statement that will make long-term AA Nazis heads burst!  I don't obsess about my next drink, because I know it's an over-rated activity filled with empty promises.  Our republic has been hijacked by a handful of selfish billionaires that have demonstrated over and over again that they have no morals and no conscience left.  Yet, we keep following them just like the lost souls listening to The Wolf Of Wall Street.

There's a good chance that our leaders are nothing other than alcoholics and drug-addicts that are all dressed up in expensive suits (that give them the appearance of credibility).  What's really incredible is that with a failing economy and with failing health, the public continues showing up and giving money to these people.  We have held on to old traditions that are no longer serving the best interests of the American people.  Those of us that aren't out of control drunks and drug-addicts must help our neighbors regain consciousness.  Without some intervention, the majority of U.S. citizens are lined up for slaughter by unethical men without consciences. Today is a good day to change this. Together we can find a happy medium that creates a healthier and happier society.

A handful of selfish billionaires have purposefully drugged-up and mind-controlled the American public. It's time for us to rescue ourselves. It starts with refusing the daily doses of liquid anxiety (coffee) followed by nightly drinks and hours of TV programming. We are being badly outmaneuvered in this weakened state. Do what the fastest and smartest people are doing to get what they have. Refuse the zombie diet and you'll stop looking and feeling like those other Walmart shoppers. It is this simple, and you can do this.

# Chapter 7 – The zombie apocalypse has already happened

Our enemies would prefer that we remain slightly sedated, hopeless, and disorganized as a group. This way we're much easier to control. Slow drunken zombies are the zombies that I want to be outrunning if I'm taxing the dumb bastards without representing them at all. Definitely not, fast smart zombies. Have you been in a Walmart lately? Seriously, if you were a billionaire genius walking down the aisles of Walmarts across America right this minute, what do you see everywhere?

Are there mostly fast smart zombies or slow stupid ones? The zombie apocalypse (change) has already happened. In the eyes of a genius you are likely one of them. This is the part where an accurate mirror is being placed in front of your face and you say, "Awww crap! I'm one of the zombies!" It's ok, so was I for a very long time.

Wouldn't you prefer running your brain and heart on full power again? Has your memory gotten better or worse since you were a teenager? It only became painfully obvious to me just how blind I had once been after completely removing alcohol, fluoride, and TV from my daily routine for several months. The increased perception, peace, and love felt towards humanity are well worth a few weeks of total weirdness. You'll begin to look and feel better within weeks, not months.

Remember, you are reading words I've written. You are not seeing the positive nature of my face to face interactions with people every day in the real world. How we treat people that aren't paying us money is what really counts. This book has spread to other people one person at a time, starting with strangers that are interested in something that I have.

Would you guess that a 300lb crazy cat lady rambling on about a book that she wrote would have much success? Walking proof of positive results is how you spread an idea to your neighbors. Since 2008 the U.S. economy has crashed, and the American zombies have done nothing to make things better. I would argue that the masses have done nothing, because the masses are mostly addicts (zombies).

Only addicts stay in abusive situations and do absolutely nothing to get out of it. It's about damn time that we the zombies get back our brains. Refusing magic drinks and cure-all pills will give us back the balls and true spirituality that we need to make things better.

Clearly our leaders on TV did not stop millions of Americans from losing good jobs, houses, and often families that got blown to bits by the financial storm starting on September 11th 2001. We have taken a severe beating as a country and need to stop whining about our sad plight to our drunken friends that can't help us get out of this. If this economy has wrecked you too, then find someone else that also got wrecked but has managed to put themselves back together again with improvements. If you lay down with whooped dogs, you get flees.

We must fight for each other because the leaders on TV aren't fighting for us. That has become clear. People wearing expensive suits on TV are just as likely to be alcoholics that have drank away their consciences as your drunken next door neighbors. The only difference is that one of them is wearing a really expensive suit and likely has multi-millionaire parents. When are we going to stop being tricked by the guy wearing the most expensive suit on TV?

When is it enough for you to try a new strategy at life? I know that I had enough of a beating about three years ago. That's when I then adopted the high consciousness diet and the light in my soul got turned back on again. I refuse to go back to being a self-sedating average American.

I don't buy the same illusions that flawed people wearing expensive suits on TV are selling to all of the other defeated Americans. These con-men are never going to suddenly start telling us all the truth. It's simply not how they're wired. It's about time that someone breaks the spell that has been cast upon their victims. We all deserve the maximum level of free will possible while here on earth. Americans value freedom, right?

As a group our consciousness has been purposely lowered to make us more docile slaves. Would rich men sabotage the brains of the public by intentionally selling us a low-consciousness diet? Only under the influence of mind numbing prescription drugs and alcohol would an entire country allow a few rich assholes to be our leaders.

It's about damn time to start waking up the zombies. Our entire country seems to have been sucked into the same cult, the church of the holy bottles. It doesn't work to improve your life, and it never will. It has wrecked our bodies and made us poor. The church of the holy bottles makes its priests and ushers wealthy while the rest of the congregation slips further into poverty.

As long as it's an orange bottle with a Doctors name on the side, then it's a guilt-free escape from reality that must be done daily in order to take your daily ass-kicking. The completely defeated citizens of Cleveland Ohio were such a shining example of this. You're either sedating yourself daily via alcohol or pills, or not.

Then there's the equally ridiculous daily worship of the other type of bottle for those classy intellectuals that simply like the taste of wine, (daily) and no less than a bottle at a time. Never has the human ego masked an excuse for a daily drunk better than a semi-wealthy wine drinker. These are perhaps the proudest and most delusional of all of the walking dead in America. Wine drinking alcoholics are still alcoholics.

If you get buzzed every single day then guess what, alcohol may have control over you. It got me for awhile, until my own life-changing realization of that very same truth. Alcohol had gained control over my life, and my behavior. Once I realized it, I then decided to do something about it. Strangely enough, I had an overwhelming urge to walk over and unscrew the TV cable chord from my wall. Everything has changed since then.

After living with and growing to love an entire family of rednecks in Georgia I've gotta say, at least beer-drinking rednecks are halfway honest with themselves when accepting that they are alcoholics. They at least admit that they need their daily buzz just to function. College educated business professionals have woven a web of self-deception that seems fortified by the pride that goes along with an expensive college degree. Both blue collar and white collar people are equally vulnerable to getting caught by the church of the holy bottle. Either way, a drunk is a drunk.

The church of the holy bottle destroys self-respect, ruins good relationships, and perpetuates bad ones. Nothing great comes from the path of least resistance. I think that it's about time to start resisting the daily habits that our billionaire slave owners would love to see continue. They do not care about us and prefer that we keep seeking alcohol and pills for escape. Why? The escape never works.

While using their solutions for our problems, we become the perfect victims for assholes to feed off of (for life). How many current alcoholics do you know that claim to be victims? How many Americans claim to be victims and are receiving some form of a victim relief check? You're either on the take from a corrupt government that you despise, or not.

If I have to be a zombie and there are hundreds of millions of us in the United States, then I choose to be a fast smart zombie. When I bite, people get smarter and healthier. They begin to take ballsier actions and stop acting like subservient dogs that are dependent on food stamps.

This is truly the zombie disease that billionaires are the most terrified of, the spread of consciousness from one freed slave to another. All of this time, the greatest fear of rich men around the world has been the spread of knowledge. The Gnostics were pretty well wiped out of existence by the Knights Templar. With knowledge comes fearlessness. Large corrupt empires can't have that spreading in small towns and villages around the world.

My bite contains logic, not brain killing ignorance like the T-virus (TV) strain of zombie that currently dominates the U.S. population. For analogous purposes, unless you are a billionaire, then you must choose to be a fast smart zombie or a slow stupid one. We're all allowed to regain or surrender as much of our free will as we choose. Others cannot do this for us. The decision is ours to make.

Albert Einstein once stated that you cannot solve problems with the same level of consciousness that created them. How do you raise the consciousness of millions of people? You identify a very small set of behaviors that have a huge impact on the human brain and then, you change them. The result being increased brain activity and the ability to solve problems that used to baffle you (AA jargon). This

113

is how consciousness is boosted. Pills from your doctor will <u>not</u> do this for you. Just look at all of the walking examples around you that have chose pills to address their problems.

There are a few movies that are excellent analogies for why it is time to raise the consciousness of the suffering public. They are: Rise Of The Planet Of The Apes, Rise Of The Lycans, Day Breakers, and Warm Bodies. All four of the previously mentioned movies beautifully illustrate the super wealthy keeping the masses under their control. Each movie illustrates why the masses must free themselves from the control of evil men. Only while we remain slightly dumber and constantly sedated can the ruling elites maintain their edge.

Each movie portrays a weaker slave class that finally gets woken up and takes back power from corrupt leaders. Remember, a single person cannot physically control millions of people that are equally as intelligent as themselves. The super greedy few that own our politicians and therefore us, must keep the masses in a zombie-like state for the game to continue.

A horrible parent that wants a small child to stay quiet and occupied could simply hand them an I-pad and a sippy cup of apple juice spiked with Jim Beam. This is pretty well what smart phones, flat screen TVs, and the religion of pro sports has done for former grown adults in America. The majority of working class adults perform their jobs and then are immediately sedated and entertained into a near retarded state of consciousness.

Once the average American can see lies, they become a Lycan, as in the movie, Rise of the Lycans. Don't vampires wear amulets around their necks for protection? Somehow the dumbest zombies amongst us seem to be falling for a similar trick. Sociopathic assholes will tattoo crosses on themselves or wear them around their necks. Incredibly, it works as an invisibility cloak for them to rip off zombies without startling the poor dumb bastards. Nazis wore crosses too while slaughtering their way across Europe. A cross around a person's neck means nothing about their moral character.

The truth, love, and logic contained in this book are like a shot of steroids for your soul that will make it easier for you to start doing what is right and honest. In the movie "Rise of the Lycans" there was

114

a victim class and a vampire class that ruled over them. There were a few members of the peasant class that wore large collars around their necks. One of them with a collar bears a striking resemblance to Jesus. The character's name is Lucian, and he wanted to revolt. As in, revol-lucian, does that make sense?

Rather than remaining a servant of the vampire class for life, Lucian made a key to remove his mind-controlling collar that had kept him weaker than the vampires that he was once enslaved to. Once he had the collar off, he then gave the key to other slaves to allow them to unleash their own true potentials. What exactly was it that Jesus was doing with moronic ancient people during his time?

I would argue that he was reasoning with indoctrinated people using sound logic and breaking through a lifetime of fear-based mind control. Jesus revealed to people that God is within all of us, and that assholes in ceremonial suits requiring weekly offerings (taxes) for protection are frauds. If you've read the entire new testament, that's what it's all about. Jesus exposed the sham of the government and its citizen mind-control systems during his time.

The Roman emperor and future kings made an example out of Jesus by placing images of a crucified man that dared to expose the kings fraudulent control system. Do you understand what this book is all about? The roman authorities crucified Jesus because his words inspired the peasant class to seek true spirituality from within, rather than look to the priesthood for protection. Jesus empowered people. Whether his character was flesh and blood like the rest of us, or just a fictional character, he gives us an ideal to strive for. Ideas create reality.

The small statured man in "Rise of the Lycans" is able to catch the ears of the peasants. His words made sense and helped common people to realize the terrifying truth that all dictators fear; that the ignorant masses are more powerful than the small minority of elites. We don't need the vampire class of humans (politicians) to protect us. As a group, we're already far more powerful than all politicians and billionaires combined. We simply have to realize it and start working together to unveil the current control system that's been keeping us poor. What do you think that this book is doing in your own head right now? You do have the choice to remove your own mind-controlling collar, and will have the knowledge of how to do it.

# Chapter 8 – How television and sedatives have been used against us

I reference movies because our population has been conditioned to spend hours upon hours in front of a screen that, as David Icke says, "Tells us a vision". Tell me, is the TV telling you your own vision or somebody else's? Our brains make powerful connections based on what we see and hear from these screens. Have you ever heard of a type of screen that is able to hide something bad that's coming? What do you call it?

The ruling Elite that vainly attempt to quench their unquenchable thirst for money and power have successfully used our TV's against us as a smoke screen to hide their true intentions. This is a tough pill for the human ego to swallow. Accepting that we have been tricked into mentally weakening ourselves for a lifetime sounds horrible, but that doesn't mean that it's not true.

Your ego doesn't want to accept that you've been played like a fiddle. Our freedom has been slowly taken away by a well orchestrated set of circumstances and illusions. None of this has been by accident.

Human beings showed the elites just how powerful TV and movies are at controlling mass populations of people after the movie "Jaws" was first released. A Hollywood produced movie portraying an oversized man-eating shark with a taste for human beings was able to scare millions of Americans right out of the water. People actually stopped swimming at ocean-side beaches for years following the fictional movie. To this day, many grown adults fear going into the water due to that movie.

Wizards use a staff made of holy wood to cast spells on ignorant people. Aren't there staffs in Hollywood that cast spells on people now? Surely you know grown adults now that are still terrified of swimming in the ocean because of a movie from thirty years ago, right? Logic can be easily destroyed and abandoned by the magic of Hollywood.

Showing a few rich and greedy men already lacking morals or a conscience that kind of power was too good to pass up. If you were a bad guy that had the resources to produce a movie or a television show that would get millions of people to behave <u>exactly</u> how you wanted them to, could you pass up that opportunity? How many Starbucks were open for business in the United States before the TV show "Friends" came out?

Go back to the year that "Friends" first showed really good looking and funny people hanging out at a coffee shop and drinking coffee. How many Starbucks were open nationwide back then? Fast forward to the year of the final episode of "Friends" and see how many Starbucks were in operation. Television drives trends. More importantly, it drives behavior. We might as well be monkeys watching a video, and then mimicking the behavior.

If a group of wealthy men were intending to create a demand for anxiety relieving pills and increased alcohol consumption to make the public dumber, would they use a TV show to sell nighttime coffee consumption? If you waste all of your time learning checkers while rich assholes are playing chess, then you deserve to be their bitch. If Hitler were to produce a TV show to sell liquid anxiety to his target audience, then he'd probably call it Friends too.

Most of us that do have consciences don't want that much power and don't want to control and manipulate the whole group. Life has taught us that power corrupts. As a result, most of us decent people have completely avoided politics, haven't we? We have seen too many other people that started out with good intentions, but later got corrupted by temptations that none of us could resist.

As human beings, when we get power, it tends to go right to our heads. I think that was the entire point of the "Lord of The Rings" books and movies. Human beings have a very difficult time handling large amounts of money and power. The more we get, the more that we want. It's like trying to fill up a black hole. It cannot be done. How many miserable rich people have you met during your lifetime?

One of the greatest illusions ever pulled off by the elite (via our TV sets) is the illusion of choice in a two party political system. Both parties are paid for and owned by the same small group of super

118

wealthy elites that share a common interest, to stay in power. Picture a Presidential debate on television as nothing more than a giant puppeteer under the stage playing his right hand puppet against his left.

Only an addict that has had his consciousness dimmed much like the lighting in a strip club would buy the illusion that choosing one president or another will make any difference in what kind of changes get imposed on the zombie public. The system is toast and we all know it. It's like an old car engine that has 280,000 miles on it and has lost compression. We're not getting any further by pouring the miracle-in-a-bottle thick honey-like substance into it. It's done, and needs to be dismantled and rebuilt. We are like a whole country of retarded children attempting to ride a dead horse.

It's time to get a new vehicle or start riding the bus. Will I be sitting on a urine-smelling bus with a bunch of half-dead people while millionaires fly past us all in their Mercedes? Hell no. I actually sobered up and I don't feel like being part of the victim class of America. Did I have to seek out a group of other people that had done the same thing to escape their sad situations? Yes. I found other people that had escaped addiction, and I followed their advice to break free. My new life goal is to empower poor Americans and to drive the vampire class of Americans crazy.

The world has changed in many ways and we must adapt using logic, common sense, and principles of freedom. Americans must raise our consciousness now in order to provide a democratic solution that actually addresses our current challenges. Old belief systems that have been corrupted by greedy billionaires must be replaced. Somebody needs to pull us off of the corpse (a corporately funded political system) and give us all a big hug.

After umpteen presidents and huge shifts of power in our congress and senate, we have to be brain dead zombies to not see that our entire political system has been hijacked by the world's elite. We live in a fascist dictatorship that's all dressed up as a democratic republic. It's not. Corporations and world bankers own our asses. Our own TV tells us that congress has a 10% approval rating. For congress to still be employed by us makes no sense.

Our protections from government have failed us, and we are failing ourselves. The "will of the people" is no longer being served. This is the truth, and we know it. Actual solutions to this problem are being uploaded right now. World bankers and our sell-out politicians have stolen from the wrong group of people. Our ancestors have booted greedy assholes out of power before and so will we. Resistance to tyranny is ingrained in our DNA.

When the zombified public starts raising their consciousness back up again, the dingy strip club lighting gets turned back on bright. Then our politicians will begin to start looking like the skanky prostitutes that they really are. What do you think these guys look like when you take them out of their thousand dollar suits? Put them in a pair of shorts and a white tee-shirt (with no TV makeup on) and they start to look like Walmart people to me. Screw their infinite supply of future promises that never come true. We are better than this and can find better people to help run things. In fact, 99% of us that actually do run factories manage business and do all of the actual labor are already running things.

What would you think of a grown man at your regular 9-5 job that was covered in TV makeup? I'm pretty sure that most of these politicians would look like selfish and lazy people with the same bloated bodies as the rest of the train-wreck addicts in America that we also have no real respect for. Why do you think bars and night clubs are kept so dark? It's to maintain the illusion that makes sick people look good.

We go to dark places and consume consciousness killing alcohol, so we'll buy the illusion. Aren't we placed into a weakened state of mind when we're sitting at home intoxicated in front of our TVs? When people sober up the next morning, suddenly, the perfect looking model that we met the night before while buzzed in a dimly lit bar, transforms into a heavier and more wrinkled body double that aged ten years overnight.

We're all being kept drugged up and sedated, so that we'll keep buying the illusion that these guys on TV are better than us. They're not. Their actions prove that they don't care about us. Congress has a 10% approval rating from us, the public. Somehow we haven't already fired them all. This makes no sense.

We can't keep walking around in drunken stupors anymore. It's not working out for us. It's as if the whole country has buried our heads in the sand, and you know what happens to our asses while our heads are buried. We've become addicted to anti-depressants, alcohol, and the impossible pursuit of obtaining everything that we see on TV. The super wealthy that do understand how to manipulate us via TV programming don't view the public as equally valuable people. Instead, they see targets. What part of your body do you think they're aiming for?

Are you getting the zombie metaphor yet? They don't use guns to shoot for the head. They use TV, alcohol, drugs, and anything that renders us all brain dead. The few want the many, to stay as dumb as possible for the rest of our lives. That way, we'll stay poor and hopeless, and they get to own all of us.

The way that the public can piss off as many billionaires as much as possible, is by unplugging ourselves from our TV programming. Do you like the idea of millions of Americans behaving in a way that drives terror into the hearts of billionaires? I do. In fact, the less that we fear them, the more terror they will begin broadcasting on TV. They've got to keep us in line somehow, even if, they are secretly funding the same terror groups that are used to pass additional controls on an increasingly disgruntled American public.

Billionaires funded al-Qaeda to destabilize the Middle East. Then, when our own U.S. troops began posting pictures on Facebook stating, "I will not fight alongside al-Qaeda" and, "I will not train al-Qaeda" things began to turn against some evil government planners. These soldiers had written on cardboard covering their faces (while in uniform) overseas. Our own troops had to flat out refuse to train the same murdering scum al-Qaeda that was attacking them in Iraq.

Remember when Obama and John Kerry were trying to convince the public that we had to attack Syria? That's when our own U.S. troops began posting pictures on the internet, in uniform, refusing to work with al-Qaeda. Our politicians may have no honor left, but our troops do. So, the solution that the greediest human beings on earth came up, just a year later (to attack Syria) was to rename al-

121

Qaeda, and now call those <u>same</u> guys ISIS.

Alex Jones has been explaining how the scam works for years (backed by documents) and has not been thrown in jail or kicked off of the radio for defamation of character, or slander. As Alex Jones frequently says, the Billionaire architects of our government think that you're so dumb, that they fund ISIS, and then after ISIS attacks, our own government gets to put more cameras on our streets, and tax us heavier, to keep us safe from the very threat that they created in the first place.

The human brain cannot defend against repeated lies on TV stated as the truth. When combined with alcohol, anti-depressants, and a constant drip feed of fluoride (known brain inhibitor) into our blood streams we're turned into obedient zombies. This brain-deadening cocktail has held the public at bay for decades.

Meanwhile, the rich have been living with increasing levels of decadence while the rest of us struggle to pay for rent, food, and gasoline. Do you get that the appearance of people on television that tell us how to live, and what to be thinking about, is a lie? They don't look anything like that in real life without tons of TV makeup on. It's an illusion, and we are delusional for as long as we think that it's real.

It's about time that the curtain is pulled aside to reveal the wizard of OZ (the president) for what he really is. A pathetic group of little old white men have taken absolute control of what they see, as an otherwise lost heard of idiots. Do billionaires have the right to take advantage of a country of drunks and drug addicts? Yup, until you swallow your pride, seek real help, and actually sober yourself up, you deserve to have a bunch of rich assholes continue to dominate you.

Our doctors are just as guilty for throwing drugs at all of us to solve practically everything. We continue to get less and less healthy, in spite of taking more and more medicine (drugs). Doctors too, have been bought-off by the same billionaires that own the President, Congress, and Senate. They sold us out and deserve to lose their wealth.

The President is merely the spokesperson and fall-guy to take the blame while billionaires control us all from behind the scenes.

This is the truth. If the voters want to see reality on TV, we would all demand that no makeup is allowed anymore. This way, we can see the real people that we've been obediently trusting for years.

News anchors are just reading a script, and in the name of making $200,000 per year, would you have any motivation to question the content that you were reading? David Icke perfectly calls our TV reporters what they really are, NEWS READERS. The only thing that questioning their teleprompter (speech controller) will get them, is a pink slip. Do you think that News Readers want to lose $200,000 per year jobs and end up stuck in the trenches with the $9 per hour front-line zombies?

What we don't realize is that we (the public) can demand changes like this and the people on TV have to honor our wishes. Or, we can stop watching them. If we stop showing up, they will cease to exist. Checkout the movie "Surrogates" with Bruce Willis. Watch it, and you'll get what spending all day stuck in front of a screen has done to most of us. The amount of youth and vitality that can be gained by abandoning TV watching is incredible.

Our group accepts or denies the world that we live in. If you want to see scary looking bloated messes on TV that have sworn allegiance to the government that bribes them $200,000 a year; then remove the caked-on makeup that hides the real people delivering us the news. Are there good looking people that support rich evil men? Sure, but there are plenty of alcoholic scumbags that push the government agenda too. They would look a whole lot different without the magic of TV makeup.

I dare celebrities to start a zero makeup truth movement on TV. After all, the rest of us in the real world aren't covered in TV makeup, are we? This would be like a game of no makeup chicken on TV. Unhealthy people covered in makeup, is like a badly burned cake, covered in frosting.

All of the celebrities that want the American people to see reality, would have to sacrifice their own pride in order to expose their enemies for the frauds that they really are. Bill O'Reilly, Candy Crowley, and Oprah all look a lot different without an hour of reality defying makeup. Heck, half of the grown women in America are paving over reality with a barrage of daily makeup. It's an illusion to make them look healthier than they really are. The little kid from The Sixth Sense sees dead people, and so do I. When you stop following the zombie diet, you'll begin to see the difference between the living, and the dead.

I'm guessing that the zombies at home would seriously consider sobering themselves up, if they saw these people for an entire week, with no makeup on. If we turned on the TV and saw Oprah, Donald Trump, and the rest of the richest people on TV with zero makeup on, I'm betting that it would freak us all out pretty badly. We would be like zombies seeing our own true reflections in the mirror for the very first time.

With no more TV makeup, we would all see each other more accurately. Healthy people would still look full of health, and the unhealthy would look….wait for it…..wait for it, not healthy. This way the dead can keep listening to the dead, and the living can start only paying attention to the living.

Stephen Colbert is perhaps the ballsiest guy on TV that would actually issue such a challenge. I believe that he is trying his best to wake zombies up using satire. It's ok to be a zombie. I once was, but I woke myself up and so can you. If you want to look better, feel better, think faster, and experience the good things in life, then you're in luck. The hard drive in your own head is being defragmented right now.

Billionaire's egos justify why they are entitled to control all of us using television programming. Do you see how a few human beings that have amassed a great deal of wealth could crown themselves kings and start making decisions on behalf of the rest of us without our consent? Would a small club of billionaires be beyond using secret forms of manipulation against their target audience?

I was once one of their hopeless zombies. Then one day, it occurred to me that I had lost self-control. I turned off my TV, started reading books, and stopped drinking the same things as the least healthy Americans do. Perhaps when my older brother with the 150+ IQ (that read books constantly in high school) stopped using fluoride toothpaste, it was for a reason. I remember being a little kid, and thinking it was strange that my teenage brother was brushing his teeth with nothing but water. Perhaps he had stumbled onto the handicapping effects of daily fluoride use.

What does fluoride have to do with any of this? The Nazi scientists discovered that after putting a very small amount of fluoride into the drinking water (1-3 parts per million) at the concentration camps, that the prisoners stopped trying as hard to escape. Fluoride was proven to be an effective brain sedative. It's no wonder why your kids are being prescribed legalized speed (Ritalin) so they can pay attention in class.

The Russian dictator Joseph Stalin also used fluoride in the drinking water in the Russian GULOGS. The latest Resident Evil movie worked in some Russian zombies for a reason. Most scenes in movies are not put together by mistake. Sometimes movie scenes are arranged in a subtle way, so that they are directly absorbed directly by your sub-conscious mind.

Stalin found that his government could reduce the number of prison guards by 75% after fluoride had been introduced into the inmates' water supply. There are literally thousands of studies confirming the negative brain effects caused by fluoride exposure. What do all Americans do twice a day every day? More amazingly, we all force our toddlers to put something in their mouths that says, "Contact poison control if product is swallowed" right on the side of the tube. We do this because we were taught to by people that we trusted. Do politicians run the government, and does government send out the health guild-lines to our schools?

Would politicians and billionaires introduce a daily dose of something that made us all just a little dumber, without us knowing about it? Simply YouTube water fluorination, and see what you find. How many super wealthy people do you think drink city water straight from their tap? Fluoride-free distilled water can make an incredible difference. A gallon of distilled water per day can transform an acidic overweight body into a healthier slimmer you.

Would you like to gain the concentration and clarity of thought to write your own book about something that you care about? By removing a few known brain inhibitors, you can supercharge your own brain. After doing so, you can begin accomplishing things that were once considered to be impossible for you. Parasitic politicians don't want you to become a better problem solver. They would prefer that you drink diet soda, eat fast food, pay them taxes for protection (from terrorists that they sent money and guns to) and keep your mouth shut.

Are you aware of expensive whole house water softening systems used by many wealthy people for their own houses? If thousands of dollars for clean water is simply too much for you, than what about 65 cents a day for a gallon of distilled water? What other mammals on earth ingest fluoride to protect their teeth? Has it ever occurred to you that some of the smartest people out there may already be avoiding fluoride altogether? This is becoming common knowledge, and only the most stubborn of the commoners will be the last ones on board.

Why does every tube of fluoride toothpaste say to contact poison control if a pea-sized drop of their toothpaste is swallowed? If it is so poisonous then why on earth are we putting it in our mouths every day? This makes no sense, and that's why other countries have outlawed public water fluorination. Why do our city leaders keep insisting on dumping fluoride into our city water supply? Are the local governors and city council members more or less wealthy than you?

Why is fluoride the main ingredient in some rat poisons? We use rats to test many chemicals on due to a similar reaction to how things affect us right? German scientists figured this all out a very long time ago. Those that are truly in the know avoid using fluoride in their own food and drinking water (all while telling the voters that it's all totally safe).

The fluoride in your toothpaste also absorbs through your gums and has the same effect of inhibiting brain function. So please, brush up tonight. Keep that minimum wage job that is keeping you poor while some wealthier asshole works less, and stays more comfortable than you.

Don't question if any of this is true and don't look into it at all. Trust your loving government officials because I'm sure that they love you a lot. Don't change what you've always done because things in your life are going so well right now. Our country is in great shape, and the citizens appear to be getting stronger and healthier by the day.

We all get told the same things over and over again from the time that we are kids, until it becomes fact. Even, if the fact is a lie. That is until one day somebody finally comes along and exposes the lie by proving their counter arguments against it. As adults, until the majority of us are convinced, the lie continues to be known as the truth.

Are the majority of Americans really smart people? No, we accept that fact. The average adults are pretty infantile (but not you of course) just all of those other people at the grocery store today. Past examples of humanity's brilliance: The belief that the world is flat, Santa Claus, the Easter Bunny, cigarettes are good for you, asbestos is a safe insulator, hiding under your school desk will help protect you after a nuclear blast, x-ray machines used in the early 1900's to measure shoe size are safe.

We all have fallen for tons of stupid ass ideas as an entire group. Please have some intellectual curiosity and stop accepting the fabricated historical account. There's not even any real history on the History Channel anymore. The real History has been moved to H2, and your poor butt probably can't afford that cable package.

Our owners don't want us using past knowledge to solve our current problems. Instead, we are forced to watch teams of tattooed dirt bags wearing all black buying and selling junk from desperate Americans in the spiritual Mecca of Las Vegas Nevada. A whole country of retards is very easy to manipulate. I either am going to help wake up the brains of millions of zonked-out people, or get crucified by a cheering crowd of morons one day. I am very comfortable with either outcome. Either way, I won't be stuck in this "Idiocracy" for the next thirty years.

Billionaires have bought all of the land, water, and resources in this world. Forbes magazine just released a list of the world's wealthiest billionaires in 2013; there were over 400 of them. That's 400 Billionaires that are walking around on planet earth right now and dominating 7 billion of us. That's the best we are doing with the pussy-ass version of God that they have trained us all to believe in. We are chumps.

A millionaire is about as important to a billionaire, as a homeless person is to the rest of us. Please picture a pile of 1 million dollar bills dumped in your front yard. Then, multiply that pile by 999 times, and visualize just how much land that pile of loose singles would actually cover. That is the wealth of one billionaire, and it's all worthless paper backed by nothing. In fact, each billionaire doesn't even hold all of that paper; it's just a number on a computer screen. There is no vault of gold, and no big pile of paper. Sadly, it's all just numbers on computer screens that are loaned out to idiots that happen to rinse their mouths with poison twice daily.

It takes the wealth of 999 millionaires, to add up to the wealth of a single billionaire. So, millionaires, if you want to survive the zombie apocalypse, then you better start waking up the zombies as fast as you can. Otherwise, they will one day be used on you, just like the Nazis were used on the wealthy Jewish people in Germany. Human beings can be trained to blindly follow orders, no matter how insane those orders are. This has been proven in recent history.

Videos of police brutality in the U.S. right now, in the year 2014, ought to be enough for you to put aside your old favorite toothpaste and try something new. I was handcuffed in front of a gas station less than a week ago, in February of 2014, because I had the same haircut as some ghetto thug that they were looking for. Surely the type of person that authors a book is worthy of handcuffing first, and identifying as the wrong guy later.

After spending a few minutes in cuffs and surrounded by cops, the head detective made it all ok by telling me, "The good news is, we're taking the cuffs off". After that, they let me go so that I could enter the gas station and purchase two bottles of non-fluorinated water. For zombies that don't realize what deep shit we're all in, this ought to make you unplug your cable cord right now.

Which houses and pantries are still going to have food in them, if the elites cut-off the food supply of 50 million zombies on food stamps? Have you ever faced an army of hungry people, 50 million strong? There aren't enough guns and bullets to win against those numbers. The zombies will always win. Just last week, I was detained like a farm animal for the crime of faintly resembling a white guy with a short hair cut. Looking at my face and speaking to me for thirty seconds was simply too risky for half a dozen armed police officers.

If there is one thing that rich people get, it's eliminating your competition, right? If you have 500 million bucks and your competition has only a million but better ideas than you; would they use a bunch of brainless zombies to haul you away after making up lies about you on TV? History has already answered this question. Suddenly, the Resident Evil movies and the fictional Umbrella Corporation, starts to make perfect sense.

Waking up the brains of our neighbors is the key to our groups' survival. Our military and police are good men that mean well. The vast majority of all police, military, and civil servants are good people that mean well. Please help unplug them before you get handcuffed first, and identified later. This really did happen to me.

We know what a great track record human beings in positions of power have regarding telling the truth to the people that they rule over. As in, they make the rules that you and I have to live by, but they don't. Does that sound about right? How long must this go on before decent people start reasoning with their neighbors? Good people will follow bad orders if they're on the zombie diet.

If I woke up one day only to realize that I was a slow stupid zombie, by God I would find a fast smart zombie and start doing exactly what they do. The movie "Warm Bodies" explains the zombie metaphor perfectly. Helping other human beings and feeling empathy for them is the key to our recovery.

The human heart can do amazing things. When triggered, our hearts release a tremendous source of energy that evil men can do nothing about. Whether you know it or not, this book is opening up connections that will get your heart pumping again. We all know that feeling of intense love and the courage that it gives us.

If you believe in God, then perhaps all of the zombie movies have been God's subtle attempt to reason with us. An attempt from God to show us what we are becoming, (in an exaggerated fashion) so that we can reject it. Does that make sense? Pro-humanity millionaires that refuse to put on TV makeup would definitely help the American zombies to realize that TV has been a huge lie. Millionaires that have 30 years left to live need to realize that young idiots, pose a huge threat. Injecting reason and logic into their heads is a good idea.

An American zombie may gain some awareness by seeing other wrecked celebrities without their normal suits and makeup on. The good news is, we can reverse the negative effects, and transform back into healthier people again. All that we have to do is decide to unplug from the daily TV programming. We have no problem at all looking at other people's beliefs in foreign countries, and pointing out that some of their beliefs are insane. Handcuffing the wrong person without first questioning them is not a good sign.

Any outside observer can easily see the harm being done to us, but we're blind to it. It's not fun to accept that we have been duped is it? Perhaps it's time you investigate a little and as you do, you'll likely see that more of this book will ring true than you ever expected.

Do you really think that going a few months with no fluoride toothpaste and only drinking distilled water is going to make your teeth fall out? Have you really been trained to be that fearful not to research something on the internet that's not already accepted by the flat world zombies? These people don't know shit about anything. Why would you worry about what they think? Why were we all told as little kids that a fictional character named Santa Claus exists? Average Americans are not exactly ahead of the learning curve.

If you are too scared to Google search "fluoride use by the Nazis" then I have two words for you, woof, woof! You've been well trained by your billionaire trainers. Get back in your cage and eat what you've been trained to eat, drink what you've been trained to drink, and believe what you've been trained to believe. Be a good dog and do what you're told by the nice man on TV that you spend hours a day starring at (like a monkey watching television). Meanwhile, healthier people are out and about moving around in the real world.

Be sure to drink four or five cups of coffee that make you just anxious enough to reach for some alcohol or sedatives at night to relax you (make you dumber) each night before you fall asleep (pass out). If this at all sounds familiar, just know that you're doing exactly what

130

your owners want you to. The coffee that the masses are addicted to is no more of an accident at causing you to reach for brain-deadening sedatives daily, than the free pretzels that are put in a cheap bowl at the bar to make you buy more drinks. Be a good monkey and take the bait that will make you thirsty for more nightly brain damage.

Billionaires want you drinking daily because you are much easier to screw over without any retaliation if you're drunk all the time. Deep down inside drunks know that they are drunks and have lost a lot of respect for themselves. We've become a country of sheep with no self-respect left and assholes are sheering the shit out of us.

The American people have become like millions upon millions of cowardly lions just waiting for someone else to come along and hand us some courage. Dorothy just showed up, and you're reading her book. Only her is a him, or she is a he, or something like that. Courage is being installed right now and when you're finished reading this book, you'd better get some bigger underwear because your balls are about to get bigger. Imagine the corrupt politicians freaking-out because a software update for human beings to make them both smarter and braver has finally been created. You're running the upgrade right now.

Try going without any sedatives for an entire month and you tell me if you're not smarter, braver, and don't have a better working memory. People that ingest coffee after 5pm and are surprised that they need sleeping pills (that are basically a pill-form of alcohol) in order to fall asleep every night, this, is a retarded behavior. It is keeping you dumbed-down and weakening your ability to remember shit. If you stop taking these brain numbing pills or drinks before bed every night then your memory will begin to improve quickly. How are you supposed to solve real problems in real life if you memory is shot?

Young people don't respect old people that cannot operate a dvd player; nor do politicians and billionaires respect drunken adults that cannot legally drive a car on a daily basis (because they're drunk). At the very end of the remade "1984" movie, the character Winston found himself locked up in an institution. The defeated slave readily accepts his daily shots of gin with a few drops of some chemical added to it that seems to keep him hopeless and docile. The authorities had also trained Winston to accept and repeat that 2+2=5, showing that with enough repetition all logic can be abandoned. Common Core.

Even bold lies can easily be accepted as the truth (by people that sedate themselves daily). There are also constant alcohol commercials on TV that remind you to sedate yourself (just in case you had forgotten). The message is repeated to all of us that still watch TV, no less than 100 times per day. If you want to see real live zombies at the grocery store, then simply stop sedating yourself for an entire month. Remove TV, quit drinking, quit using fluoride, and you'll soon have the perception and speed that the newly visible zombies don't.

# Chapter 9 – Facing ugly truths we've been trained not to investigate

Believing that jet airplanes crashing into buildings causes the steel-framed structures to implode into a giant pile of dust, is just as ridiculous as saying that 2+2=5. To not research 911 Truth, is to piss all over the graves of the founding fathers of this country and everybody else that died under the false pretenses of the 911 attacks. Three buildings were demolished that day not two.

I'm sick and tired of near-retarded adults policing the rest of us from explaining the 911 magicians trick to the rest of the non-retarded group members. Some of you have the intelligence to perceive when you're dealing with a sharp person, and some of you don't. At some point, the sharpest people in America need to stand up at town hall meetings and lay their asses on the line by speaking the truth in front of large crowds (of not-so-bright people). Frankly I don't give a damn if I get torn limb from limb by an angry mob of complete idiots that are still defending the governments' version of the story.

Donald Rumsfeld was telling Congress that two trillion dollars was missing the day before 911. The two trillion dollars was not spoken of again following the 911 attacks that occurred the very next morning. How convenient for Mr. Rumsfeld and the Presidential administration at that time. Look and see if this is a verifiable and factual statement.

Contempt about any new information being presented to you in this book or any other, prior to your own investigation, will keep you trapped in everlasting ignorance (Herbert Spencer). As someone that briefly wrestled with a drinking problem, I now understand exactly why and how people get seduced and trapped in the vicious cycle of addiction. We do it just to cope with the harsh realities of everyday life in a world that is becoming increasingly less reasonable to live in.

Life is not easy for those of us that have had to work for a living. Having the additional stress of the 911 attacks on top of normal problems was simply too much for many sober adults to handle. So, what did many of us start doing more of as the US economy has slowly eroded away? Only a few years after 911, Weapons of Mass Distraction were shipped into the US in the form of flat screen TVs. I don't care who you are, you'd have to be a robot not to get seduced by a brand new 50" flat screen in your family room. I know I did.

The now critical nature of the present economy (not only in the USA, but worldwide) calls for us to pull it together. We have become a country of drunken pill-popping sheep being led to the slaughter by politicians that don't care about us at all. We must help one another to sober up, and turn off our TVs because they've robbed us of our health. It's time to restore sanity as a country. Our survival as a group now depends upon it.

We must start holding ourselves accountable for our own selfish actions and start helping our neighbors. If the whole country goes down, I've got news for ya, you'll be living in the mess! Then, all of those zombie apocalypse movies will make perfect sense (way too late). We don't have to go down that road and I don't think we will. We can turn things around. Our billionaire slave masters that have been terrifying all of us for the last 10 years have taken too much. I've had enough of being afraid.

Start having some compassion for the group, because we're part of it. Only a handful of super greedy billionaires (about 400 people worldwide) are counting on us to remain drunken, divided, and sedated while they live like kings. Our Republic that was formed with principles of freedom has been thrown out the window. I intend to do my part in helping bring decent people back to reality.

Whenever I die and my soul continues on in a new existence, I want to do so with a clear conscience. I want to have lived a life that speaks my truth. Even if I get ridiculed, outcast, or killed for attempting to give courage back to a country of cowardly lions and pill-zonked zombies, at least I tried.

I will not behave in the manner that unethical billionaires want me to. There is no honor in that, and we are not dogs to be trained. I would rather have this brief ride in a human body get ended prematurely by corrupt men attempting to silence me, than bow down to men whom worship money before God. Living a lifetime that defends good people rather than patriarchs is the way that I want to be.

134

We are all constantly asked to ignore our God-given consciences just to get by. Over the course of a lifetime we have been conditioned to cold and heartless. Do you think that it might be time to start listening to that conscience that tells you to do what is right?

When we finally break our mental chains of addiction, fear-based control systems (that only empower the rich) will crumble. We will finally raise our level of consciousness and start saying no when rich assholes start making unreasonable demands upon us. Once that happens our God-given consciences will be operating as they were designed to.

We will naturally know the difference between right and wrong, and do what is right. Not, what is convenient, or what will appease the rich asshole standing in front of you and making threats. Once we remove the very unnatural inputs of TV, alcohol, and not-give-a-shit pills, (sold to us by our TV) things will change for the better.

Stop living under rules and conditions that our leaders do not follow themselves. The whole slave and master relationship can be ended. After unplugging yourself from the same brain drains as the other zombies, something amazing will begin to happen. Strangers from all over will begin listening to you. Your words alone will carry more power because you'll look and feel better than the other docile people all around you.

Each day as I'm adding the final touches to this book, more and more people are engaging in conversations with me. That something that is different about me (and how to get it) is being given to you right now. It's going to give you more energy, more fight, and more heart. These are things that we all deserve to have more of.

To regain our God-given conscience, is to regain the highest level of freedom available here on earth. The dictators on earth know this, and they are throwing everything that they can (ISIS) at the public to keep our consciences turned-off. Greedy politicians prefer a fearful public. When the public stops following the slow zombie diet, it will be checkmate. They don't think it can happen, but I do.

How do greedy billionaires keep people's brains turned off? Simple, feed them a diet of stress, fear, TV, fluoride, coffee, alcohol, anti-depressants, sleep-aids, and obesity causing foods. Human bullies want you to be dumb, docile, and with a low self-esteem, so that you will continue to take their abuse and do nothing about it. Greedy billionaires use television to convince millions of working-class people to believe that we are powerless. Nothing could be further from the truth.

Once the majority of Americans come to believe that we have the power to declare an election a farce; then real change can begin to happen. In a country that has seen millions of good people lose everything, it's time that we push back. We have the power to fire elected officials that are clearly not serving the group.

When it comes to our high-level government officials, (and the banking executives that own them) we outnumber them by nearly a million to one. That's one million (currently sedated) cattle-like people for every one wolf-like politician. How on earth in a republic have we not fired all of the corrupt officials already? This makes no sense. Where did our self-respect go? I'm guessing into a toilet after drinking it away.

In "1984" George Orwell completely realized the tremendous threat that television posed to the masses when utilized by government. It's fair to say that Mr. Orwell was ahead of his time. He saw that future tools of indoctrination would transform previously intelligent citizens into primitive sheep-like adults. What kind of dog did Mad Max have? We all love heroes that are equally as viscous as the bad guys and only reluctantly decide to battle for the meek, due to what's been taken and cannot be replaced.

Go online and find the movie "Conquest of The Planet of The Apes". Watch that movie trailer and then ask yourself, are the contrasting lives of upper and lower class Americans really that different? Do you notice that heavily armed police are used in the movie to defend the slave master humans from the only slightly less intelligent servant Apes?

Redbox sprouted up everywhere after 911 and removed the opportunity to walk past and rent movies like this one. Screw having cats and dogs that can be trained to serve you as your personal pet when you can have much smarter servants that can do more complex tasks. America's upper class could take advantage of moronic people to become their new personal slaves (and they have).

Most Americans have become little more than well-trained and TV programmed servants. The rich stay rich (and don't work at all) and most of you continue kissing their asses and groveling to them just like the servant Apes in the movie that I won't shut up about: "Conquest of The Planet of The Apes". When a conquest has been completed, you end up with a bunch of poor and pathetic conquered people. Look around, it's already happened.

Using the technology of the future (which is now) to completely mind control only slightly dumber people, could be done. All of our movie stores were slowly phased out in the years following 911 because you don't want a bunch of damn dirty Apes watching old movies that perfectly illustrate what is happening to poor Americans right now. Elites of the world simply weren't satisfied with having cats, dogs, and pathetic spouses to completely dominate.

When the world bankers pulled the plug on the U.S. economy in 2008, they made a stupendous mistake. They left alive millions of people like me, walking around their newly formed prison without bars. You see the prison is so high tech, that the bars are merely mental. Much like in The Shawshank Redemption, it didn't take long for old Andy to walk through the prison unmolested by the other inmates or guards.

When you're facing a life sentence, then what's a few years? Then there's the issue of the meticulous nature of people like Andy. You see, when Andy was young, his report cards would consistently come back with comments stating that he was conscientious and diligent. Once locked up, Andy finally decided to abandon the alcoholic escape that had contributed to his failed marriage and unjust imprisonment.

With constant sobriety, the meticulous mind of a person like Andy must have something to keep it occupied. Mindless inmate labor leaves an immense amount of creative energy leftover. The ego of the completely crooked bible-wielding warden (the 1%) was far too blinding for him to imagine that Andy was able to document the warden's criminal activities and then distribute the truth to the public (placing the warden in checkmate).

1% of America, it's time to surrender from your positions of power (that you've abused) and face the legal consequences, or grab your favorite gun and a bullet. Any day now, the very police, military, TSA agents, or your very own personal security guards may come walking up to you, and place you in handcuffs for crimes against humanity. Ideas create reality. The internet that was likely designed to monitor and police us all has instead become an impossible-to-stop spread of information. Low-level people are now exposing high-level scams. The truth resonates with people. Lies and corruption are being exposed daily at an ever-accelerating pace worldwide.

Orwell knew that with well-planned propaganda, that corrupt leaders would manipulate the masses with ease. Billionaires own all of the TV stations and have the final say of everything that we are allowed to see. The propaganda is beginning to fail. I am pretty sure that the actual teachings of a dude named Jesus Christ got him crucified by the Roman government, alongside of a couple of other revolutionaries. Back then it was only one enlightened man and a small group of disciples that quickly disbanded when things got ugly. Now, there are millions upon millions of God-fearing people exposing corruption all over the globe.

Jesus had flawless logic (just like Spock) and a large conscience that the Roman government could not corrupt with money. So, they had to kill him to stop him from spreading an enlightened way of thinking (heightened consciousness) to the masses. Regular people were starting to listen to him in spite of the fact that he didn't have any money.

You can't have a reasonable person that is able to point out the flawed logic in a corrupt system walking around and removing fear from the common man. Our organized religions have been infiltrated and corrupted as well. Pastors of mega-churches are corporately friendly and politically correct (while their congregations become poorer and poorer). Great job preachers! Sell-out preachers that have taken dirty government money to avoid this brutal job market won't escape the karmic hammer that universal law promises them.

When is the majority (that does believe in some sort of God) going to stop following the orders of men who keep getting caught lying to us? They don't even believe in simply being good. Yet, we keep allowing them to set the rules over the rest of us. We pretend that they are God-fearing people while their actions and their bank accounts tell another story.

The masses have to stand up in numbers to dishonest men. If only one person jumps off the ground in a sports stadium, nothing happens. However, if fifty thousand people all jump off the ground at the same time, then the whole stadium shakes. This is an appropriate time in history to peacefully shake the stadium. Will crooks take swings and a few shots at an awakened public? Yes, ensuring their arrests and removal from power. It's worth it. Let our scummy politicians and bankers lash out at the public for broadcasting the truth.

Our politicians have been caught red handed for millennia taking advantage of their power and ignoring the well-being of the people. It is time for this to stop, and it is time for humanity to evolve spiritually. Spiritual people are not fearful, and will not follow ridiculous orders coming from evil men.

Do you get why dictators would not want the masses to obtain true spirituality? There are some religious fundamentalists that say, "God, God, God" and still turn out to be racist, ignorant, selfish people (regardless of how holy they claim to be). That's not what this book is about. This book is about eliminating hypocrisy within yourself. Rub the truth in the faces of all of our abusers. We have all been postponing some very necessary confrontations in our lives. Do you want to end up like millions of dirt poor Chinese factory workers that avoid confrontation at all costs?

Once your conscience has been boosted, and your brain has had corrupt programs eliminated from it, a stronger and more spiritual connection becomes possible. This is more so your own personal journey to getting connected to all that is good within you. One thing that real life experience has taught me is that organized churches still have plenty of customers that seem to have no conscience left at all.

Nearly all of our churches stay locked up and empty six days a week. This proves that helping the needy is a bottom priority for all of those beautiful and empty buildings. Those churches could be housing the homeless, and feeding the needy. There is a clear difference between boosting consciousness and being religious. Organized religion has left plenty of room for hypocritical money-worshipping zombies.

A lot of happy people that have raised their level of consciousness did so by tackling their own addictions. They turned off their TV, and stopped seeing everyone else as separate. We are on this ride together. Finding common ground and happy mediums is a good place to start. We share the same land, water, and air with each other. Once your own inner spirituality gets turned back on again, fear, hatred, and greed just seem to melt away. They get replaced with tolerance, patience, generosity, and a general love for all of your fellow neighbors.

We can even forgive the billionaires that currently own everything. We just don't have to keep them in charge of all of us any longer. It is they that will have to learn how to let go of some of their control over others. If you've been sucked into the insanity of addiction like I once was, it's ok, it happens to the best of us. Life is meant to be lived, and we cannot learn without making lots of mistakes. When we find ourselves totally lost, beat down, and defeated, for God's sake, surrender. Not to evil men, but to God.

Admit that your way isn't working anymore, lay your pride aside, and admit total defeat to God and ask for help. Prayer does help, but must be followed by positive actions. Help will come from other people that have recovered from similar circumstances. They do exist, and there are tons of them out there. You're not alone in this.

The peace that is unleashed after truly sobering up, telling the truth to others, and finding peace with God is a truly profound experience. Going at life alone is a terrible and painful strategy. There are literally billions of people sharing this planet and we need the help of not only God, but the help of each other. Each new kind act towards a stranger makes looking into the mirror a little easier.

Love for other human beings (and humanity in general) is the greatest gift that God has put into this experience. Nothing in a bottle, no pill, and no drug can outdo the awesome power of love. Like a giant tidal wave in the ocean, love can level any man, woman, or child, and reduce us to rubble. Or, it can transport us straight into heaven on earth. The choice is ours. Choosing only cats and dogs to love, is like staying in the kiddie-pool next to a warm clear ocean.

For me, love is a wave that I have ridden many times. I will continue to try to catch the next wave until the day that this body stops breathing. That is my hope. Love is God, and God is love, and love is good. If you're not here on earth to love other human beings, then what are you doing here?

Our human brains may never fully be able to comprehend what God and love truly are. I'm thinking that little kids can probably do a better job teaching humanity about God and love than our TV sets have done thus far. All I see on TV is that alcohol and not-give-a-shit pills will duct-tape our soulless corpses back together just enough to keep going back to that horrible job that you hate, so you can buy the stuff you don't need, and continue relationships that are making you so happy that you have trouble facing them without daily sedation.

Shitty boyfriends, girlfriends, and spouses are really going to love this book! For all truly shitty relationships, this book is the beginning of the end. When consciousness gets raised, shitty relationships get ended. There will be short periods of uncomfortable change followed by long lasting fulfillment and relief. I know which path I'm choosing.

Consciousness gives people a combination of balls, brains, and restraint not to unnecessarily harm others. We all deserve to be treated with respect and dignity now, today, here on earth and during this lifetime. Only parasitic people (that want countries full of cowardly slaves) would train lower-class citizens (that do follow the rules) of their organized religions (crime) to suffer terribly today for future promises tomorrow.

The most common thing about assholes claiming to be religious is that they are always making you future promises that never come true. In the meantime, they need your time, your energy, and some of your money, even though they live in a bigger house, drive a nicer car, and eat more expensive food than you. Their kids get to attend expensive schools and get better jobs while your weekly offering pays for it all. I think that God got cut out of the deal. George Carlin had a very similar bit. It's not that George was pissed-off at God, just at stupid congregations and their greedy preachers. Most of these preachers need to start using their empty churches to house the homeless and feed the poor.

Rich people that control these organized religions follow none of the rules. Fat selfish religious people that live like kings now while their neighbors slave away for 60 hrs a week aren't fooling God. A church person with no self-control is still powerless over their addictions (including money) no matter how many times they mention the name Jesus Christ.

After the big crash of 2008 the American dream has turned into the American nightmare. For many still suffering, the only exceptions are those brief escapes from reality via drug and alcohol induced stupors. Millions of Americans have lost their jobs, houses, and can barely afford food and gasoline to commute to jobs that have only gotten harder and don't pay enough to live on.

If this were not the truth, then fifty million Americans wouldn't be on food stamps right now, but they are. At the same time, the unemployment rate is supposedly at less than 10%. What a huge joke that statistic is. We all know that the true nationwide unemployment rate is much closer to 20% and is not improving.

Good people that have always attempted to follow the golden rule are not immune to the traps of addiction in this post 2008 economy. The same billionaires that created the financial collapse are now selling the public (that they see as nothing more than trainable primates) a barrage of drugs, alcohol, and lies via TV. They want to keep the entire herd distracted, confused, and docile while the American dream circles the toilet bowl.

Billionaires would rather eliminate us and open up the borders to provide cheap third world slave labor than do what's right. In fact, that's happening right now. 20% unemployment, no problem, let's bring in 30 million more unemployed people from south of the border.

142

I would rather spread upper class logic to third world people. Let's ruin our potential replacements worldwide by educating third world people with sound logic. It can be done.

When you turn the word God around backwards, you end up with the word Dog. Human beings will only allow themselves to be treated like dogs after they have lost all spirituality. Sometimes lots of really smart people develop the same problems due to a terrible economy, does that make sense? Huge numbers of Americans have joined a group of people with similar problems, sought help, and put their lives back together again. During the Great Depression, millions of people died of malnutrition and health problems that go along with being poor and frequently drunk. It may be that time again for millions of poor Americans that consider themselves to be victims of our current economy. It's time to seek help.

Global elites have no problem watching former middle-class Americans self-destruct. My response is to refuse self-administered euthanasia and to begin fixing broken human beings as fast as humanly possible. I am damn good at fixing things and making them go just a little bit faster. Old things can be fixed and do have value.

There is great value in both old machines and in older people. For the most part, a few common parts become clogged-up over the course of time. A 200 Horsepower vehicle can sit for too long and be deemed worthless by a rich guy that can't fix anything (and always buys new). Many of you reading this will quickly tell me that you've gotten too old and it's too late. While reading, I've already taken apart your vehicle, cleaned out an old carburetor that was completely clogged, and am putting things back together again. Also, I removed the power robbing governor that was in there too. It turns out that it was just put in there so you'd keep accepting the next round of lies every four years while you get older and poorer.

There's an account of Abraham Lincoln visiting Charleston South Carolina just after the civil war had ended and the slaves had been freed. While President Lincoln was walking through the streets, a black man bowed down to Mr. Lincoln and without hesitation President Lincoln bowed back to the black man. Honest Abe told the former slave, "You don't need to bow down before any man, only bow down before God". Imagine Morgan Freeman's voice saying, "You damn right!"

We must bring ourselves to admit that our government and financial system are both totally corrupted and operated by the same small <u>minority</u> of criminals. They want us all to bow down to them (and to our own personal addictions) and become their servants. For those of us who want actual positive change, we must <u>stop</u> doing the same things daily. We must communicate to our friends, family, and neighbors about the lies that we all have remained in denial about.

Things in the U.S. will not get any better until we face the truth together. Our manipulators only exist for as long as we continue seeing our neighbors as our enemies. We are all better than this. We must come to believe that hundreds of millions of Americans (and billions of people around the world) can have rewarding lives that are governed by love, logic, and common sense. Not just, my country, my race, my religion, or myself.

It's ok if we have gotten lost along the way during all of the excitement of this ride that we call life. We must learn from our mistakes and quit doing what's no longer working for the majority of people that are generally good. Millionaires often forget that their decisions to make them more money are often hurting real people. Deep down, most people are good. It's only the TV that has programmed people to believe and behave otherwise. When that powerful mind altering device is abandoned, you'll be amazed at how much better you'll feel.

We must renegotiate a more mutually beneficial relationship for our group. It starts with sobering ourselves up in order to regain self-respect. Average Americans must come to an understanding that it is totally normal for the human egos of millionaires and billionaires to get corrupted by money and power. As a result, even the best of souls can temporarily lose their connection to God (anything good and honest) and that's ok. Their souls also came here to learn. We are not here to punish them, but we no longer have to continue allowing them to victimize the whole group. Assholes only behave in a certain way for as long as the people around them allow it.

Stop doing business with unfair people. Stop repeating the same daily behaviors that have kept us trapped in ignorance and in misery. When we change our own actions for the better, then assholes can no longer manipulate us (because we won't let them). Once we have tackled personal demons, it's much harder for others to dominate us. Predatory people get easy meals out of addicts.

Removing TV, drinking only distilled water, using non-fluoride toothpaste, and flushing out bowels filled with years of processed foods will begin to allow clean fresh fuel to reach your brain. The difference between a dead broken-down vehicle, and a beast of a classic, is a needle-sized hole in each carburetor. I've already cleaned your carbs (while you were reading) and put things back together again. All you need to do now is start putting in good fuel and you'll be amazed. Mental walls that were put in place by assholes are now gone. Your very own processor is now coming to more logical conclusions that will directly benefit you.

# Chapter 10 – Taking back our power, searching for truth, and restoring our health

The true power is (and always has been) at the bottom of the pyramid. We have simply been tricked, trained, drugged-up, and fed cheap drinks on purpose, to not realize this. A relative handful of wealthy men have made us believe that they hold all of the power. They don't. In fact, they never have. It has always been nothing more than a well orchestrated illusion that has been programmed into the public's belief systems. The illusion is being shattered right now.

We need to realize that we are indeed spiritual beings that have no reason to fear death. To make life better for the majority, we must not fear losing our lives while fighting for the freedom of our group. Kings and politicians have feared the enlightenment of the masses for thousands of years. They know that if the masses all get really smart, then we will see no more need for the elites (parasitic people). We are now at the point where we clearly agree that our Congress and Senate are providing no protection for the American people.

Some people will sacrifice us all for more money. Why not dust yourself off like old Harrison Ford, and punch out a few Nazis before you die. Thousands of Nazis did come to the U.S. following World War II (via Project Paperclip) became citizens, and were absorbed right into the military industrial complex that President Eisenhower warned about when he left office. Our Senators, Congressman, and the President all answer directly to the same group of globally reaching corporations (and the billionaires that run them).

When we do die (if there is a heaven) and the angels pull up a review screen of how we did, then I certainly don't want to see an image of myself cowering in fear and quietly conforming during a criminal takeover of my country. Wouldn't you like to fight against a few old Nazis and their control freak offspring before you die? Or, are you going to just conform and become part of a world that's been the dream of World Bankers for 100 years?

America is home of the free and land of the brave right? Then why are the majority of Americans being ignored and are experiencing a declining quality of life? At the exact same time, a minority of billionaires are making all of the rules that govern our worsening lives. Good people are being dictated to and we all know it. This is a spineless way to continue existing.

We must take back our power and realize that we determine the fate of our own lives, not a few rich a-holes with zero concern for the group. Our sheer numbers cannot be beaten when we work together. Every zombie movie ever made illustrates this very point. The numbers always win! Whatever direction that we the zombies decide to go, we go. Other people have been steering us, and it's time that we start steering ourselves again. Everyone reading this is gaining a greater level of self-control. The power to create a more positive timeline for your own life has already been increased. Think of it this way, multiple power supply wires to your brain that had been cut by the controllers of our society, (via TV programming) have now been repaired.

Stop watching TV and you're cutting the control cord between you and the manipulators of our declining society. Our society is declining fast right? Each time you plop down in front of your TV, it's like pouring sugar into your new freshly cleaned out gas tank. The carburetor that I just took apart and cleaned gets quickly re-clogged, and you remain a non-threat zombie to the world banking elites. Keep your TV off, and refuse to pay attention to it. The additional brain power from the repair work that's already been done will become obvious.

Remember Egypt? Did Mubarak leave office, or not? The masses ask and they shall receive. We just need to keep our brains turned back on, and our souls connected back to good (God). Clearly Sunday church and 20+ hours of television per week has not produced a world full of enlightened people. Perhaps it's time to start trying some new daily behaviors and a new strategy to turn things around on a nationwide scale. Each one of us does make a difference in this battle for a fulfilling lifetime.

Why is raising the consciousness of the average American so extremely vital? Well, we are kind of getting our asses kicked as a group. Forty to fifty million Americans receiving food assistance is not exactly a sign of a healthy economy. If you're fat and happy and really don't care about those other people, then you'll change your mind real quick when their food stamps get cut-off.

You now have the will to refuse the things that have artificially lowered the brain-power of the masses. With the new neural pathways that now exist, if you <u>choose</u> to <u>not</u> pour sugar into your freshly overhauled brain, then a few awesome things will begin to happen: Fearlessness, peace, unconditional love for mankind, a conscience that will automatically do the right thing, forgiveness to others and the compassion to help them, forgiveness towards yourself for being human, appreciation for this life, and gratitude for this learning experience. Are these things worth working for?

If the path to obtaining them simply starts with unplugging your cable cord and refusing to pay attention to TV wherever you go, will you try it? There is a reason that both Neo and Morpheus in the original Matrix movie are standing in front of a TV with a big pyramid on the back of it. Can you believe the incredibly paper-thin electrical wire of control surrounding our belief systems that TV programming is?

We are like 300 million cattle returning to jobs that we hate and spending lifetimes in fear due to just one little electrical wire going into the back of a voluntary (Government approved) hypnosis machine. The same wire might as well be plugged into the back of your head, just like in the Matrix movie. How many cattle (awaiting slaughter) will remain in the field when three small electrical wires separating them from freedom are turned off? They must first see a cow breach the fence without getting shocked. When the other cows realize that the fence has been turned off, (and have gained knowledge of the upcoming slaughter) it doesn't take long for a stampede towards freedom.

The proposed "high consciousness diet" found in the pages of this book offers far more benefits to Americans than the "norm" diet has produced. Do you want to be one of the American food stamp army? I don't, and God help you if you do. Isn't it about time that we stop doing what everybody else in a suffering herd is also doing every day? Unplugging your TV, is like unplugging the electrical fence. All this time our completely corrupt control system has been hanging by a paper-thin wire. The all-seeing eye can simply be unplugged.

Perhaps repeating the same daily routine as 50 million food stamp cattle, is not a good idea anymore. Stalin amassed an army of citizens on food stamps too. It was not a good time for that group. We do not need to repeat what the Russians did because we can learn from their mistakes. I don't want to be huddled in a cold room sharing one potato with my entire family. That type on non-sense was accepted by an entire country of people (not that long ago). Billions of people are now living in poverty rather than standing up to their oppressors. This is a fact. Everyone reading this now knows how to cut the electrified fence that's been protecting our loving Politicians, Bankers, and 1% from the zombies.

I would argue that the "norm" daily behaviors of Americans have produced millions of slow-moving, slow-thinking, and fearful people that are submissive to unfair leaders. Our group keeps on repeating all of the same false premises from TV. Our TV sets and smart-phones have all been used to shock our psyches, and keep us all in line. Watching buildings implode on 911 was the ultimate electrical shock.

Afterwards, we all readily accepted cattle-like treatment of ourselves at airports and in our homes. Suddenly our phone calls are listened to, and our emails are swept for suspicious words. This is no different than what Russian citizens dealt with under Stalin's control. Everything there was watched and listened to, just as it now is here. We literally allow ourselves to be corralled, searched, and processed like criminals within our own country.

We repeat ridiculous premises like: 911was pulled off by guys with box cutters, NORAD just happened to have a full stand-down that same day, and the buildings weren't demolished using a controlled demolition. Somehow people actually believe all of these statistically impossible coincidences occurring on the same day. The electrical fence surrounding the field of your mind has been cut, its power is off, and you don't have to plug it back in again.

These same zombies are also oblivious to the fact that the Supreme Court has granted corporations equal value as a person has.

This is mass insanity, suffered by a mass population that was victimized by a massive PSY-OP. As in, a psychological operation carried off by a third party (not bearded guys in caves that practice crossing monkey bars). Only a planet full of talking Apes would buy such a completely rubbish story. How on earth did we all go along with the story for so long?

I admit that I accepted the televised and politician-approved version of the story for a while. I also believed Al Gore's global warming movie for years, but later changed my mind. After actually hearing out the counter arguments presented by sane and logical people, I then admitted that I had been tricked. I now accept the more logical version of reality that scientists and engineers support after reviewing the actual evidence. This applies to both global warming and 911. Process that one you old Fox News watching conservatives.

I also refuse to believe in Santa Claus or the Easter Bunny. Sure our politicians are super honest with everything else, but on this one issue of 911, I refuse to accept their groups' consensus of reality for any longer. They also had a consensus to create the TSA, The Patriot Act, and Obamacare, didn't they? We're dealing with very classy individuals that really love us a lot. They would never lie to us in order to exert total control over the group and make tons of money during the process.

Also, as of June of 2013, the Supreme Court has overturned an amendment to the constitution that was part of the civil rights movement to guarantee equal voting rights in all states for minorities. In other words if states now want to implement totally racist voting registration rules they now legally can, without federal penalty. Perhaps old white people are about to lose their ability to vote in the next big election. Suck it old people, you shouldn't drive so slow (just kidding).

It's called karma old racist white folks. Looks like 30 million immigrants from Mexico are about to start voting for new laws that support death panels for old white people. No expensive medical procedures for old people and free healthcare for poor foreigners. Obamacare! I guess hiring the cheapest lawn crew with a whole team of illegal immigrants (rather than paying Jimmy from next door a fair wage) is finally coming around to bite you in the ass.

Fat smug old men collecting social security that frequently tell me, "I'd hate to be your age, you're screwed" don't quite see the chess board that I do. Bill Gates is on video stating that one less old person having an expensive medical procedure could mean ten more teachers get jobs. Soylent Green. It's all about going green, and the lobotomized 25 year-olds are only concerned about inheriting the Gran Torino (while living at their parents house and working for $8 an hour). The chessboard is grand and Fox News has merely been an effective pacifier.

Old people in America today are equally in as much danger as Jews just before young Nazis began loading them onto trains. I've lived in Florida for a few years now. The old people here are as happy as clams to live like kings while slave-like wages are all that are offered to the people now serving them. Old people greatly underestimate the complete lack of empathy present in TV hypnotized young adults. I can just see TV trained 25 yr olds (previously unemployed) loading up the trains for $14 an hour while texting.

All the chess pieces are in place, and I'm trying to unplug you poor bastards as fast as I can. Both the young and the old are being set up for disaster. The concentration camps for non-party supporters won't have bars though. Instead, TV-programmed old people are unconsciously walking themselves into hospitals and being processed by unconscious hospital workers that are blindly following new Obamacare (anti-senior) protocols.

Granted, most TV hypnotized old people are far too proud to unplug their TVs, and far too fearful to stop administering their own daily tranquilizers. The roads sure would become safer and traffic sure would move faster. Alright alright, "Hey old people and hospital workers, you guys are about to participate in a well-organized and very subtle genocide". If you don't want to participate in a world that the architects of Obamacare are building, then unplug yourself. Remove the TV programming from your operating system.

Both Republicans and Democrats are standing aside to let the powers-that-be legalize 30 million third world people. These new Americans can start voting with all of the superior logic and

151

bargaining abilities that their former third-world country has taught them. Once again, old white people with money, you wanted cheap labor today and forgot that they may be voting away your rights tomorrow. Tomorrow is here, and you're still alive. The old can start sharing with the young, and the young can refuse to support death panels.

The hardest part for millions of addicted Americans is going to be admitting that they are addicted to anything in the first place. As a former drinker, I can tell you that when people finally walk into the rooms at AA meetings, we're often the last person to realize the truth. Our human ego is blinding. Highly intelligent people with proven track records of success are just as likely to develop substance abuse problems as anyone else is.

Our egos lie to us and keep telling us that everything is ok, while our personal situations keep getting worse and worse. This is exactly what the billionaires that have rigged our political system want; they want us lying to ourselves about our own personal problems and <u>failing</u> to address them. They want you to fear straying away from the "norm" due to fear of public ridicule. TV is their primary control tool.

Fear of public ridicule is a tremendously powerful mechanism. It has prevented the public from figuring out the massive scams that have been successfully pulled off on us all. If you say something to a friend, family member, or co-worker that differs from the televised version of the story (version of reality that all the politicians support) you are likely going to get called a conspiracy theorist (thought criminal).

Doesn't that term have a negative connotation? The super wealthy want you to stay in line with the accepted beliefs of the other zombies that will automatically attack you if you threaten their existing belief systems. The programmers of the zombie public must find this to be hilarious when watching a smart loving human being get yelled at, for saying something intelligent to a hypnotized person. This happens on a daily basis here in the United States just like it once did in Communist Russia and in Nazi Germany.

Over the course of time, intelligent people just start drinking more often to prevent themselves from actually saying something smart (and getting attacked for it). This definitely happened to me in Cleveland when I attempted to bring up the third New York City sky scraper that was demolished on 911. After commenting that his shirt was missing the third building demolished that day, a friend of mine wearing a memorial to the twin towers quickly went into attack mode.

The once friendly fireman that had always greeted me with a smile quickly turned to anger. He yelled at me, "don't you get started with that shit" pointing his finger at me with rage in his eyes. All of our past positive interactions had been thrown out the window and the once loving man had been replaced by a programmed attack dog. Maybe he thought that armored cops wearing riot gear were going to storm into the bar and pepper-spray him in the face for even being part of such a conversation. We've been trained like robots, and I'm breaking the programming right now.

The otherwise kind man was defending which version of reality, the government approved version, or the critical thinkers' version? It was a sobering experience for me. This is likely how it was for Germans questioning Hitler's version of reality as the Nazis slowly rose to power. The people had been hypnotized, and it was very hard to break through their programming. Could this happen in a whole country of Americans that in all other instances, we call morons?

Billionaires want you to repeat all of the "norm" daily behaviors that have gotten America into our present physical, mental, and spiritual health, (sad state as a group). Why? Because we're becoming dumber and cheaper labor that cannot negotiate for ourselves as well as we used to. Does that make sense? To them, you are asleep, unaware, unawake, and totally unconscious of their manipulation of you. The billionaires owning America want fearful primates that follow orders.

John Carpenter made the title of one of his movies called "They Live" featuring Rowdy Roddy Piper. It's not exactly the Shawshank Redemption, but the movie does have a very relevant message to it. They (billionaires) live while you sleep. You're simply a pawn on the chess board of life that rich a-holes completely control. I really don't like the idea of being another person's programmable pawn.

There is a five minute excerpt from "They Live" featured on Youtube that illustrates the main point of the movie. It's very relevant to today's economic and spiritual conditions around the world. It basically shows a man that sees the world as tell-a-vision and billionaires owning everything intend for us to see it.

The movie shows what happens when we raise our own level of consciousness, and how our perception of reality changes. The man found glasses allowing him to see deeper into reality, so that he would stop getting scammed. This book is creating your own pair of glasses. You will still have the choice to put on the truth seeing glasses or not.

If we boost our own level of consciousness, then the blinders for seeing the world are taken off. There are some very true statements made in this short movie snippet that deserve five minutes of your attention. It is gravely important to understand that the tiny minority of billionaires that have bought off our politicians do not care about the well-being of the masses.

The cheaper that the available labor pool gets the better! Screw your family, your friends, and your kids, all in the name of their personal profit. Universal law allows them to slaughter us if we lack the will to save ourselves. That's how they see it.

The reason that they have gotten away with screwing us over so badly with decreasing amounts of lube for the last twenty years is simple. Increasing amounts of TV, and what it's been selling more of, prescription not-give-a-shit pills, alcohol, and a declining quality of life that we are all told we can do nothing about. Do you really think that going from a twenty-nine inch tube TV in 1995 to a 50" flat screen in 2010 is going to decrease the amount of time that we spend consumed by a box in our living rooms? It certainly got me.

My own father still fails to free himself from the TV that was brought home to him from one of the most vampiristic relatives in our extended family. Why would anyone in their right mind keep a gift from a Godless relative that worships only money? Once again, that flat screen TV that is hooked up to a cable box is like a radio-active vase in your family room. You can't see the damage being done, but it was put there by your enemy and your time is being stolen by it. We're not here forever.

Maybe that's why shoppers are referred to as consumers, because their free will has already been consumed by the TV that programmed all of their wants. We must unplug the television, review the actions of our leaders, and start treating their words with as little value as everything else that's being sold to us by our TVs. The results are astounding when we finally break free from the exact same daily behaviors that have moved the herd of American zombies into a complete state of apathy.

The elites may be doing just fine, but we have been beaten senseless, and are starting to act more like trained Apes than people. We need to stop kissing the asses of other human beings that cannot seem to stop themselves from eating all of the food, and hoarding all of the resources. Gluttons are not good leaders, and decent human beings should not fear upsetting those whom have clearly lost control.

Have you been to walmartpeople.com yet? Isn't it about time that we get some tiny smidgen of self-respect back for ourselves? If you take some of these people on television out of their expensive suits, and remove the caked on makeup, then some of them deserve no more credibility than Walmart people seen rolling down the aisles in their scooters and spandex. Take away the suit, the hair, the makeup, and the script that someone else wrote, and you start to see a trained person that's following orders.

Our news casters and pro athletes are more like performing carnival chimps, than actual independent thinkers. Most of us working class slouches have more freedom to do and say exactly what we want than our idols on TV do. I don't envy their circus performer existences. Their owners have a much shorter leash regulating what they can do and say while they're out in public.

Do you understand that TV sells all of us an illusion of who is credible? If you would like to see the world with an incredibly increased amount of perception, then you must first change the daily behaviors that have been obstructing your vision. Does that sound like an experiment worth trying out? The good thing is, if you're completely new view of the world isn't what you wanted; then you can simply return to the old behaviors that were keeping you oblivious in the first place.

I am guessing that most people reading this will be quite pleased with the increased brain power and over all sense of peace that the high consciousness diet will deliver. Speaking of diets, the bulging waist lines of Americans have only gotten bigger over the last thirty years, haven't they? Is it fair to say that the mountain of health advice delivered to the masses through TV, magazines, and the internet is failing us?

When exactly do the ignorant zombies start noticing that we've turned into a country of physical train wrecks? Take Donald Trump out of his really expensive suit and put him in a pair of gym shorts and a tee-shirt, and Walla, Walmart shopper! Do you really believe that if there's a God up in heaven, that the angels will say, "Well, you've just spent a lifetime being fat, fearful, dumb, and drunk, welcome to heaven!"? It's a confusing sentence, I know, because our logic is really that retarded.

If there are any higher spiritual beings in the entire universe, is it more likely that after you die, having lived a life of being fat, fearful, dumb, and drunk, that the angels would say, "Dude, really? Dude, you just like, totally slept through the last fifty years of your lifetime and carried out the bidding of sneaky rich people. They used your TV to hypnotize you dumbass. We tried thousands of times in thousands of different ways, through thousands of different people to wake you from it, but you kept shushing all the divine intervention attempts away. You kept telling people that you got this! So, when would you like to go back?"

Perhaps it's about time to start telling your ego (your addiction's lawyer in your own head) to shut up if you aren't 100% happy with the human being that you see in the mirror each morning. Part of raising your own level of consciousness is re-building a healthy self-esteem. This doesn't involve you being drunk, high, or on not-give-a-shit pills in order to feel good about yourself.

Intoxicating (filling yourself with toxins) yourself into a delusional state of being each day, so that you can lie to yourself that you like who you are is not going to impress any higher spiritual beings. If they do exist anywhere in the entire universe, then perhaps they are watching and waiting for us to do something good on our own. If advanced beings are watching over us, then they would be looking for an ounce of discipline from each one of us before providing us some assistance and inner peace.

If you're over weight then perhaps it's time that you acknowledge that the "normal" diet has created a herd of self-hating zombie-like cow-people. We sooner attack a thin person in our own delusional dialog than get honest with ourselves about our own loss of self-control. We've started defending the insane behaviors that we now share with the growing sub-species of cow-mericans. Is this rude to fat people? Yes. Are many fat people rude towards the rest of the world while walking around with almost zero self-awareness left?

The American dream has become the cow-merican nightmare. It's about damn time that we break the spell, and start restoring ourselves into the dignified human beings that we deserve to be. I promise that eight diet cokes a day replaced with eight glasses of distilled water will allow you to drop the extra weight faster than any lies sold on TV. Unplug your cable box, throw away all the alcohol, and find rooms full of other people that also abandoned their own daily sedation. Find healthier people your own age and do what they do.

Has it ever occurred to you that oppressive and abusive owners would want lots of Americans with poor body images and low self-esteems? They will put up with worse wages, and take more abuse without quitting a job. Terrible employers need unhealthy and miserable human beings to take their crap (that do nothing to stop it). It's very profitable.

That was the story that was painted all over the sad city of Cleveland Ohio. Only a few rich a-holes had hoarded all of the profits and offered a miserable existence to the drunken tattoo-covered slave class. The majority of citizens there accepted a pathetic existence of poverty that was perpetuated by their own self-medicating addictions. The whole city was a giant prison with no bars.

Underpaid employees that have drinking and drug habits are ideal in oppressive job markets that are looking for spineless cowards. Addicts will stay in horrible situations without walking away from the abuse. Most of this book was forged in Cleveland, Ohio, so I'm not afraid to mention it. Thank God that the people there were unable to turn me into another defeated wage slave that says, "it is what it is" without attempting to make things better.

If a person hates them self enough then you can treat them like rubbish and they won't leave, because they don't have the confidence to do so. I did leave, and there are plenty of other better jobs offered to me outside of Cleveland Ohio. Unfair employers depended on masses of cowardly zombies that lacked the self-respect to leave that town.

Right now, some sad slave in Cleveland is asking another one, "Whatever happened to Max"? I experienced a revolution in consciousness. The same type of change would end the Great Recession of 2008. Nothing would be more terrifying to our fearless politicians and billionaires than seeing a nationwide boycott on TV watching, alcohol consumption, and prescription drug use. Without those mental chains an entire country could regain a better quality of life in a matter of months, not years.

The vast labor pool of zombie Americans that have accepted ever worsening labor conditions in the U.S. could be gone in a matter of months, not years. This is the elites' worst fear, and we could easily make it a reality. Perhaps that is why our borders are being opened up right now. The really rich want to keep their cheap mindless labor.

As a result, employers have been able to slash wages nationwide with very little pushback from an army of discouraged (not brave), hopeless (not confident), and delusional (full of shit) addicts that think things will magically get better if we just keep doing what we've been doing (insane). The American zombies have been looking for our politicians to make good on any of their promises (insane). What an insane premise that is for an insane group of defeated people.

Do you want to be a programmed slave? I don't. So stop playing the game the way that the billionaires have arranged for you to. We're hopelessly hypnotized by a box in our family room that has

158

made them wealthy and us poor. I'm breaking through the programming but you must choose to put good fuel into your own operating system. Then, refuse tomorrows programming. Stay unplugged.

A friend of mine whom also stopped drinking informed me about a book that helped him go from 265 pounds down to a healthy 185 in a matter of six months. The book is called, "The Primal Blueprint" and very clearly explains why Americans have gotten so out of shape. Once again, I ask, when you're not drinking, high, or prescription-pilled into oblivion, do you like the person that you see in the mirror?

It's time to tell your ego to shut up and ask yourself am I the adult that I envisioned growing into when I was a little kid? If your answer is no, then why not make some changes that will piss off rich people? Do you really want to be their perfect trained slave for life? Would billionaires distribute a food pyramid that is totally upside down and backwards to set up the masses for failure? Does that sound more like par for the course?

To me, rather than calling them our government officials, they are Ape Management. Watch "Conquest of The Planet of The Apes" and this will make perfect sense to you. The movies were never about apes, nor separating blacks from whites. It is much more about social class inequality. The mental controls used by an abusive upper-class gave them a false sense of security.

The movies illustrate how rich and poor have been further divided as our technology has advanced. Sadly, the corrupted ego of a rich a-hole will justify an oppressive slave-like existence of the poorer people (employees) that serve them. If you're born into a rich family then you deserve an easy life (while those whom work for you suffer).

Wealthy Americans have been trained to ignore poorer people (that are now suffering all day long). Ape management believes that lower-class Americans deserve their suffering; even if they are kind, sober, work 50 hours per week, and believe in God. This is flawed logic. It's time for a change in Ape management. Watch the old Conquest of The Planet of The Apes and you'll see what I'm talking about. The very diet of poor people is designed to lower their IQs.

Hot pockets and cheap beer would kill anything (including brain cells).

You do understand that working class health nuts are not the people who have designed the food pyramid that is taught in public schools? Does it make sense to you that perhaps the reason that the majority of American adults have become over weight is because we have been following a flawed belief system? Would you believe that it was designed to create more manageable citizens?

There are appropriate moments in history for civil disobedience. Are you the type of person that is going to continue repeating the same behaviors as the other stupid zombies in Walmart? Do you want what they have? I assure you that they're not writing books or coming up with a plan to get us out of our slave-like existences.

Why would you keep copying the least healthy people? Stray away from the "normal" routine that millions of submissive Americans do every day. Perhaps it's not a great idea to share the same daily behaviors of moronic people caught on "Jay Walking" that are unable to name the Vice President. Stop going with the crowd, because the crowd has become a little embarrassing.

If things have become a mess in your life, then alcohol needs to go. If you're not an alcoholic than what's the big deal? If you do want enlightenment yet your knee jerk reaction to the previous sentence is to say, "Don't mess with my alcohol" then you might be an alcoholic. Jeff Foxworthy ought to do a "You might be an alcoholic" bit to jackhammer that point home to his audience.

Normal people that aren't addicts don't say "Don't mess with my alcohol or pills". There are entire countries that barely drink alcohol or take prescription pills (legalized drugs) at all; their levels of overall happiness are actually higher than ours. The U.S. is not ranked as the happiest country in the world. In fact, we're not even close to the top of the list. Look it up on your smart phone, Google it.

When I stopped drinking daily back in 2011, my body dropped twenty pounds within two months from simply removing the daily alcohol. People don't realize just how bloated they have become. To summarize the amazing nutritional book "The Primal Blueprint" it's all about your body's insulin response to grains, sugars, and high carbohydrate diets.

What exactly do you think beer has in it, things that are good for you? Is that why crazy rednecks and construction workers that drink ten beers a day end up looking like mutants from a post-apocalyptic pirate ship? We all see the wrecked bodies of friends and family members that have tried to hide their long-term drinking problems. They're wrecked. Is that what you want to end up looking like, a leathery half-mutated pirate?

The food pyramid that has been taught to our group is totally upside down. Our bodies will quickly improve if we eat how the hunter/gatherer humans were eating thousands of years ago before we got office jobs and developed big fat asses that came along with them. Our bodies are genetically programmed to react to the types of foods that we eat each day.

Nearly everything that we've been taught is wrong. Bill and Hillary Clinton along with the Obamas don't want you to be skinny, smart, and strong. They much prefer having fat dimwitted cow-mericans that have short life spans and allow them to milk the crap out of without protesting. Don't be easy food for the upper class to leech off of.

The elites want to keep you hooked on three different expensive prescriptions all of which make you fatter and dumber. Now they are taking poor people's tax returns to pay for the same Obamacare that is used to pay for your daily sedatives. The state wants all citizens to suffer from anxiety, run to your doctors for help, and then get prescribed a lobotomy-in-a-bottle. I'm sure you'll be a great Walmart worker in our awesome new global corporation with one global currency. Of course there will still remain a small ruling class of snobby rich people (with no empathy left) just like in The Hunger Games.

We've all been trained to eat foods that actually make our bodies store fat rather than burn it for energy. Do you agree that the average American has become significantly heavier during the last thirty years? Lots of grains and processed sugars that we have been suckered into eating daily (due to the food pyramid) have caused us to

161

store more fat and burn our existing muscle. Those of us that have always completely disobeyed the food pyramid have ended up being the healthy minority. What a joke. The result being that most Americans are starting to look more like "Norm" from the TV show "Cheers" rather than normal human beings. Do you really want to live in an entire country full of male and female "Norms"?

I witnessed a co-worker drop forty pounds in three months by drinking a gallon of distilled water daily while eliminating all soda. It's all about your body's insulin response to the types of foods that you are eating. Exercise has a whole lot less to do with our weight than we have been trained to believe by our Government approved guild lines. Diet soda ruins your health. Please stop drinking it for God's sake. Fat people love diet soda. If you want to stop being overweight then stop drinking diet soda.

Do you get that our own government would set up its own citizens for failure? All to sell us prescription drugs and super expensive hospital stays that have made the health care industry wealthy and the American people sicker? Would wealthy men do such a thing? We all know the honest answers to these questions.

Start coloring outside of the government approved guild lines. If you want to get thin and feel good about yourself again then stop following the food pyramid that was created by our pyramid scheme government. The guys at the top get rich, and everyone else below them gets used and screwed-over during the process.

Ignoring the problem is not making the situation any better. At some point, those of us that are actually healthy must start helping those who have obviously lost self-control and are suffering daily. It's time for an intervention. It's time that Americans begin helping each other to face the truth by not being afraid to speak it. What do you think is happening inside your head right now?

Allowing completely delusional people to spew lies in front of you all day long without speaking up and correcting their lies perpetuates a society that is full of sick people. Look around, that is what we've become. The fewer healthy have become afraid to speak truth in front of the sick group. What a cowardly way to live. Live like a coward and you'll earn the fruits of a coward.

If we start making fat-bloated-zombie checkout lanes at the grocery store, then fat bloated zombies will begin to realize, that they are fat bloated zombies. A society that allows the sickest and laziest people to live the easiest lives is headed for collapse. Southpark has an award winning episode called, "Raising The Bar" that shows what we've become. Youtube it.

If we don't change fast, in about five years you'll start seeing Mexican lawn crews cleaning up after the post apocalypse battle. Instead of noisy leaf blowers strapped to their backs, they'll have flame throwers that are used to clean up bloated Americans that were deemed "Not useful" by President Hilary Clinton. By then, those of us that didn't transform into 300lb blobs of negative energy will be welcoming the Mexican lawn crews of death. Front line wage slaves that are currently working full time and serving rude unemployed fat people know exactly what I'm talking about.

After spending five more years of working 50+ hrs per week to support unemployed monsters of selfishness on "disability", those of us that have not been cheating the system will gladly stand aside and allow poor foreigners to handle our oppressors. Fat people, you're pushing your luck by insisting that young healthy 18-45 year old Americans slave away for 50+ hours per week (to live in poverty) while you don't work at all. You're not our kings and you're not the victims in the current arrangement.

Billionaires know how long term situations play out. Fat Americans are being set-up to be later attacked. Not by me, but by younger and healthier people who are desperate for work and not too bright. To avoid being part of this nightmare scenario we need to start addressing our own problems now.

This book is about regaining control of your thoughts, your actions, and your power. Far too many Americans have had their power taken away by the well-organized efforts of an evil minority. Millions of Americans have been mind-controlled to believe that we are powerless to determine our own level of happiness than our government officials (official assholes).

Addiction free people won't try to con-vince you that they are victims of life. They actually tend to believe in the laws of cause and effect and understand the concept of personal accountability. Let's become strong self-sufficient people that can't be oppressed.

We must now raise the collective consciousness of the zombie public. If the group thrives then we get to thrive within it. If the group suffers then we also suffer. We are all part of the same group. We must help to turn the brains and consciences of millions of people back on.

Do you get that we are completely unable to spread (sell) enlightenment to all of humanity if we (not you of course) are spending hours a day in a drunken and TV hypnotized stupor? Do you get that the people around you apply no value to the words of a drunk, a pill-popper, or an over-eater that obviously suffers from low levels of self-control? People buy things from people that they want to become.

If you want to sell enlightenment to the ignorant masses, then you must first become an attractive spokesperson that has something that most people want. People respect people of action. We love super heroes because they are a force to be reckoned with that possess strengths beyond that of the common man.

In a country full of drunken TV hypnotized men and women, a sober person now possesses a rare level of speed and self-control. Visualize a fat pill-addicted person that collects unemployment. Then, imagine that they have a super intelligent 155lb chimpanzee that does all of their chores for them. Is the chimp stronger, faster, and able to escape from its abusive owner if it chooses to leave?

As a human being gets deeper into addiction, their ego creates a corrupted version of reality. Eventually, a fat, weak, and drunken person begins to think that they are the dominant animal when standing in a room with their 155lb servant. Nothing could be further from the truth. The stronger and faster servant could beat its oppressive slave owner senseless at any time. The only thing preventing the faster and stronger servant from escaping an unfair lifetime of servitude, are the mental chains that the owner class has carefully put into place since childhood. When you spend a lifetime allowing others to do all of your heavy lifting for you, don't be

164

surprised when your slaves one day realize that they are stronger and faster.

The new Rise of The Planet of The Apes movies have nothing to do with chimpanzees. When upper class Americans become too drunk, and too delusional to realize that they've over-stepped the boundaries between right, and wrong; then poorer Americans (the majority) will re-assert control. The only question is, are you joining team drunken slave owner, or team Ape? Stop hurting other people all day long (in the name of money) and please join team humanity.

The Ape class (working class) Americans that are currently working 50+ hours per week (just to survive) are faster, stronger, and much greater in numbers now than ever before. Poor Americans far outnumber the comfortable reality that is falsely portrayed on TV. Wealthier Americans absolute refusal to raise wages (for the now huge lower class) has been a huge miscalculation. When the old "Planet of The Apes" movies were first made, there was a much more even wealth distribution in the United States. That has changed. Hypnosis via television programming is the only thing stopping a nationwide revolt from the stronger and much larger lower class.

The middle class has always provided a buffer zone to defend pampered rich people, from barbaric wage slaves. The buffer zone is gone, and the rich have mistakenly attempted to lock up equally smart middle class people in the same cages with the mega-powerful slave class. Back in the seventies, people worked full time, and could afford houses, cars, and families with the average wage. This is no longer the case.

The metaphor between servant chimpanzees and lower-class Americans was much less obvious at the time when those movies were first released. Like 1984, I'm assuming that the author of those scripts had foresight into the future use of mind control and technology to further clamp down on the working class. Please rent "Conquest of the planet of the Apes" and you tell me if you understand the true message of the movie?

Everybody nods our heads politely and pretends to listen to unsolicited advice being given to us by people that are clearly less physically healthy (to any outside observer). Have you ever observed a wildly unhealthy person giving health advice to a physically and mentally fit person? I know I have. Fat sick people love to dole out health advice to skinnier healthier people. This is like a toothless zombie groaning at a fast smart person that can punch them in the face and run out of the room before the zombie figures out what hit them. They call me fast Meeks.

What do we call an over-weight person that is dumping a load of unwanted health advice onto a much healthier and physically fit person? Delusional, right? At some point, a person's health gets so bad physically that they lose all touch with reality and they begin to view the world through a fun house mirror (provided by their own corrupted ego). On some level, many Americans have lost their sanity. Was that not also the case in Nazi Germany? What about the completely poverty stricken masses of North Korea today, are they sane people? Are they brave?

When somebody's ability to think clearly is intentionally impaired on a daily basis via drinking or popping pills, then that person's entire perception of reality becomes diluted. Does that make sense? When you dilute a drink, does it become less strong, or more? Anyone that is a functioning alcoholic must understand that their own perception of reality is functioning at a diluted (weakened) capacity.

If you're a functioning alcoholic, then you have a weaker grasp on reality, than a sober person does. Would you like to have a stronger or a weaker, grasp on reality? If your current belief system has produced an unhealthy and unhappy you, then perhaps it's time to install a new operating system in your own head with a much stronger processor. This is not some far out fictional theory; it can easily be done starting today.

# Chapter 11 – Understanding logic, and how our brains work

Think of the human brain as nothing more than a biological computer. Many of us have desktops or laptops, right? By now, most of us have owned multiple computers that operated using the best and worst operating systems available to us at the time. It is not that long ago that we had to wait and wait and wait for our computers to simply load the next web page.

At some point, most of us have gotten a computer virus that made our computer stop working correctly. Snoop Dog would call that catching an S T Dizzle! Cheap whores in real life and on the web will throw a wrench into your processor. Think of this book as an anti-virus program to clean out our brains after years of dealing with our cheap whore politicians and their virus infected speeches.

Let's talk about what happens when your computer processor gets infected by (affected by) a virus. We all agree that a computer processes information, right? We type in a word that we are seeking information about and the computer quickly delivers us the data that we requested. Computers are programmed to perform tasks that solve problems. For instance, the simplest computer that we are familiar with is a calculator and on it 2+2=4.

A properly running computer can sort through vast amounts of information very quickly and deliver us the answers that we are searching for. Have the American people been finding the answers to the problems that the politicians and the news casters have been telling us about for the last ten years? I would argue no, our situation has only grown worse.

As a group, we keep asking questions and have failed to get any good answers from the people that we have entrusted to be our best problem solvers. The rest of us just aren't smart enough to run our own lives and that's why we have the government in the first place, right? When a computer gets a virus, it stops working correctly and fails to provide us with the answers that we are looking for.

Sometimes our computers crash completely and don't run at all, but more often than not, the computer slows down. Have the brains of the American people not been slowed down drastically? Many of us have seen pop-ups about corrupt files on our computers. We also see corrupt politicians popping up on our TVs. Most often, we simply ignore them, so long as our computer is still running.

The computer in our heads is still running (even if it has slowed down a lot) due to years of drinking and drugs. Drink beer daily to tolerate retarded logic on TV, and from all the brainless people that now surround us each day. Sedating ourselves every day via constant mind altering drinks and pills has become the only socially acceptable way to cope with living in a retarded society of hypocrites and fools. Most Americans do currently act more like trained Apes, than loving and logical human beings with strong consciences.

We are faced with two terrible choices, be a heartless slave owner that throws crumbs at pathetic poor people below you. Or, be part of the pathetic lower class that accepts shit treatment all day long, for unlivable wages. Screw both of these choices, neither is honorable.

Both groups are completely blinded by ego and are being pitted against one another by the billionaire architects of our society. Both sides are operating with virus infected egos. Both groups can get bent, because we are bringing the middle class back in America!

A clean computer that is virus free is able to easily zip to the next web page at lightning speed. When you ask a virus free computer what 2+2 equals, it processes the information quickly and accurately just as it was programmed to do. The modern computer is a marvel of engineering that can perform a myriad of complex tasks while storing a ton of old data (memory).

What else has a memory, and what do we use our own memory to help us to do? Our memory helps us to make decisions and solve problems based on past experiences. What happens if we cannot remember things from our past mistakes? Does this make us better or worse at solving the simplest of problems?

People with shitty memories become shitty problem solvers. Is your memory good, or is it much worse than it used to be back when you were a teenager? What do you think that this book is doing for your memory right now?

How many Americans have a hard time remembering very simple things? We haven't exactly gotten smarter and better at remembering what we were taught in grade school, have we? Ironically, smart phones are creating dumber people by the day. Thanks a lot Steve Jobs. The Patriot Act takes away freedom, the Justice Department protects politicians, and Smart phones destroy intelligence.

Now I have a boss that cannot remember the simple principle of sharing that he was once taught as a kindergartner. Instead, sports scores and his family's well-being is all that his virus ridden processor is capable of caring about. We've been robbed of our consciences and good people are suffering as a result. Most of us are hurting others daily without even being <u>aware</u> of it.

I don't want my own personal comfort to come at the expense of somebody else's miserable existence. No one else should have a lifetime of poverty imposed on them so that I can live like a king today. Back when there was a middle class, moderation was considered reasonable. Being extremely rich or poor isn't practical. Somehow, extreme assholes have programmed the public to believe that only two extreme choices now exist. This is <u>not</u> true.

The human brain is a bio (living)-logical (running on logic) computer that operates using logic and rules that have been programmed into our brains (belief operating systems) throughout our lives. From a young age, ape Training Videos (TV) has been conditioning the belief systems of an increasingly stupid group of adults. We are trained to believe that, if you do this, then that will happen. We watch thousands of repetitive behaviors on TV that are absorbed by our sub-conscious (which then controls 95% of our behaviors). If we spend hours a day watching rich assholes on TV, we then begin to mimic their behaviors (without even thinking about it).

Our brains are using logic. After being programmed by our parents, teachers, and the environment around us; we then come to conclusions based on the existing programs that we have been conditioned to believe in throughout our lives. One child may be taught that if he works very hard at his schooling and gets good grades, then he will get to go to college. Another child in the same high school may be taught by his parents that school is unimportant, because that child will be working on the family farm.

Clearly a child's parents can program certain beliefs into their own child's brain through repetition, can't they? The human brain can easily be programmed to respond to particular situations in totally different ways (depending on who does the programming). As a country, we've unknowingly allowed ourselves to be programmed by assholes on a mass level. They have done this using our TVs against us.

One child is trained by his parents that all Jews are evil and that he must salute SS guards in the streets. He is then told the same thing by his teacher (trainer) at school, and gets laughed at and ridiculed by his classmates for simply questioning this belief. The radio news caster casually makes comments about filthy Jews when the same child turns on his favorite radio show. This child is growing up in Nazi Germany. Entire countries of well-intentioned citizens can be completely trained to believe just about anything. We are no different and have already been subjected to an equally large amount of programming.

The young German boy's brain was programmed to believe that Jews are evil. The masses (group consensus) in Nazi Germany had been trained to believe that Jews were inferior human beings, and that Adolf Hitler (politician) was protecting the best interests of the German people. Countries of people can be programmed to believe lies that negatively affect their attitudes and actions towards innocent third parties.

Through repetition, the masses of an entire country believed Hitler's words (lies) to be the truth. In reality, the masses had been tricked by a small group of corrupt politicians to obtain an evil minority's objective. Would a politician use a huge lie via TV, using constant daily repetition to steer public opinion? History has already answered that question. Are Americans in the year 2014 that you see out in public every day any smarter than the German citizens that Hitler had tricked? We all know the likely answer.

Germany had suffered greatly after the end of World War One. The German economy had gotten worse and worse over the course of years. The German masses had become very poor, disgruntled, and hopeless. Does any of this sound familiar?

Do you think that the German people drank more or less alcohol, as the economy slowly declined? Please don't tell me that you believe that the U.S. economy has improved since 2008. The actual unemployment rate is around 20% and 50 million people are currently on food stamps. New high paying jobs from emerging industry are not popping up, unless you're a tattoo-covered 300lb fat guy living in Las Vegas.

If human beings get treated in a degrading manner for a long enough time, eventually, they begin to feel like victims. I would argue that the German people had been beaten into a lower level of consciousness that made them more vulnerable targets for Hitler's words. Politicians do attack the psyches of the American masses through speeches on TV.

When economic conditions are that bad, for that long, for that many people, we then become sitting ducks for the next con-man that comes along. We begin to seek frequent escapes from reality that end up making us even weaker and more vulnerable to getting suckered. Do we know of a country that has millions of down and out people that fit this description? Are these same people beat-down enough to accept a Nanny State?

Aren't Germans and beer drinking synonymous? Isn't Germany world renowned for its beer? Isn't it true that the German people have a reputation for loving there beer? What other country can you think of, that just so happens to drink beer like water, and takes great pride (on TV) in a life-long love affair with beer?

Trust me, I've been there. I've used the cure all solution of affordable silver cans at the end of hard work weeks for years. Eventually, I found out why they say that a silver bullet is how you can kill an aware wolf. My once weekly escape somehow turned into a daily habit. In less than a year, the things in my life that meant the most to me quickly deteriorated. My go-to solution for stress had somehow become a powerful daily seductress.

The only things that mattered to me the most when I was drinking daily were my TV remote and a supply of silver cans to last me until bedtime. Television and too much beer is how billionaire a-holes have successfully turned wolves into well-trained and passive dogs. I can attest as a former problem drinker that over the course of a decade, alcohol slowly separated me from my conscience. The daily temptation of a drink was always followed by another and another until my backbone was gone.

Over use of sedatives turns off all natural spirituality (something that we are born with) and can cause the best of humans to do or say the worst of things. It kills our conscience and we all know it, but we aren't ready to face life sober, not yet. Not until Jesus Christ himself reappears. Then you'll finally start acting brave again, right?

We refuse to stop today, because a bearded man from the clouds is supposed to come down first. Only then, will we try to sober ourselves up. This is a bullshit life strategy if there does happen to be a God that is waiting for humanity to show some courage.

Having no personal accountability is exactly what the Nazis depended upon while they slowly took over and controlled the drunken German citizens. Nothing here in the U.S. is really any different. Look no further than magic pills and bottles that have reduced our country into a bunch of cowardly lions running our mouths from our couches while drunk.

Have you not seen examples in your own life when alcohol was used as a conscience killing substance? Do you get that America has become a beer-drinking nation of which the economy has been rocked, just like pre-Nazi Germany once was? This isn't about Americans becoming Nazis, it's about our actions as human beings becoming worse, and worse, and worse, without us even being aware of it.

We're half sedated, all of the time. If you don't think that anti-anxiety pills are keeping you partially sedated, all day long, then you're delusional. We've become a country of drunks and pill-heads. Our elites have successfully chemically neutered both American men and women.

172

Our stress relieving solutions of alcohol and drugs have successfully robbed the United States of America of our conscience. More importantly, alcohol clouds our awareness of the root cause of our problems because our own egos lie to us. I have met entire rooms full of spiritual self-respecting adults that had once done terrible things to their own friends and families while trapped by the insane influence of alcoholism. Many of them quit drinking and became better people. Some don't. Like any other brand of church or cult-like club, AA also contains plenty of hypocrites. My advice is to find a few good sober people, tackle your problem, and eventually leave the rooms.

We've become a country full of drunken hopeless idiots (not you of course) that were promised a better life, by a great speaker. Please remember, things didn't turn out so well for the dumbed-down and drunken German citizens. I think any human being with a functioning brain can admit that America has not seen the hope and change that we were all promised back in 2008. Being on food stamps for the rest of your life and working minimum wage jobs is a pretty horrific outlook for former middle class members. Things have not turned out very well for our group. I'm betting that some of the German citizens that lived through the Nazi era wish that they had been tipped off and snapped out of the spell that they were all under. Pulling a drowning person that's already underwater and is slipping in and out of consciousness daily, is not a bad thing.

We are not living in Stalin's Russia, and the smart former middle class is not going to get silently shipped off to Siberia. Do you get why this book has been written during this time in history? America is in deep shit and no politician on TV from either party is going to dig us out. The true architects of this mess have us digging a ditch just like Cool Hand Luke, only to fill it back in tomorrow. I will not dig my own grave. We've all been intentionally overstressed and overwhelmed so that our brains stop working.

Turn off your TV, stop taking sedatives, and find other people that aren't addicts to help you do this. Stop being run around by assholes all day, and regain your own self-control. We cannot repeat mistakes made by whole countries of people that were turned against each other by corrupt politicians. It has happened here in America.

The consciousness of our country has been lowered, and we must recover together without turning on our neighbors like our greedy owners would love to see happen. The politicians do not care about us, and their actions have made that perfectly clear. We must sober ourselves up if we want to get out of this mess. Massive battles are not won while drunk. Nobody taking heavy duty pills and drinks can think their way out of a paper bag. We've been tricked by solutions prescribed by the friendly man in the white coat that's been paid off by our elites. Politicians now want to manage the ignorant masses like cattle and sheep.

To be drunk, high, or on pills, is to carry out the will of your enemy. We are all much harder to manipulate if we are sober. It's very hard not to get really pissed off, if you get treated like a worthless slave while maintaining continuous sobriety. Try it, and your heartless bosses will begin to fear you.

Do you want to be manipulated by other people to carry out their own selfish agendas? I don't. Drugs and alcohol slowly erode away a person's conscience. Over time, this causes us to behave more like dogs blindly obeying authority, rather than acting like loving human beings with a functioning spine.

Americans have become addicted to these weapons of mass manipulation. It's time that we stop allowing ourselves to be chemically sedated by our opponents. Do you want to be part of the docile zombie herd, or one of the early defectors that has discovered the high consciousness diet?

# Chapter 12 – We've become slaves that are addicted to our own mental chains

It's not easy to break away from these addictions. First off, who wants to admit that they've lost control over anything? Not me, but have you ever known somebody else that was clearly addicted to something and wouldn't admit it? Breaking out of addictive insanity is not easy, but finally the pain of $3.50 gas and 20% nationwide unemployment is doing it. We are waking up and finally facing the truth.

We can't afford to keep doing the "norm" any longer; it's not working for us. Things are going badly on a nationwide level. We cannot follow in the footsteps of the drunken German people that got trained like dogs to carry out the evil agenda of a few greedy men. The Nazi Germans were walking around in a semi-trance and were completely unable to be reasoned with. Americans today are in an equally deep trance right now. These very words are penetrating and dismantling that programming, so you'll cease to be just another compliant Nazi.

There were once greedy assholes that wanted to rule the entire world, right? What about now? Are there still groups of men and woman that may have organized efforts to achieve world domination? Adolf Hitler wasn't acting by himself. There was a group of wealthy men (bankers) that helped to fund the Nazi's efforts. The German people were unable to see the direction where Hitler and his financial backers were taking their country. If the people back then had known exactly where they were headed, then they wouldn't have gone there.

We are better than this, aren't we? If you are saying "no", that you're not better than the Nazi Germans then may God shine down on you, and forgive you. Perhaps then you can forgive yourself for simply being human. Life is not easy, and we all deserve second chances to do something good before we die. What matters the most is how we finish this game, not how we have played it up until now. When we fall down, we get back up, and keep fighting just like Cool Hand Luke. Even rich assholes will begin to respect us if we have the balls to stand up to them. We can't fight them drunk. We're too slow that way and would be like Forrest Griffin fighting Anderson Silva (UFC). Youtube it.

We have been systematically trained to keep waiting for somebody else (outside of ourselves) to come down and save us. In the meantime, we are all getting our asses handed to us in a completely corrupt system that is run by evil men in a well-organized fashion. We have waited and waited for the words spoken by our ever-so-honest politicians to come true, but they never do.

How gullible do we all have to be, in order to believe that a girlfriend that got caught cheating on us 100 times but promises us that this time things will be different? Boy have we been stupid. When we're finally ready to admit that we've been had, then things can start to get better for us all.

Please grow some self-respect and kick our cheating politicians to the curb already. They don't deserve to be in charge of us for a minute longer. They've had more than enough chances to help our group, and have failed us miserably while their own lifestyles have remained the same. We know this is true. We all have to work longer hours for not enough money to afford a decent home and healthy food. The elites still get to go golfing at the country club each week. This arrangement is far from balanced.

We have been stuck in an abusive relationship that no self-respecting human being would stay in. Only a drunk or a drug addict would lack the self-respect to call a liar, a liar to their face. If something is true, then none of us should fear saying the truth out loud. Otherwise, we are cowering down (acting cowardly) before liars and cheats.

If there is a God looking over our actions, do you think we would be rewarded or omitted from receiving help if we act like cowards? When a person gets caught doing the same shady things over and over again, while their partner remains loyal and honest, then the relationship is abusive. Let your asshole slave owners get pissed off and attempt to punish an entire group of already pissed off workers.

Why do people stay in abusive relationships? A low level of consciousness is a good bet. What does that mean? When your consciousness is at a low level, you are unable to see or face the truth. Your ego lies to you about why you continue to stay, and you make up excuses for the other party that is abusing you daily.

Perhaps you're allowing yourself to get treated like garbage for money. Do you know anyone that hates their job, but keeps going back because it pays well? In that case, money has become your highest power, and you outta replace the word God with money, because that would be more appropriate.

Once you're willing to accept degrading treatment from others in order to get money, it's only natural for your own level of self-respect to drop. Then you must drink and drug (like a stripper) to keep your conscience from doing its appropriate job (to get you into a healthier situation). Face your oppressor and confront the wrongs that they are committing against you. Or, you can run to the nearest bar after work and then return to your awful job the next day for your next round of beatings. After you die, perhaps you'll get an award saying, "Biggest Pushover On Earth".

A person's conscience will tell them that being treated like garbage is wrong, but our conscience can be silenced very easily by using alcohol and pills daily. This is how American wages have gone down the shitter so fast without us doing a thing about it. Can you begin to see the key in front of you that's going to get you out of your own crappy situation?

Prescription anti-depressants people, they are being over-prescribed. Aside from documented chemical imbalances in less than 10% (go back a few decades, when America was healthier) of the general population, the rest of us are totally full of shit. If you weren't already diagnosed by your early twenties with legitimate mental illness, then you're probably just one out of fifty million Americans that were completely sold-out by your doctor.

Pills that make you feel nothing while your spouse, or job, are treating you like garbage are no better than drinking or doing illegal drugs. They too are shutting off your God-given conscience and are preventing you from escaping your own daily abuse. Druggies, alcoholics, and prescription anti-anxiety (fear) pill poppers make the best victims when it comes to treating somebody like crap, and having them do nothing about it. Their logic has been weakened, and greedy assholes love that sweet cheap labor that drunks provide.

Once we're addicted, we lack the capacity to give-a-shit while being abused on by others. Do you think that the life situations of people taking these mind numbing substances have gotten better or worse since the great bank crash of 2008? If the most important things in your life have gotten worse or disappeared completely, then stop. Seek help to get off of unnecessary pills and drinks.

Leave the giant parade of over-medicated losers that all share two things in common, a government handout, and a victim mentality. Nobody feels sorry for you, except for your drug-addicted-self. The pills clearly have not solved your major life problems, have they?

If I'm a greedy billionaire (World Bankers, CEOs, Board Members, and Crooked Politicians) then I would want as many of those pill-poppers and alcoholics as possible. Those in the business of screwing over people for money love doing business with a country of drunks. Labor rates are the lowest since the great depression, and a country of drunks is too brain-dead to adjust for inflation.

Billionaires don't want you so drunk that you don't show up for work anymore, but just enough so they can treat you like crap. Employers want to keep Americans right on the edge, without you quitting or having the courage to confront their shady behaviors. Any former employer of mine knows that when they acted shady and decided to piss on my feet, then I've called them out on it. If bosses act shamefully then speak the truth regarding their shameful behavior, and let them feel uncomfortable.

The sneaky slave owners in America are playing dumb regarding these solution pills and alcohol that are constantly advertised on TV. That, or they're on them, and we now have drunks and drug addicts running the world. They only pretend to not want the masses to drink too much or take too many pills. It's all a huge lie. The Elites of America absolutely positively want a country of functioning alcoholics and pot-heads, because they do the most work for the lowest wages possible. I suppose Billionaires may be doing the same with low-level Politicians.

Drunks and addicts will run their mouths outside of work all day long about telling off their bosses, and then stay longer in shitty jobs for shit wages than anyone else does. We all know how human beings respond when authority figures tell us not to do something, don't we? Back in the 80's, our politicians on TV came up with the ultimate mind fuck on America, "just say no". U.S. prisons had been privatized and set up for profit. Politicians suddenly had the ability to become share holders for privately owned prisons, and wouldn't ya know it, those prisons got filled up to capacity. The war on drugs was launched at exactly the right time to fill up those newly privatized (for profit) jails.

People tell us <u>not</u> to do something, then, we do more of it! Just to spite them. Billionaires figured this out a long time ago, and have been using reverse psychology on the public for thousands of years. Is it possible that our billionaires have out-smarted the zero-dollar-aires now watching Ape training videos for hours a night? We literally are watching a repetitive Training Video that shows us where to pawn all of our stuff.

Our wages are falling too short to simply afford the necessities of food and rent. Like any other drunk or drug addict, rather than confront our abusive employer; we decide to get drunk more often, and start to pawn all of our stuff. You know, the more reasonable and intelligent way to cope with our slave owners, I mean bosses. Fat tattooed assholes have never had it so good in America. A country full of addicts is very easy to fleece.

If I just gained 100 extra pounds, covered myself in tattoos, and started wearing all black every day, then I'm pretty sure that a line of defeated Americans would start forming in front of me. Then I could simply pile up their stuff, and then sell it back to them later for a lot more. Have you ever wondered why the poorest Americans that are on food stamps are still able to afford the largest flat screen TVs? Is it possible that billionaires wanting slave labor have replaced physical chains with televised programming?

Americans are constantly drinking alcohol and taking drugs (prescription or illegal) that reduce their brain function down to a level too low to legally drive a car. Think about people that you have known that were close to mentally retarded, and still, received their driver's license. The bar is not exactly high for driving a car, is it?

Think about senior citizens that cannot remember what they ate for breakfast, are unable to work a DVD player, and cannot promptly remember their own kids names, and still, they too, are able to drive legally. I would argue that an out-of-it senior citizen and a drunk driver operate motor vehicles in a very similar manner. Both parties are suffering from impaired judgment and a lack of motor skills. The brains of senior citizens that have trouble driving cars are operating in a diminished capacity.

Drinkers and pill poppers must become aware that they are reducing the power of their brains down to the level of an 85 year-old white man (who hates black people) that cannot solve simple problems. Do you really want to share the same amount of brain power as a racist 85 year-old man that can't drive a car in a straight line? I don't. This is perhaps the least reasonable segment of our population. All of which, receive a government check and watch Fox news all day while eating like horses. Sure 21 year olds with young fresh brains can drink often for a few years, but older people with older bodies can't, it makes them near retarded. Old people in America are now proud of reading the news paper, going to the store, and taking a crap (all while their country is being demolished).

Many anti-depressants and alcohol significantly reduce brain function and lower a person's consciousness down to the level of the mentally impaired. We've established that moronic people can still legally drive cars. Yet, alcohol and some prescription not-give-a-shit pills are reducing our abilities below that already very low bar.

If you're doing this to yourself multiple days a week, or worse, every day, then what do you think it's doing to your overall problem solving abilities? Do you think these mind numbing substances are making our daily problem solving abilities better, or worse? The billionaires that have hijacked our political system and turned it into a dictatorship, want the American people to stay as drunk and as out-of-it, as senior citizens that are just shy of nursing homes.

Corrupt politicians want you using alcohol and pills in an insane attempt to escape from reality, because the escape never works. Criminals remain in charge, and we accept whatever the next round of bad news is. You will always wake up in bed the next morning, reach for coffee, and return to your shitty job for your next round of beatings. What magnificent creations of God we've become. How proud the angels above must be of our daily drunkenness, fearfulness, and apathy.

As soon as you get home from work, billionaires want for you to crack open a beer, or light up a joint, so that you'll return to your terrible job the next morning. Our greedy owners want us to keep coming back the next day, without even putting up a fight for better working conditions. They don't want you to be pissed off enough to go find something better, or organize your co-workers to demand fair treatment. Please have another drink and turn on your TV programming, just like all of the other minimum wage workers and unemployed people. Stay poor, and stay down.

It's all been designed so that we lack the time, energy, or self-respect to escape our plight. Instead, billionaires want you to be in a beer-induced stupor, in front of your TV for hours every night. Your owners have you captured for two to four hours of conditioning, before you return to your abusive existence the following day.

We readily accept the television programming that they have carefully prepared for us to advance their own selfish agendas. The TV is used to program, the human that is sitting in front of it. Please YouTube "TV is mind control" and watch a few videos that explain how we are conditioned like dogs to behave accordingly.

The flicker rate of our television is about 30 frames per second. The human brain can only last a few minutes at that rate of stimulation before your critical thinking ability is completely turned off. You then become a trainable ape that dresses itself, can talk, and does chores for slightly smarter owner-class, all day long. They stay richer, and you follow orders.

After just a few minutes in front of your TV, your natural ability to think logically about a news story is shut down. You become just another chimp watching Training Videos showing you how to behave. You continue absorbing news content without questioning its validity. Politicians and billionaires would never use a device in your own home to manipulate you without your consent, would they? They love you so much, and want you to get a piece of their wealth.

Just picture a space ship that has a force field shielding it from space debris. Then, picture your brain having the same type of force field that shields it against bullshit presented to you by politicians that have been caught lying to you hundreds of times in the past. That natural force field is shut off within minutes of sitting in front of your TV. So please, keep starring at it for hours a day, it's good for you.

The alpha waves in your brain transition into a more suggestive state while watching TV. Would power crazy billionaires take advantage of that kind of power? Even the best of souls are defenseless when subjected to just a few minutes of television.

We are watching other people on TV lie, cheat, and steal for money all day long. Watching repetitive images of others doing heartless things in order to drive a nicer car, and have sex with better looking sexual partners has no effect on how heartlessly you'll treat real people in the real world. Did God really put us all here on earth to treat each other like shit, all in the name of money, cars, and sex? Is this the meaning of life?

How many products have you bought that you didn't know existed before they were presented to you by your TV set? I've bought tons of things that my TV sold me. Admitting that you've been tricked is a lot easier when someone else admits it to you first. I too, was a victim of the same scam, and was used by others for years of my life.

Today, I look and feel very different from the morbidly obese Americans that watch hours of TV per day, and take their daily meds (drugs). All, so that instead of recovering, they can collect their disability check, and drive a beautiful new car. These poor souls have failing health, and due to their meds (drug habit), many of them are unable to achieve an orgasm. Our bodies are our true vehicles for experiencing life, not our shiny cars. You are not your car.

Orwell wasn't bullshitting us when he wrote about the government one day setting out to abolish the orgasm. All of you suckers that got conned into taking a form of Prozac know exactly how close to home this statement is. Watch "Equilibrium" to see what's being taken away from us. Feeling nothing at all is much worse than experiencing the non-medicated ups and downs of being alive.

Very few of us are so dangerous without meds, that we must be tranquilized by our government-approved sellout doctors. All of which, drive nicer cars, and likely have a bigger houses than you do. Their patients all get fatter and sicker, while they stay rich.

One of the most powerful beliefs drilled into the operating systems of our American brains, is that, as you acquire more money, then you then suffer less legal consequences for breaking ethical rules. Get enough money, and you can buy your way out of just about anything. This is a prime example of a TV programmed belief. Our group can change real life outcomes by simply holding rich criminals accountable.

How many bankers got locked up after they lied, cheated, and stole from the American people? If they don't have to follow any of the rules, then I have the right to be a complete asshole to them when I see them out in public. I've always made it a point to let huge assholes coming into my place of business know, that they're not welcome. Over time, this creates a more positive environment to work in.

I don't accept asshole behavior in front of me, without letting the person know in a very polite way, that they're behaving ridiculously. If someone wants me to help them, then they have to behave appropriately. As a result, they either stop coming in, or change their behavior and start acting more like decent human beings.

Due to my own lack of fear, their bad behaviors go away, and I am left with a more reasonable environment to work in. More customers begin frequenting my place of employment, because there are less assholes around stealing all of the businesses time. I'm very friendly to customers that are polite, and reinforce polite behavior.

The lower class in America must realize that when we stand our ground with our oppressors, then we will begin to raise our own quality of living. There are more of us, and if we call them out in a group effort, then they will nearly always back down when confronted with the ugly facts. Don't be afraid to do what's right, but please, get some sobriety under your belt first. Our lives will begin to get better again when we start to show some balls that are paired up with sober judgment.

We did watch the entire Banking and mortgage industry nearly collapse in 2008 due to blatant, in-your-face fraud, didn't we? Then, to any critical thinking person's astonishment, zero punishment came to the millionaires and billionaires that had designed and executed the banking schemes. These mortgage and derivative scams decimated the net worth of millions of good Americans, including myself. I quickly went from middle class, to empty beer cans.

Where has true justice in the United States gone? Do we have no self-respect left in us to simply call out the politicians as a group, and fire them all? They are not the guys that are running our power plants and growing our food. By all means, they are expendable, just like a poor wage slave like me is. The world wouldn't blink if all Banking criminals and politicians were fired and stripped of power tomorrow.

We might as well call them out, and take away from them, what they have already taken away from too many of us. If the whole group decides that the money of a few rich assholes is no good wherever they try to go, than there's nothing that they can do about it. There are more of us, and they are in the wrong, please don't forget that. They did get caught purposely selling products to others that they knew were horrible, but claimed to be good.

They have not yet seen justice, and we have suffered greatly due to their selfish actions. Crimes were committed. If our legal system has failed to punish them (and it has), then we the people can bankrupt the bankers, that bankrupted us. Many of us had families that were broken apart while our assets vanished. Bankers that made those decisions that wiped the rest of us out, ought to experience the same loss of financial comfort. Police, military, and riot control, why on earth are you defending the bankers that have delivered poverty to all of us?

There were paper trails, emails, and phone conversations, all of which would provide more than enough evidence to prosecute hundreds of banking criminals. Nothing has been done to that effect, not yet. Remember, there is a seven year statute of limitations for such cases, and the masses are still suffering from the scam.

Only by delivering the message via TV, could such a magic trick be pulled off successfully on the hypnotized public. The Bankers clean out our life savings, jobs are lost by the millions, and we do nothing. What a bunch of cowards we are. That, or your TV has had you walking around under the control of somebody else.

Like a bunch of brain dead zombies, the American public has continued on, completely unfazed by the revelation that, if you're a banker that gets caught committing fraud (a criminal offense), then, you do not get prosecuted and sent to jail. The super wealthy bankers also own our legal system. Do you get that hundreds of American bankers should have been prosecuted for committing fraud, and then sent to jail, but they weren't.

The American people did nothing, aside from watching a tiny fraction (of a percentage point) of our population protest on TV, and promptly get pepper-sprayed in the face by trained morons, for the criminal act of telling the truth. Do you get that the television has trained a couple hundred million people to believe that, if you're an average American speaking the truth and asking for justice against criminal bankers, then you will get pepper-sprayed in the face? We were all trained to stay home, and stay quiet. It worked.

Do you think that Americans are more, or less likely, to protest against criminal bankers again after seeing those images? That was an Ape management TV training program (and it has worked beautifully). Quit complaining about what's not fair and, "go home!" (movie reference).

Do you get that Billionaires get to choose what "news" images get burned into our brains? Do you get that watching protestors get brutalized and arrested will modify the behavior of the group to stay home and keep your mouths shut you damn dirty apes! It worked on me. Did it work on you too?

I don't want to get pepper-sprayed and arrested for telling the truth in public about criminal bankers, do you? Watch Conquest of The Planet of The Apes, and you'll see just how far along our present day society has been moved in that direction. This is mind control 101. It's very simple logic that anyone can understand. Computers can be programmed, and so can we. Rich bastard programming is being broken right now.

If you stand up to corrupt bankers and try to draw attention to their criminal behavior, then they will send armed guards with very low IQ's to pepper-spray you if the face and then arrest you. The result, we all keep our mouths shut and begin to behave like the cowardly lion from the wizard of OZ. The sheep programs are being over-written and deleted right now.

The old Superman movies with Christopher Reeves said that superman fought for truth, justice, and the American way. America's reputation has become so bad following the start of the second Iraq war, that the recent 2006 Superman remake had to remove the phrase, "and the American way" from the movie. We need to start taking ownership of the negative feedback that Americans traveling abroad have been experiencing for a decade.

If our politicians and military leaders have used good men and women to wage wars under false pretenses, then the American people outta know all of the details. After all, it's the working classes' children that are getting killed overseas while the politicians' children live country club lifestyles. Foreigners are getting frustrated with the American people because we keep buying the lies that our politicians have been selling us via TV (hypnosis). End the programming by refusing to watch it. It's that simple.

The rest of the world that's not hypnotized by American television has been seeing a more accurate version of reality. They have been attempting to reason with the American citizens, but we haven't been listening. Most of us spend all of our energy at work all day and then quickly sedate ourselves when we get home to avoid facing the large scale problems that have gone unchallenged. Not challenging an increasingly evil system is not going on my gravestone.

Have you ever seen examples of citizens in other foreign countries that have been taught false beliefs by their own government? I know I have. How about the Communist Russians, the North Korean people, and the Nazi German people? All of these were once decent people that had been deceived by well organized politicians. Many of Joseph Stalin's citizens completely worshipped him, and he wasn't exactly a nice guy.

Governments can easily train their people to believe whatever justifies their actions. If you don't want to be mind controlled then you're going to have to refuse the mind control diet of the average American. Presently, it appears to be working really well.

If you want to regain something that the group is clearly lacking, then maybe it's time to try a new strategy and unplug your cable box. Once you've broken free, the zombified public will begin gathering around you like rednecks around wrestling rings. Once you have their attention, you can deliver your payload. One by one we can transform fields of sheeple into fields of wolves. Please watch Rise Of The Lycans. At this point, the ending of that movie should make perfect sense to you.

# Chapter 13 – Muzzled and caged American super heroes

The American public is all wrapped up watching "reality" TV and professional sports, all while drinking and smoking ourselves into oblivion. When was the last time that we saw a professional athlete speaking out against political corruption? Weird how all of our real life super heroes seem to be completely satisfied with our government, the politicians, and the entire 911 lie. They aren't exactly opening up small businesses to employ their fans that can no longer afford tickets to their games.

Our pro athletes are nothing more than the caged (totally separated from the public) performers that we see featured in the Russell Crowe movie "Gladiator". I would argue that pro athletes enjoy much less freedom than an average American does. How so? The amount of time practicing, training, traveling, and performing, that pro athletes are obligated (forced) to do, in order to get paid by their owners.

Then their owners give them the ridiculously Orwellian title of, free agents. When there's nothing really free about their existence. I have much more free time than they do and I <u>don't</u> want the deal that they have negotiated for themselves. In this pivotal time in American history, pro athletes currently mean <u>zero</u> in the equation. In reality, Pro athletes are the world's most distracting pawns.

Does an average Joe not have the ability to eat as much food, have as much sex, and have a roof over his head also? The only difference being, that the average Joe actually has a lot more free time, don't we? The Average Joe also has much more free speech than pro athletes do. Our pro athletes are more like traveling circus animals that have lost the gift of speech. I don't want what they have.

Did it ever occur to the public that very wealthy men may want to separate the fastest, strongest, and most disciplined humans from the rest of the herd? Working alongside pro-athletes would encourage (give courage to) the average Joe wage slave. We all get a lot braver when we are working alongside other strong, fast, and brave people. Confidence is contagious.

The reason that pro athletes have not been speaking out against corrupt bankers that have purposely crashed the US economy into the ground, is because they too, have owners that would ban them from the league. Our athletes fear losing their money, (their true God) for speaking on behalf of the public. Stop watching paid-off people that don't care about you.

Do you remember Maximus from the movie "Gladiator" turning the crowd against the Emperor? Do you get that even our millionaire pro athletes have been silenced and politically neutered by their billionaire owners? If that wasn't the case then somebody would be speaking out on behalf of the fifty million Americans on food stamps, but they don't.

These super strong men should not be our heroes, because when it comes down to displaying some real balls, they have none. They are owned, and they are just as fearful of their owners, as the rest of us are. Pro athletes could wield a great deal of influence over the masses to bring about positive societal change if they weren't terrified of losing their money, but they are. They are just as trained to keep their mouths shut as the rest of us.

The American people worship pro athletes like Gods. In return, not one multi-millionaire pro athlete walks away from their owners, and fights on behalf of the fans that fill the stands. I challenge any famous pro athlete that supposedly believes in God to start fighting for the true best interests of the American public (instead of staying silent due to fear of their owners).

It's a total joke that our strongest, fastest, and most determined Americans, all have owners that won't let them speak out on behalf of the rest of us. Instead, blatantly obvious corruption by bankers and politicians goes completely uncontested by our idols. Do they really worship God, or money? When it comes down to helping millions of suffering Americans, our pro athletes do nothing but distract us.

We all know the truth, but none of us wants to face it. Otherwise we might have to improve ourselves instead of vicariously living our dreams through some other guy on TV (that doesn't give a crap about us). Both the pro athlete and Joe six-pack are equally terrified of defying their billionaire owners. The daily drunk and our pro athletes mean nothing in the equation for positive change in America.

If even a single one of our pro athletes stuck their own neck out on behalf of the American people to prevent a second great depression, it could cause the tides to turn for the better. Our pro athletes are like caged animals, well fed, and well groomed, but still forbidden to speak out against the politicians and bankers that rub shoulders with their true owners. If the sports fans really wanted to get their heroes attention, then perhaps an empty stadium on game day would do it.

Our pro athletes have been rewarded (bribed) millions of dollars for their hard work (servitude), dedication (obligation), and their God-given gifts (steroid use). If this book ever makes it into the hands of a pro athlete that has always praised God, I ask, how bad do things have to get for the millions and millions of fans that have worshipped you as their hero? Please grow a conscience to fight on the behalf of God fearing people, rather than your billionaire team owners that own you. They (team owners) own you (pro-athletes).

Will any pro athletes ever walk away from their owners that treat them like muzzled race horses? I'm not holding my breath. The absolute silence of our pro athletes will surely be rewarded with silence regarding their existences in the world history books. Sports records will become completely irrelevant if the United States falls apart like the former Soviet Union already has.

One of the more disturbing things about professional sports and their power to distract the masses, is that Hitler outlined how pro sports would be used to do just that, distract us all. To truly learn from our past, we must examine our history. Adolf Hitler became a master at manipulating millions of people to behave in the manner that he wished.

The History channel has recently shown lengthy programs about Hitler's takeover of the minds of the German masses in an effort to prevent history from repeating itself. That's History channel 2. The primary History channel has been reduced to "reality" TV featuring: Pawn Stars, Counting Cars, America Pickers, and Swamp People. Surely watching those shows (while getting drunk) will educate us all regarding world history.

We need to accept that a minority of super wealthy assholes have bought off our politicians and neutralized our most physically gifted human beings (pro athletes) from fighting by our sides. Our strongest, fastest, and most fierce competitors have been paid-off to stand aside while corporate dictators shipped millions of American jobs overseas. This caused millions of Americans to lose everything while the top 1% has grown much wealthier. This is a fact.

The biggest victims of this massive nationwide scam have done nothing in response, except run to the gas station for more beer, and to their doctor for some guilt-free not-give-a-shit in an orange pill bottle. When are the good guys that have tens of millions of dollars going to start speaking out and putting their lives on the line? If there has ever been a time in recent history that divine intervention was needed, this is it.

There is divinity within all of us, but we aren't going to find it if we're constantly drunk or zonked-out from prescription pills. Our doctors have betrayed us. Deep inside of every human being is a voice of right and wrong, a conscience. Many of us, including our pro athletes have had that conscience silenced. That's being changed right now.

Our lives thus far may have taught us that doing the right thing and telling the truth may not prevent bad things from happening to us, but that doesn't mean we should stop. Perhaps it is meant to be that our souls get really lost in the dark, in order for us to crave the light once again. We need to humbly ask God for some help. We all have great potential. Let's stop watching others be great. We have an incredible capacity to create change. We can change the world and make it a better place to live in. We can become human beings that pro athletes are impressed by.

# Chapter 14 – Find true spirituality and fear will cease to control us

Take a second to stop and imagine that this whole thing that we call life is just a game that our souls volunteered for before birth. Then, in order for all of our souls to learn as much as possible on a spiritual level; we also agreed to forget who and what we really all are, a conscious being, having a human experience. Does that sound possible?

The veil of forgetfulness would truly allow our souls to embark on "dangerous" missions in the darkest of places in order to test our bravery, or lack thereof. If everybody knew beyond the shadow of a doubt that we all have indestructible souls, then this ride would not be that exciting now would it? Have you ever worked at a family owned business where the children of the owners were employed alongside non-family members?

Were the children of the owners more, or less, worried about getting fired for slacking off than the non-family members were? Do you get that human nature is to "get away" with what we can? Therefore, if we knew for sure that we have immortal souls that will continue to exist after death we wouldn't take this game so seriously, would we?

Do you think tyrants want you believing that you have an immortal soul on a learning experience or not? Wouldn't a tyrant prefer that people believe that we are all living in a "one shot" godless human life that will cease entirely when we die? I'm thinking that tyrants want us believing in the "one shot" deal.

They would likely want you to believe in a random accident of intelligent life that only occurred here on planet earth in the entire universe. That way, you remain controllable when guns are pointed at you. Do you get that a tyrant's greatest weapon against vast numbers of human beings (that could easily overpower them) is a lack of spirituality? This results in an intense fear of death that serves tyranny well.

People lacking a belief in an afterlife (or worse, the trained belief that you're going to hell when you die) greatly _fear_ death.

Shame on the ruling elite! Organized religion (crime) has been used to condition the public to live lifetimes of fear. The ruling class (that follows none of the rules) then gets richer in the process while the ignorant public pays them taxes for protection.

All rich church people that take money from poor people while failing to provide practical job training, education, and 7 day per week food and shelter (given that there's a building that was constructed using church donations) ought to be banned from going to church. That, and they should shoot themselves in the heads for using God as a money making scheme. If you've constructed a church building using donations from less fortunate church members, and don't use that same building to house them after they've lost their jobs and homes, then please remove yourself from this game.

Churches are supposed to be like long term insurance policies when the shit hits the fan in real life. People do lose jobs, houses, and spouses. If the church isn't there to help put back together destroyed people, than what's it there for? The vast majority of churches stay locked up and empty, for the majority of the time. Thanks a lot church Dicks. Didn't Jesus Christ himself frequently cuss-out the church people of his time for their hypocrisy?

Shame on the masses for falling for this trick for so long! Strong evidence of advanced beings has been put into writing by ancient cultures and has been disregarded and discredited by our kings and their priests for thousands of years. Kings have sold humanity the most convenient version of reality in order to rule over us all.

If a historical event can undermine a king's authority over the public, then they make it disappear from the historical record. Would our modern day politicians do such a thing to stay in power? We all know the answer.

This is our opportunity to be thankful and grateful for everything that we have learned from the game of life. Please don't cuss-out God for letting us explore in the universe on our own, without constant help. This is the same free will that we all want so badly. We all want to do what we want, without others telling us what we can, or cannot do, right? Free will is important. Your TV had been used to steal it from you, and it's being returned right now.

193

Last time I checked, America stood for freedom, liberty, and independence. Most of you remember the phrase, "taxation without representation" right? I would argue that both organized religion and the federal government have done the same thing to a bunch of TV brainwashed talking monkeys.

Haven't you ever seen a small toddler swat away their parent for trying to help them do something new? When the toddler predictably gets hurt after trying the new activity on their own, they then turn around and cuss-out their parent for letting them get hurt. This is exactly the same behavior of the average suffering American that's crying out for a politician to help.

The politicians and churches may have collected taxes and church dues for a lifetime, but have no intention of providing actual food and shelter for suffering Americans. They are much more likely to recommend that you pawn away all of your belongings at the local pawn shop. Politicians and church officials worship money and their own personal comfort, not God. Otherwise, they would start becoming less rich, in the name of helping their fellow man to get back on his feet again.

Zombies, please shatter your delusions that church preachers and politicians are going to help save you, they're not. Unplug your TV, and start saving yourself now. Do you get that human beings may be very much the same, in that we may have asked God for a human experience with no help, and now that we are here on earth getting our assess kicked, we turn around and cuss-out God for allowing us to get hurt? Would we do such a thing?

Do you get that we cannot have it both ways if we want to learn new activities on our own? If earth simply is a training ground for young souls (and a school that we will eventually graduate from) then perhaps it's time that we start standing up to the school bullies. Perhaps the lesson to be learned is that if you don't stand up to a bully, then you deserve to be bullied. The bully is simply doing their job.

Also, if you see others that are weaker than you being bullied, then have a conscience, and stand up for your fellow man, rather than turning a blind eye to save your own ass. Only men and woman without consciences (cowards) sit by silently while the weak and the innocent get bullied by evil men. A world in which it is every man for them self, is a world that attacks itself, and suffers under constant conflict.

It only makes sense that when you find yourself in a very dark place (and cannot see a positive thing) to seek light. When you find that light, you then become enlightened. This is the journey from a low level of consciousness where you feel powerless, to an enlightened level of consciousness (where you are at peace with God). At that point, you cannot be bought, sold, or scared into doing the bidding of evil men any longer. You will be free.

Do you get that a corrupt political system would invest a lot of money to steer the masses away from a high consciousness diet? How else are millions of people going to be manipulated (man being polluted) by fear and greed, if the people do not fear death, and can't be silenced with money? Tyrants can't rule over large groups of highly enlightened people. Too many people will sacrifice themselves to protect the God-given rights of the group.

Seeing is believing, right? How many times have we all heard that expression? This is where the billionaires (that see the American people as little more than a large herd of well trained cattle) have got us by the brains! Television (Tell....A.....Vision) shows the masses exactly who is in charge, and tells us a vision of what to think about it. The people that control what is shown on TV, then control what we believe in. They choose all predictable human reactions, only if, you watch their programming.

If you own the media companies, and have billions to spend on television programming, then the masses see exactly what you want them to. Does that sound about right? The public is seeing and believing exactly what the owners want us to. Refuse the programming. We all can choose to not watch TV. Then, billionaires lose their ability to control our thoughts, beliefs, and opinions.

Which person is more likely to worship money over all else, the common man, or the billionaire? Since the advent of TV, the masses have been programmed by those whom worship money, not God (the greater good of humanity). Do you get why the moral values of America have gotten worse as the amount of television that we watch has increased?

As a group, we have been set up for failure by an invention that allowed dictators and tyrants to tell us, their visions. When such a powerful device got distributed to the masses, we never had a chance! For a while that is, until a little thing called the internet popped up and allowed the sharing of information freely. Neo flying through the Matrix is simply a person that's spreading information on the internet.

Billionaires and the governments that they control are now censoring the internet, go figure, but the masses are not all brain dead morons. We can see why the sharing of information online is now being controlled. Facebook and YouTube videos absent of profanity and vulgarity are now frequently being deleted. If you don't believe this, Google it! Truth cannot be restrained forever when billions of people worldwide are involved in the game. We all have power in this game.

I have personally had non-profane videos deleted from my Facebook timeline as if they never existed. Many Youtubers have also been blowing the whistle that their personal videos have been removed. I was always under the impression that Americans valued freedom of speech.

The other recent revelation on television is that everything that we do on the internet is now being monitored by the NSA, for our safety of course. Meanwhile, millions of people have their credit cards stolen by Target, causing a huge mess. Yep, let's make everything electronic, because there's no way someone can cause chaos in your life if the power goes down, or someone hacks into your account.

The same super wealthy that pay for everything on TV are also paying to have the internet regulated and more truthfully, censored. Would rich greedy control freaks do such a thing? You bet your ass they would, they have, and to this day, they are.

The American people outta be out in the streets and at politician's front doors over this issue, but we're not. Why? The actual level of ongoing internet censorship is not being televised. The closest thing to the truth that we get from TV these days comes from comedians; They have become our modern day philosophers, telling us truths about our own reality that are so absurd that we must laugh rather than cry. Comedians know what huge trouble our country is in.

Throughout history there have been philosophers that have attempted to define the meaning of life. These men and woman have shared the common goal of seeking truth and obtaining knowledge. When a philosopher has invested a great deal of time and energy to gain a better understanding of life, and acts with great wisdom and love, we then call that individual enlightened, don't we?

An enlightened person sees deeper into situations and acts with wisdom. An ignorant person reacts without thinking, on a daily, monthly, and lifetime basis. Ignorant people become pawns for the men and woman that control the chess board of life. Perhaps comedians have become our last line of defense in their attempts to reason with us and remove our blinders. They use comedy and logic to speak the truth about the world that we now live in.

Nobody wants to be played like a fiddle by other human beings that are capable of manipulating them. Many of us have been forced to do things that we know aren't right in the name of money. We have been asked to do these things by wealthier men that are holding food and shelter over our heads as a threat. If we don't comply with cruel orders, then we eventually lose our job and our romantic partners. We've been managed (man...aged) by fear, not by love and courage.

I am not a fearful person. I haven't allowed evil men to age my body as one of their hopeless and obedient financial slaves. The Wealthy have offered us (the public) deals that say, if we are willing to hurt other lower-class people, then the wealthy business owner will pay us enough money to afford adequate food, shelter, and entertainment to attract a decent companion. Screw that deal! I wasn't born on earth to spend a lifetime screwing over weaker people for money.

The normal deal has become to accept degrading treatment of yourself or others, in exchange for enough money to live. Those people with the highest levels of consciousness end up with two terrible choices in a corrupt system:

1- Lower your own consciousness with alcohol and drugs to "play ball" with the slave owners.

2- Refuse to compromise your values, and suffer the financial consequences for being ethical in a society that is now run by unethical billionaires.

Does that sound about right? Screw both choices! I'm creating a new option for the group right now. Ideas create reality.

Our TV hypnotized women are not reinforcing good behaviors of American men. Just like in ancient Rome right before the fall of that empire, many women have been reduced to trading sex for financial stability (in order to avoid this brutal job market). American women are just as guilty as the men for the sad state of affairs we're all in.

We know that wives have been encouraging doggish husbands and boyfriends to simply drink away their consciences in order to do "whatever it takes" (rip people off) to pay the bills. Women don't care how the bills get paid (or who gets hurt in the process) while their husbands make enough money for a nice comfortable lifestyle. If there's ever been a time in American history when a large percentage of American women looked the other way, (in the name of money) this is it.

If God is keeping tabs, then the laws of cause and effect will still apply to all of us. People like "The Situation" become millionaires, and Michael Hasting and Edward Snowden are enemies of the state. This mentality is right out of the pages of 1984. This needs to change so that our children can work in a society that rewards hard work and honesty. Not, the cowardly behavior of abusing yourself and others in order to save your own ass today. If life is some sort of a spiritual test, then these souls will not graduate.

How are higher spiritual beings supposed to respect us if we don't even respect ourselves? If we want God to step in and give humanity some divine intervention, then perhaps we outta start by doing some good deeds first. Try showing God that we actually believe in a spiritual hierarchy of which billionaires are not at the top.

Letting your spouse hurt other people all day long, while plugging your ears and closing your eyes is not going to get you into heaven. My best guess is that you'll be asked to repeat life again until you act with some dignity. Prescription pills and alcohol that make lying to yourself about your shady partner's actions are the root cause of your apathy, along with the current TV programs that you're running on. If you watch it, then you're programmed. Refuse to watch TV, and you'll regain your conscience. This is how we're being played.

If humanity is the most spiritual group of beings in the entire universe, then would somebody please shoot me in the head. I do not believe that's the case, but any chance to work in a little more suicide humor shouldn't be wasted. Good parents do not reward (reinforce) the bad behavior of bad children do they? Why would God be any different?

The ruling minority know that repeatedly showing ignorant behaviors get rewarded with sex and money is a great way to plant corrupt files into our belief systems. Your computer catches a virus from viewing the wrong web pages much like your brain can be infected with bad files sold to you via TV programming. All of this has been created to sway your beliefs in a manner that benefits billionaires.

Having a screen in our homes that has been proven to alter our brain waves (placing the viewer in a hypnotic state) is a quick way to catch a virus that will slow down the processor in your own head. This only makes the existing problems in your own life seem more unsolvable. You're often being sold alcohol and pills in a desperate act of coping.

TV has been taken over by corporate interests. A high ranking national defense official on Stephen Colbert recently stated that he hasn't watched TV for the last 20 years because, "It turns your brains into cotton candy". Colbert sarcastically defended TV. The government official then recommended that the audience read a book instead.

My best guess is that any congressmen or senator that would propose that TV is mind control to the American public would be

199

found floating in a river somewhere from an alleged suicide. Perhaps it's time to "Kill Your TV" as a popular YouTube video recommends. That's what I did, and the results are miraculous!

There happens to be a huge problem that is not being addressed regarding the complete impotence of spoken moral advice from parents and religious leaders vs. television programming. Sorry church, but you're getting your ass handed to you by the TV sets in nearly every home across America. Our country is now full of drunken brainwashed idiots that keep showing up the next day to their miserable corporate jobs.

Tons of corporate zombies "require" prescription anti-depressants (not you of course) just to keep showing up for your weekly soul draining. Has it ever occurred to you that maybe you're depressed because you've been acting like a turd? If you've read this far without suffering an aneurism, then this manual just may be the turning point where things in your life start to get significantly better.

If you did suffer an aneurism before making it this far, then congratulations, you're dead! If your life is already really good, but you know somebody else that seems to have nothing left to lose, then perhaps this manual can help them. People with nothing left to loose are often the most teachable because their ego has taken such a beating. Only when we have nothing left to point to of value do we become willing to try a new strategy. It's the gift of desperation.

# Chapter 15 – How to unplug yourself from the matrix

The competition between religion and TV to program the beliefs of the American public (right or wrong, good or bad) has become a total joke. The spiritual struggle between a verbally spoken set of values from a measly one hour per week church service vs. four hours per day of visual televised sex is over. When it comes to forming beliefs, it's like a butter knife vs. a machine gun.

If you're a preacher that wants to vastly improve the spirituality of your congregation, (you know, the reason that people go to church in the first place) then have them try unplugging their TVs for an entire month and you see what happens. The television has slaughtered all organized religions. Television is teaching the public their current belief systems because seeing, is believing.

What is the other statement that Americans always say about something that they are verbally told but cannot see? Talk is cheap. Our brains have been conditioned not to believe what someone tells us without showing us the proof right? TV is therefore the greatest device ever created, when in the hands of a liar that can afford all of the TV time in the world. Human beings do own the TV networks, right? Are they rich people, or poor ones? Which group of people tends to play fair and operate using more ethics?

How much proof of God is organized religion showing its congregations for a measly one hour per week? Worse, during that one hour a week at church service, the preachers aren't showing the congregation anything. They are telling them verbally, before the congregation goes home and watches TV for the next 6 hours while administering beer-induced brain damage.

Church has become a brief masturbatory behavior. Can you imagine Jesus Christ, Buddha, Mohammed, or Moses performing small miracles in front of people for a measly one hour per week (only to have the people go home to a 50 Inch flat screen)? The television easily bulldozes over all of their spiritual teachings in a matter of minutes. Perhaps Christ's second coming will be him flying around the whole world in one night. He will visit everyone's house just like

Santa, smashing all of our TVs with a sledge hammer, just to set us free. A few weeks later, (after discovering that all of the TVs on earth had been smashed) billions of pale bloated zombies would slowly begin to regain consciousness. Their health nut neighbors would help to slowly reacquaint them with reality, self-control, and free will.

Remember when the Macintosh first came out, there was a TV commercial of a 1984 future, and a hero with a hammer that smashed a TV screen, YouTube it. Maybe Steve Jobs saw what his inventions would ultimately do for humanity, render cable TV, irrelevant. I remember all of these references, because the T-Virus and the brain deadening sedatives it sells aren't governing my memory.

You've heard of cars with a governor on them so that they can't go past a certain speed, right? How would you like to remove the governor that's been wrecking your ability to learn new things and retain information? The formula for unrestricting your own brainpower is being delivered right now. You will choose whether to follow the formula or not. The good thing is that you are now being offered the choice to remove these handicaps if you choose.

I'm not programmed for hours a day, because I don't watch the programming. A great church preacher talking to a congregation of TV watchers is a big damn waste of time. Remove TV programming first, and then begin removing all of the sedatives and anxiety causing habits that poor people share in common. If the poorest and least healthy people all do something, then I try to avoid sharing their failing coping methods. Heavy TV watchers believing that they're spiritually connected because they attend church, is a joke. If this is you, then you're still a zombie.

It reminds me of a scene in "Indiana Jones and The Temple of Doom" when a sword fighter puts on a tremendous display of skill with his sword, and Indiana Jones simply pulls out his gun and shoots the swordsman dead! That, is exactly what the TV set has done to the message of all organized religions. It has shot our consciences dead. However, you're hooked up to a pair of jumper cables right now, and have already been given a huge recharge.

People who truly seek a spiritual connection with a loving God, increased knowledge, and want truth above all else, must unplug the

TV chord. Television has been strangling all of our chances to take in so much, as a spiritual breath. A one hour sermon per week from Jesus Christ himself vs. TV is a waste of time. We don't try teaching calculus to our dogs, and shouldn't preach to TV zombies.

The visual power that a TV has when combined with the duration of viewing, and sheer repetition of information shown, is simply too powerful for the human brain to withstand. Once you have successfully turned it off, or better yet, unplugged your TV for a few weeks, an Amazing thing happens! After side-stepping the billionaire prescribed brainwashing regimen of those voters you hate, your own brain will literally start to get stronger again. Is that something that you would like?

The thoughts and beliefs that run through our heads all day, every day, will suddenly start to become our own again. Not, the suggested beliefs that are paid for by billionaires. The big joke about "paid" programming on TV is that, all television, is paid programming. Billionaires have paid lots and lots of money for us to be programmed. All of their programming is failing right now.

Human beings are visual and metaphorical learners. Movies are great metaphors, and are a good substitute for somebody newly quitting their TV habit in the pursuit of heightened consciousness. You will be going through some serious withdrawals when you first quit. Quitting TV is no joke! Doing something for a lifetime and then suddenly stopping isn't comfortable. However, the brainpower that gets unleashed by doing so is well worth the first week of discomfort.

Just like quitting anything else that's an addiction, you must have an attack plan. If you want to be successful, then prepare a replacement set of activities to fill the void that your TV has taken for all of these years. You must ask yourself, has your life gotten better or worse from thousands upon thousands of hours spent motionless, without being asleep in your bed?

More terrifying, what if, the billionaires have kept you asleep on your feet for all of these years? What if the key to restoring your health really is, killing your TV? What if refusing to watch any television, is like Neo being physically unplugged from the Matrix? If this is true, then unplugging people would be an honorable deed.

You can only find out what happens, by trying the experiment. Do you like the idea of a faster processor in your own head and a better body that results from hours of additional movement per day vs. TV induced paralysis? Do you really want politicians, and Billionaires to continue controlling your thoughts, your actions, and your beliefs because they have paid for the programming?

If somebody is even suggesting that I can possibly unplug myself from the matrix, then I'm at least going to give it a try. If you could be awakened to a whole new reality, would you take the red pill or the blue one? The red one wakes you up to a whole new world, and the blue one puts you back to sleep. Which would you choose given your current life situation, the red pill, or the blue one?

Removing TV, fluoride, and frequent alcohol from my diet was enough to awaken to a whole new level of consciousness in a matter of months, not years. The old feelings of hopelessness and self-pity will get replaced with peace, confidence, and a clear conscience. You will begin to see things in a brighter and more optimistic way. Over time, others will begin to want what you have.

If you are going to try to half-ass these clear-cut behavior modifications that can be changed in order to fully awaken, then you'll simply remain asleep with the rest of the voters. Essentially, you'll be just another zombie littering the aisles of Walmarts across this country. On a cake box, if there are seven ingredients and you want to get a cake just like the one on the side of the box, then, you put in all seven ingredients right? Not, just a few of the ingredients that you want to at whatever temperature and for whatever amount of time that's convenient for you. You're being told exactly how to unplug yourself from the controllers of our society.

There are proven recipes on the side of the box, and within this book. If you follow the directions perfectly, then you get the desired cake. In this case, more brain power and better health. If you refuse to follow the simple directions because your ego keeps telling you that you, will do things your way (which has resulted in your present life situation) then you will not get the cake on the side of the box, nor any more brain power than voters of the other party that you despise.

Refusal to follow simple directions results in failure to achieve the same results. There will be a void created by removing these habits from your daily routine that must be filled with new activities. If you want higher consciousness, then out with the old, and in with the new.

When I finally surrendered to God and humbly asked for help, within days, something inside of me guided me to walk over to the wall, and unplug my TV cable. Much like in this book, another person then posed the question to me, "why is it that you are constantly altering the state of your mind with drugs or alcohol"? Like many other people, I had no clue. I had never thought about it before, until that exact question was posed to me by a complete stranger.

It was then suggested to me to attend a local AA (alcoholics anonymous) meeting, and I was told that it may be able to help me. At that time, my ego had been beaten down to a level of reasonableness. I took the advice of the stranger, and went to an AA meeting the following day to tackle my addiction to alcohol. Only after complete destruction of my personal life, had it become apparent to me that taking new actions was necessary. I wanted to escape the hell that I was in at the time, and was willing to try something new (anything).

After being a top performer in my high school class, honor roll college student, and excelling at a young age in the corporate world in sales, I had quickly established a track record of success. Very early on in life, things had gone well for me. Prior to complete catastrophe, my own over-inflated ego would never have allowed me to admit that I, had developed a drinking problem, but I had.

Our ego believes the lies that are paid for by billionaires, and programmed into our brains, while we watch (are hypnotized by) TV every day. Only when my life became a terrible disaster, did I admit complete defeat and ask for Gods help. I did not run to a church, I was in no condition to run anywhere, I was beat. I admitted it to God, and said, "God, I surrender". Help appeared shortly thereafter.

To this day, I am extremely thankful for walking into a room full of spiritual (not religious) people that greeted me with smiles and laughter on the first day that I met them. They seemed to have consciences, and I wanted what they had. Most importantly, I was

205

willing to follow their directions. They didn't judge me for my mistakes, because they had made similar ones in the past.

Don't most of us want something more, or something better out of life? I know I do. So, much like in high school, college, and at jobs, I asked lots and lots of questions. Within my first week in the AA rooms, a man about my age that I had never met before handed me a book. The man had handed me the Big Book of AA which will confirm or deny for any person whether or not they are an addict.

The large blue book of AA acted like an anti-virus for my own false beliefs at the time, regarding my own drinking habits. In a matter of days, like magic, my desire to drink or use any mind altering substances melted away. This was the turning point when my own consciousness began to turn back up to the God-given levels that we are all born with. Greedy men have fought so hard to keep us all subdued. It's time that we walk away from their scams, and regain our self-control.

I can only describe what happened to me as a miraculous spiritual awakening. That, is how it feels when you begin to get your consciousness turned back <u>on</u> again, it feels good. After a lifetime of having the goodness (connection to God) beaten out of you, wouldn't it be nice to feel some innocence again?

People start to feel better, just by having you in the room with them; People of faith that is. The other bazaar effect that happens as the goodness inside of all of us (our conscience) gets turned back on again is that people that are angry with God or totally worship money seem to flee the room with fear. It's as if assholes are naturally repelled once you've removed yourself from the zombie diet.

Abusive people and frauds don't know what it is, but they are naturally pushed away from high levels of consciousness. Those of us that unapologetically wield the truth, wield a hammer that evil men will always fear. We must simply swing it. If you have any belief at all in some sort of higher power beyond human beings (God), then perhaps the idea of spiritual armor could one day be accepted by you.

If there is one thing that frauds in our lives fear the most, it's the truth. Perhaps it's time that we all start speaking the truth wherever we go. Frauds will have nowhere to feel safe. If we are good God fearing people that have always longed for a world where the good guys are running the show, then perhaps we should stop kissing the asses of wealthy men that clearly lack a conscience. Failing to call out frauds on their lies to their faces, is simply perpetuating their existence. Super rich men treat the public like worthless dogs, because we allow them to.

Remember, bullies rely upon our fears and anxieties. It's about damn time that you stop doing things that cause you anxiety, starting with your morning coffee. This is one thing that many of the stupidest and most fearful Americans share in common with each other. Of all of the stupidest people that you know, how many of them drink coffee every day?

If you don't believe me, just survey all of the fattest and dumbest people that you know, and ask them if they drink coffee every day or not. Then find the most intelligent and physically fit people that you know, and ask the same question. Before you throw this notion out of the window, try it for three weeks and see if you don't feel less anxious.

Our vain attempts to relieve anxiety via alcohol and pills, only lowers our own level of consciousness. This makes us easy pickings for the ruling elites to victimize. When you finally stop trying to outrun the truth, and start pursuing knowledge, things start to get better. Why on earth would any self-respecting human being continue walking in ignorance as a lowly "voter" in a crooked system? The keys to enlightenment, empowerment, and a better life are being placed on the ground in front of you. You will choose to pick them up, or not.

# Chapter 16 – Secret weapons of mass sedation, and the hidden history of NASA

The water being used to make your morning coffee, and cook your food with, is another thing that the ignorant masses share in common. Communist dictator Joseph Stalin, and Nazi leader Adolf Hitler both introduced fluoride into the drinking water after their top scientists discovered its subduing effects on mass populations of people. Stalin found that the number of prison guards could be reduced by 75% after introducing fluoride into the water supply.

How many of the billionaires do you think drink unfiltered tap water in their mansions? All of our nervous systems operate using electrical impulses including our hearts and brains. We all have an electrical charge for every thought and heartbeat. Minerals and metals found in our tap water have a much larger effect on all of us, than we've been led to believe.

Anyone that knows anything about cars knows that old car batteries sometimes need water to be added to them. The water added to the battery must be distilled water (not tap water) because the minerals found in tap water will harm the battery. Any mechanic knows this. It also turns out that fluoride is not good for the electrical conductivity in our brains. Drinking fluorinated water makes it a little harder for you to concentrate and easier to control.

More disturbing is the fact that barrels of fluoride must be labeled as a hazardous waste. These barrels are then shipped as a waste product from factories, and then dumped into our treated water before it's piped into our homes. It makes all of us that drink it daily, just a little dumber. This is also true with the fluoride in your toothpaste, twice a day, every day.

In the light of certain facts being revealed to a zombie (not you of course) still heavily under the influence of alcohol, TV, pills, and fluoride, to continue on changing nothing is only possible, if we then exercise one of life's greatest sins, willful ignorance. It is very unlikely that a proud idiot, would be this far along, in this book. It's my belief that as human beings, we came here on earth to explore. We all fully have the right to purposely get as lost as we want to, for as long as we want.

We all have the right to continue on as others servants that call ourselves victims. We can continue to wait for someone else who's less drunk, less drug addicted, and more self-respecting than us to come along and save us. After displaying a lifetime of above average intelligence backed by academic and professional achievements, I've explained the fluoride revelation to my own parents. The response from my 70 year-old father (health deteriorating, diabetic and currently captured by the immense gravity of the American arm chair) was quite fitting. He walked over to the tap, poured himself a large glass of water, and drank it. I don't blame him, he's old. My father has spent a lifetime fighting hard against evil and telling the truth.

If I have ever seen a once strong, smart, and honest man reduced to a state of willful ignorance, he is it. We all, as a group have become just like him, myself included for a very long time. The billionaires that have TV programmed us all, have trained us to throw the keys unlocking our personal jail cells of stupidity and drug induced apathy, right out of our cells. That programming is being broken right this moment.

This book is my best attempt to prevent the masses from suffering the same fate as my father. He is still caged by pride, in spite of the light that has been shined on the truth by his very own son. We keep on buying the televised version of the truth that is paid for by billionaire crooks. We should be listening to people that have always been honest with us, but instead we take the word of the richest guys on TV, cause that makes sense. Rich people have never been caught doing and saying anything in order to get to the top have they?

As a child, my parents had both taught me to be uncompromising, when it came to telling the truth. My father fought many battles against crooked business men always choosing integrity, rather than compromising his honesty for financial gain. Over the course of decades, as the city of Cleveland Ohio steadily declined, telling the truth became a greater and greater liability. As corruption moves in, truth moves out. Don't give up. Keep speaking the truth and you'll be ejected out of corrupt places, or you'll clean them up.

Either way, it's a win.

Many decent adults across America have retreated to the shelter of their family rooms. We have dove into pill bottles and alcohol to avoid addressing the changing landscape of America. The increasing pile of lies referred to as, the "NEWS" has required increasing amounts of drunkenness for us to keep believing in.

We all know that we are being royally screwed by the billionaires and politicians. They lie, cheat, and steel, while we adhere to their unfair rules to avoid being jailed. It makes no sense for them to be the ones in charge of us, but on the scam continues. This will not be the case if you abandon the hopeless zombie diet. Each one of us can make a difference in this game. We all have more power than your TV has trained you to believe in.

I am not disappointed that my parents are how they are, because I got to see them do the right thing so many times during my upbringing. The city of Cleveland, much like cities all over this once great country simply wore them out. There isn't much fight left in them, but there is in me. What about you? Do you have any gas left in the tank to create a better world?

The efforts of good Americans all over this country will not get suffocated and drowned out. Politicians on TV have no problem living their lifetime as a tiny ruling class, over a country of poor hopeless drunks and drug addicts. That's pretty much what's happening right now. The recommendations that are extremely necessary for boosting your brain function are pretty easy to implement and will likely save you some money.

The water you drink daily must be heavily filtered or distilled to remove all of the fluoride. Remember, distilled water in car batteries equals higher voltage and longer battery life, right? Running a human body on dirty tap water is like running a car on dirty motor oil. The water change is not an expensive one, and your ability to think more clearly, and concentrate better will occur quickly.

There are holistic dentists out there that also disapprove of fluoride toothpaste. If you don't believe me, then Google it, YouTube it, do some research. Millions of humans live fluoride-free and they are not missing or losing their teeth. If your body contains toxic levels of it now, removing all fluoride exposure for at least a few months is a good idea. No other mammal on earth requires fluoride for their teeth. Too much fluoride has also been linked to joint pain and inflammation.

Humanity went on for thousands of years without fluoride being added to our water. Suddenly, right after Hitler is defeated and thousands of Germany's top scientists were granted immunity, moved into the U.S. to work for our government, then, the U.S. begins the process of water fluorination. It's called Project Paperclip. Look it up, Google it. The entire U.S. rocket program was created by ex-Nazi German scientists. This needs to become common knowledge, because it's the truth.

The head of the U.S. space program after the end of World War II was named Werner Van Brawn. He and other former Nazis created what later became known as NASA. Some of this information has actually been revealed by the History channel by a well done series called Ancient Aliens. Don't let the word alien put you off. We've all been conditioned via TV and movies to have a negative connotation to that word.

Try replacing the word alien with unfamiliar or unknown. In just a matter of hours this video series can open your eyes using logic and reason to reveal a different possibility about humanity's history. Our governments and the Kings have gone through lots of trouble to withhold information from the public. It's time that Americans realize that a whole lot of Nazis were welcomed into the U.S. following World War II. This again, is the truth.

# Chapter 17 - A political system, religious conditioning, and the toxic diet used to divide the masses from logic and reason

It's about time that we started uniting Americans in the United States, rather than remaining divided from the very few issues that we disagree on. There are a lot more common grounds that the masses do agree on than our TVs and the people on them have led us to believe in. How has it come to be that each presidential election divides the American people into a 50/50 split against our neighbors?

In a true act of self-defeating insanity, the winning party that takes office after every single election completely fails to deliver on any of their promises. We did not bring home the troops in 2008, things did not get better for the middle class, and the Affordable Care Act is not affordable. None of the major campaign promises made by the candidates on either side ever come true.

Pride prevents the completely dissatisfied voters (slave class) from admitting that their winning candidate has completely abandoned all values and ethics that we believed they would bring to the office. The result being, that our personal pride has kept us trapped in these four year relationships with unfaithful and abusive partners. We keep on making excuses for them, even though everybody from the opposing side is pointing out the blatant lies.

Please have some self-respect and stop believing that your politician is going to be different this time. Please don't try telling me that things will be different after this next election. Billionaires keep asking 300 million people to put-up with several more years of complete country destroying bullshit, and nothing ever gets easier for us, does it?

This sounds like a winning strategy for a country of people that are definitely not being heavily oppressed between elections. Proud citizens with their noses in the air, and their chins held high are asking to wake up on the ground, not knowing what hit them. What do you think the German citizens were like after Hitler's fall? Stubborn pride and willful ignorance sets up apathetic citizens for a rude awakening.

The exact same phenomena occurred during the George W. Bush Presidency that is happening right now under Obama. We, the voters are to blame for this ongoing abusive relationship. Our own lack of self-respect is the only thing keeping us all from firing our corrupt leaders now. They are not leading us well. We do have that power to remove all of them from office at once. We also have the right to do so. This did happen recently in Iceland, but, you'll never hear that concept on TV.

Have you ever seen somebody getting cheated on by their spouse that probably knew it deep down inside, but was too afraid to end the relationship? Do you respect people like that more, or less, for failing to free themselves from their abusive relationships? The American people have repeated the exact same prideful behaviors during the last 2 presidencies. It's all made possible by pride, fear, and a general lack of self-respect.

Both Bush and Obama got re-elected after completely disappointing their own parties fan base during their first terms. Why? Both democrats and republicans have been trained like dogs, to never vote for the other party. Keep on accepting that only two terrible choices exist, because this is the best treatment that we deserve. Shut up, and take your crappy circumstances for the next few years.

You might as well stay with girlfriend A that is cheating on you, because girlfriend B would cheat on you even more often, does that sound about right? To both politicians and strippers, money, is God. Their spiritual connection that would consider the best interests of humanity is not turned on, and they should not be our leaders. It's time that the public fires all of the corrupt officials, and installs new rules that benefit hardworking Americans. We can do this, and we don't have to wait until another election to fire a corrupt representative. They work for us, and we've forgotten that.

If Americans weren't drinking and pill-popping ourselves into the walking dead, then we would have stopped buying the delusional version of reality a long time ago. The stripper and the Politician are not interested in you. They do not care about you, and when your money runs out, they will leave you for dead and be on the lap of the next person with money to spend. This is reality. This is the truth.

These types of multiple year agreements, and the people that have been pursuing them, need to be replaced now.

The American people must have been drunk and sedated not to notice that Mitt Romney was installed by the billionaire owners of this country, as a Straw Man candidate. Why? The billionaire owners knew that Romney would lose, and that Obama supporters would still support their only choice, due to stubborn pride. Anyone with a brain knows that Obama did not bring about the changes in America that had been promised, back in 2008.

Ron Paul had stepped up and easily had the independents, tea partiers, youth, and old racist white republicans that never would have voted Obama, no matter how much they hated Ron Paul. Ron Paul won the Texas straw poll in 2011, and in 2012, for the republican nomination. He was a shoe-in for the Presidency if he had won the Republican nomination.

However, he did not support the agenda of the Billionaires that own both parties, and therefore, a much weaker candidate was picked for the 2012 election by the powers-that-be. The powers that truly control Congress, Senate, and the White House don't give a crap who the American public agrees with the most. Obama doesn't call the shots. He's just the spokesman to sell the public the next round of well crafted lies.

Are you one of the suckers that is still buying their lies? Did you really believe that Bin Laden was dumped at sea? Do you know that the entire Seal Team that "got" Bin Laden was killed in a Helicopter crash because they were telling their families a different story? We are equally as gullible as the public from The Running Man when it comes to buying televised propaganda that makes our government look like our protectors (when they're not).

Anybody with any functioning logic left in their skulls, could see that Ron Paul had grabbed the youth vote from Obama prior to the 2012 election, and had the tea party voters as well. Denying Ron Paul the nomination was absolutely positively against the best interests of all Republicans. Correct me if I am wrong, but any true Republican would always choose to have a Republican President de-throne a sitting democrat, even if, it meant backing the most liberal republican candidate, right? That did not happen, because the whole process is rigged, and has been, for a very long time.

From the point that Mitt Romney was falsely installed as the best chance for the Republicans to retake the white house, the smartest, and most critically thinking members of the American middle class had been taken out of the race. The independent voters were told loud and clear, that our billionaire owners are nominating the candidates that they want to, and that the swing voters, can suck their balls. Independent thinkers need not apply, and our election process is a fraudulent joke.

Ron Paul was denied the republican nomination, and the election process was a complete farce from that point forward. There is a YouTube video featuring a former Russian KGB agent explaining how to transition a country into a dictatorship. The video was filmed in the 1980's and clearly outlines how mass populations can be demoralized (have their morals removed) and molded over the course of a generation. I highly recommend that you watch this video, and ask yourself, has this not already been done in America?

Through television, prescription drugs, alcohol, and the fattening up of America, I'd say it's been accomplished. Do you know anyone that is badly out-of-shape, hates their job, and only seems confident when they are drunk or high? I know I do, millions of them. We're Zombies! These are the zombie Americans that will keep riding a sinking ship right down to the bottom of the ocean.

We've all heard alcohol being referred to as, "liquid courage" right? So it's fair to say that alcohol provides temporary relief from fear and anxiety. Coffee on the other hand could be referred to as, liquid anxiousness, or liquid uneasiness. People do not start downing pots of coffee in order to build up the courage to ask someone out on a date, do they?

Any former alcoholic can tell you, that over the course of time, that same alcohol transforms from liquid courage, to liquid stupidity, liquid selfishness, liquid apathy, and liquid delusion. Yet, due to the addictive nature of alcohol, people keep going back to it. People, this is an insane thought process that applies to both alcohol and coffee.

One addiction causes the very side effects that the other addiction treats. It's a very expensive cycle of insanity. Unfortunately, the downers that are used to relieve your anxiety are also robbing you of your brain power. Over the course of years, this has deluded the masses power of reason.

We have a duty to our fellow human beings, to get our own shit together. If you've been waiting for Jesus to come down from the clouds and do everything for you, then you're shit outta luck. If he does come back, it's likely that the first thing that he'd cuss everyone out over, is all of our alcohol and pills. We've become a bunch of selfish assholes.

Too many Americans have been led astray by a grossly underestimated tool of influence called TV. Corrupt billionaires have gained full control of TV content, and have peddled an entire buffet of consciousness killing substances to the public. In order to receive some divine intervention, you must first break the spell of TV. How? Unplug the damn thing as if it were an evil hypnosis machine that one of your worst enemies had placed into your home without your knowledge. Right now, there are obvious choices in front of you that can drastically change your life. These choices were not so obvious before you picked up this book.

Some people believe that God speaks to us through other people. Who is to say that the content of this book hasn't been divinely inspired? Isn't the basis of all organized religion based on words written down by flesh and blood human beings who claimed to have had divine intervention? Wasn't it only after these ancient men had life changing experiences that they wrote down lengthy instructions as a guide for the masses to live a more spiritual existence?

Wasn't it the masses that chose whether or not to believe that the instructions were an honest attempt to help them, as opposed to a dishonest attempt by their king to scare and control them? I'm pretty sure that simply writing this paragraph down on paper, and showing it to the priests of Jesus's time would get me called a heretic, and they would say, "that's blasphemy, crucify that skinny white guy!". Hopefully humanity has matured even a tiny bit during the last 100 generations, since the actual time of Christ.

I see lots of grown adults that are limping about their daily lives after years of hard work, major disappointments, and regular attendance at some type of organized religion for one hour per week. I would argue that these people are running on spirituality 1.0 vs. TV 7.0 and are a completely defeated group of people. If God is all powerful, and you greatly believe, then why can't God help you control how much you eat? If you're an overweight person, then what a weak God you have.

It's not God that has failed to give you self-control, it's the TV that has taken it away from you. The vast majority of Americans would likely agree that they believe in God, and would really like some help from said God with today's problems. Many Americans have lost so much, in such a short time; that they would like to see revolutionary changes.

Imagine that an armored guard comes into your place of business in their street clothes and demands something that your boss doesn't approve of. We pepper-spray them in the face, because they disagree with our owners, and have them arrested for civil disobedience. That sounds fair enough, right?

Only a country of drunken drug addicts would watch the 99% protesters get brutalized on TV and do nothing. How could we not demand that all of the armored soldiers and the men that gave the orders to spray not get prosecuted for terrorizing the American public? We all watched, and then quickly retreated into the safety of our houses to hide in fear, like the dogs we've become. That is, until our houses got taken away too by the same bankers that own the armed guards in the streets.

Once again, I thank the bankers for being so, so, extremely greedy. If the bankers hadn't taken away so much from the middle class, then the smartest of us wouldn't be re-programming the robot zombie lower class to attack the bankers. Billionaires (that have no consciences) blowing their brains out, because millions of poor people start turning on them, sounds fair to me.

Before you judge me, and say, "That's too harsh, it's cruel" then what about Hitler, Stalin, and Saddam Hussein? What about those college students in America getting pepper-sprayed in the faces for peacefully protesting our bankers? Was none of that brutal and cruel towards non-violent people?

Isn't the world better off if some undeniably evil men do blow their brains out? Or, should we just leave dictators in power forever, and sit drunken on our couches watching sports, just waiting for Jesus to swoop down from the clouds and save us? Correct me if I am wrong, but Jesus mostly gave people verbal advice about how to live their lives. He wasn't an action hero that flew around the world like superman, he gave logical spiritual advice.

If you're waiting for Superman to be actually standing right beside you before you are willing to actually do something brave and courageous, then you have nothing brave or courageous about you. Would Jesus respect men and woman that were only willing to do brave things when Jesus himself was standing right beside them? I'm pretty sure that Jesus would describe that as a complete lack of faith.

If the Roman Emperor did successfully construct the bible through control of the priests in the Roman Catholic Church 300 years after Christ died; Then the bible may have been edited in a way that would make all future Christians wait (without taking action) for the return of their savior while getting their asses kicked by the current government. Would an emperor tamper with history and have his own priests mass produce books that convinced the ignorant masses to wait for a savior?

This would allow for thousands of years of corrupt kings to rule uncontested. Jesus, proving that life after death does exist should have made the masses fearless forever, after the resurrection had occurred. However, 300 years later, the kings on earth at that time formulated an excellent strategy to keep the masses subdued and as guilty as hell, organized religion.

The Roman Empire wasn't about to let true Christianity spread worldwide. Orwell's 1984 had the Ministry Of Truth, and the Roman Empire created an equally corrupted Ministry of Spirituality. We call it the Catholic Church. Their bishops were dispersed across the globe

218

to exert control over large populations of very stupid people.

Surely you can agree that human beings living in the year 300 A.D. weren't highly scientific and enlightened people were they? Critical thinkers that dared to vocally oppose the emperor's brand of spirituality were jailed and killed. The crusades did happen, and Gnostics were slaughtered worldwide. It's no coincidence that Bishops are one of the pieces on a chess board, as are Knights (as in, the Knights Templar).

Here we stand 2000 years later with around 7 billion people that appear to be terrified of death, and ritualistically attending 1700 year-old belief systems that were created to control very ignorant people. How exactly would Jesus try to reason with us if he was here in today's world? Would he tell us to watch more TV, drink more beer, take more pills, and rip off anyone just to make a living?

If we want Gods help to get us out of this terrible economy and help free us from crooked politicians, then we may actually have to show God a little bit of effort. If you unplug your cable cord, tackle your addictions, and began seeing the lighter side of things, help will be provided. A lot of humbling things have happened to millions of good Americans since the crash of 2008. We had slaved away for years of our lives to finally obtain that crowning achievement that was part of owning the American dream. All of that stuff is not who we are and what we're made of. Our actions towards our group are what define us. Are we acting honorably, or not?

Like the three generations before us, we expected our lives to continue along a prosperous path with normal ups and downs. However, millions of lost homes since 2008 have rocked the psyches of our entire country. I would argue that the billionaire bankers that have eluded justice thus far have made a fatal mistake. They took away too much, too fast, from too many God fearing people without finishing the job. Rather than crushing our will to have freedom, they boosted the natural spirit within all of us.

We must surrender to God (even if it sounds ridiculous), turn off the electronic training devices inside of our homes, and sober ourselves up so that we can regain our conscious contact with all that is good within us, as in God. People, we have been separated from each other, God, and the divinity within us all. Nearly all of us have the potential to do something good for this world.

Do you see God on TV? I don't. I see a false representation of reality. I see the illusion for what it is. I refuse to accept the brainwashing funded by billionaires. Most billionaires are selfish assholes, how else do you think they accumulated that much power? It's my mission to wake as many zombies (low-information voters) as possible. This way, we can begin building a world of our dreams rather than continue living in a control freak's paradise that only tyrants would lust after. We (the public) can undo tons of intrusive control systems that have been constructed while we've been asleep. Freedom awaits the brave.

# Chapter 18 Stepping out of the frustration and into the solution

Once you've decided that just about anything is worth trying to get reconnected to God (or anything good) because things have gotten unfulfilling and you actually want help, then this becomes easy. These directions for boosting your consciousness are stupid simple to follow. Can you follow directions?

When you bake a cake, do you pick and choose which ingredients to put in it? Not if you want the cake to actually turn out like the one on the box, right? You must remove all consciousness killing substances that have been scientifically proven to reduce brain function.

Spiritual people all over the world, by the millions, are enjoying a positive connection that you will get back, **IF** you can shrink your ego, and follow the directions. It's time to get your brain operating at full power again.

**Things to REMOVE:**

- No TV for one month, did any of the ancient prophets have TV distracting them? No, once you've gone a continuous month without it, you won't want to go back, because your brain will be working much better

- No more fluoride, this means no fluoride toothpaste, and no drinking or cooking with tap water, buy distilled water, or get a three stage water filter, cheap filters don't remove fluoride, buy distilled, the health benefits will become obvious, excessive fluoride causes joint pain and inflammation, look it up

- Cut alcohol to a minimum, if this sounds terrible, and you're reasoning why you can't stop drinking, you may be an alcoholic, and that's ok. Would it be so bad to lose your own dependence on alcohol? If you are addicted, then you'll need help to do so, if you are an alcoholic, AA is the cheapest and most effective way to end the addiction and gain more freedom over your own actions and thoughts

- Stop popping mood altering pills unless you're a documented paranoid schizophrenic or a documented bi-polar person with a chemical imbalance, only a tiny fraction of us truly need to be chemically sedated at all times, the rest of us have been sold drugs by TV, that only seem to rob people of good health

- Try replacing coffee with something that health nuts use instead, coffee only causes more anxiety, and has become the "norm" of the cowardly masses. There are plenty of caffeine alternatives available at supplement stores, such as: 5 hour energy, Green Tea, or a pre-workout supplements that will give you all the kick of coffee with no unwanted anxiety, no yellowing of your teeth, and no coffee breath, don't forget to add purified water throughout the day like all health nuts do

- A gallon of Distilled water daily works miracles to detox an old body

- Eliminate diet soda, the Aspartame that's in it is terrible for your brain, Aspartame….keeps you tame. Only with the right people in the Presidential Cabinet and a new head of the FDA was Aspartame made legal (during the Bush years), severe negative health effects are documented

It's funny how coffee causes anxiousness that is relieved by alcohol and anti-anxiety pills, and also yellows our teeth. Do you remember the tooth whitening craze during the Bush Era? Lots of extra fluoride was consumed by everyone wanting to look our best, myself included. By altering these very simple activities, one day at a time, things will start to change very quickly.

Running lots of distilled water through your system is absolutely <u>essential</u> for detoxing your body and brain, so they can begin functioning at full power once again. Kids are really good at learning things, and so was Einstein even when he was an old white-haired man. This is like flushing out your car's old radiator to remove old deposits of gunk and rust.

## Things to ADD:

- Sleep, we all need it, and our brains require a good night's sleep to flush out toxins that accumulate during the day, sleep more, and you'll think better and remember more

- Exercise, you may have to actually work a little during the day, in order to be tired out by bedtime, in moderation, exercise is very good

- Positive music, find out what music the happiest people are listening to, and avoid the same music that all of the poorest and dumbest people always have on

- If you're listening to angry music, you'll remain an angry person, anger is often fear all dressed up

- Walk

- Read, reading and listening to music helps increase brain activity, while TV weakens it

- Try new activities, learning new things strengthens your brain

- Be thankful, it's amazing, but just by thanking God for what you do have, you'll feel better

- Get outside, we're not cave dwelling vampire bats, enjoy a little sunshine, this world is beautiful outside of your shelter

- Forgive, when you forgive everyone who has ever done you wrong, you can finally forgive yourself. Let the universe handle other people's bad behaviors, but don't be a doormat

- Don't stick around in bad situations to make sure your oppressor gets punished, walk away and let God handle it

- Walk away from repeat abusers if they refuse to do what's right when confronted with the truth.

- Create a plan B and exercise your right not to be their victim for any longer, ideas create reality

If you're not already walking at least half a mile per day, then you'll need to add this very short walk into your daily routine. Why? Because your body has to actually get moved a little in order to get the fresh clean water distributed throughout your system. Cars that just sit in garages and never get driven fall apart. Both cars and people start to run poorly if they sit for too long.

The radiator fluid in our cars becomes acidic and corrosive over time, much like the water in our bodies does. Both need to be flushed out on a regular basis to keep things running in tip top shape. Why on earth would you want to put highly acidic sodas and energy drinks into a neutral water based body?

Health nuts drink tons of water and look healthy, while bloated Walmart zombies poor acidic sodas into their systems all day long. You are choosing which group to copy. We all are choosing what type of Americans we are copying on a daily basis.

We all have created the body that we have. You are responsible for the body that you have. If it's in bad shape, then you can begin creating a better one today. Unless you're paralyzed from the neck down, you are determining the shape that you have. Removing TV removes hours per day of couch ridden paralysis.

Haven't you ever seen somebody pour a soda on the corroded terminals of a car battery before? The citric acid is so strong that it actually strips the calcium right off of the metal battery terminals. Just because drinking multiple cans of soda is the "norm" for the brilliant zombie public, doesn't mean that it's a good idea.

You don't have to continue mimicking insane behaviors that are repeated daily by unhappy people. New choices are right in front of you. If you choose to take new actions that result in a healthier you, then the world will begin rewarding you for doing so.

Once you have successfully detoxed your body and your level of consciousness begins to rise, several amazing things will begin to happen:

1. You will begin to have considerably more energy

2. You'll enjoy increased concentration and a boosted ability to solve problems

3. You'll feel much more optimistic

4. You'll feel more loving and forgiving towards everyone

5. You'll start to become more thankful for your present situation, no matter how little you may have

6. Abusive relationships will come to an end, out with the old, and in with the good

7. Your body will become more tuned to things that are good and bad for you, for example:

   - Your skin may break out after eating toxic foods, listen to your body and avoid foods and drinks that cause your body to negatively react

   - You'll gain a stronger intuition and naturally know when people are being both honest, and deceptive towards you, listen to your intuition

This brings us to the metaphysical benefits that heightened consciousness provides to people. Buddhist monks are said to be walking around at a higher vibration than the average person does. What the heck does that actually mean? Well, when someone is in love, or you meet somebody that is very positive, you tend to feel their energy, right? Some people give off good vibes, right?

On the other hand, hateful people tend to give off bad vibes, and other people in the room tend to sense it. Monks have carefully trained their minds to focus on positive thoughts. Their bodies respond in a positive way, due to an overall lack of stress.

Gregg Braden is world renowned in the field of metaphysics, has written multiple books, and explains on YouTube how our DNA behaves differently according to our state of mind. What does that mean? Basically, the DNA in our bodies operates at its 100% God-given capacity, and provides our bodies the most healing possible, if, we are acting in a loving manner.

The most energy is available to us, if we are kind and forgiving towards others on a daily basis. How many really selfish people do you know that have always had plenty of really nice possessions, but are always complaining about their bad health? I see plenty of them, and I wouldn't trade situations with them.

# Chapter 19 – Doing things the old way has got us to today's sad state of affairs

When we try to make deals with the devil by hoarding our own wealth and refusing to help anyone else that won't benefit us in some way; our health and relationships usually suffer in a direct correlation with our own level of selfishness. People that are living in fear and selfishness are failing to utilize the natural potential of their own DNA.

Picture a car that has dirty spark plugs and is barely running. Simply doing good deeds towards others automatically changes your plugs, so that you're firing on all cylinders again. A complete lack of consideration towards the world then results in a vehicle that is not running well. We simply have to start caring about the well-being of the people around us, and put our money where our mouth is.

Even if you've been a selfish person for decades, adopting the high consciousness diet and performing good deeds for others will still give your body a new set of spiritual spark plugs. You'll begin to fire on all cylinders once again, and you'll feel it in your heart, your body, and in your soul. The power of helping your fellow man should not be underestimated; God does perform miracles for those of us that stand up to bullies.

It's never too late to become a better person. Humanity can't seem to help ourselves, or ask God for help until we're heading over a cliff, and that's ok. It's how God made us. We don't deserve help from God if we completely sacrifice the whole group of decent people just to save our own asses. We must be willing to sacrifice our self, in order to benefit the group.

Do you agree that some people seem to get more worn out, run down, and start falling apart at a much younger age than others? Are those people that age poorly generally loving towards others or not? Have those less healthy people ever placed financial gain ahead of personal relationships? When it comes down to what actions will protect the most money, do unhealthy people generally choose the well-being of the people around them, or the most financially convenient course of action?

They choose the money, right? In return, the health of a selfish person suffers, and decent self-respecting people disappear from their lives. Of course life seems very unfair to selfish people, because other selfish people are the only ones that will keep hanging around them. Selfish money worshipping people construct an entire existence that becomes void of decent people. The only willing takers are all spending time with them for the financial benefits.

Most of the really unhealthy people that we know are always complaining about their bad luck, and bad relationships; assigning all blame for their failures, to the other party. They are always the victim of some asshole that did them wrong. In reality, most of this mysterious bad luck that "unlucky" people constantly complain about is a direct result of selfish actions that harmed others in the pursuit of the most money, and least work, for themselves.

Selfish people are clueless of the fact that reliable honest people avoid them. This would be like a shark in the ocean that doesn't understand why the fish are always swimming away from them. The problem is that America has become chuck full of selfish people. We hide at home all day watching TV to avoid rude idiots that are now everywhere.

Seeing situations for what they truly are isn't the only benefit that you'll enjoy when adopting the high consciousness diet. Your body will quickly respond to toxic foods and beverages with discomfort; instead of throwing pills at the discomfort, it will actually occur to you to avoid those foods, because apparently, they are not good for you, hence the pain. Does that make sense?

Most animals in nature would stop eating something that caused them pain and discomfort, right? If there is a God watching over us, we can't appear to be all that smart when we keep eating things that cause us pain, can we? However, all other animals on earth are missing one variable in that equation; they don't have pills to throw at their problems that some other animal is selling them for a huge profit.

People that are following the herd mentality throw pills at things like heart burn, don't they? In fact, most Americans throw pills at everything. Can't sleep, a little pain, a little anxious, you name it and there are pills for it. Have you ever stopped and considered that pain in your chest is a biological response to let you know, not, to eat something again? It will be easier to listen to your body after you have boosted your consciousness.

We weren't designed like cows and pigs that eat all day long, just waiting to be led to the slaughter by the more intelligent farmer. There are billionaires that look at us as nothing more than an ignorant herd of hypnotized zombies that deserves to be milked or slaughtered, as they see fit. The Resident Evil movies are a plea to our sub-conscious minds to stop complying in this system that we've been born into.

In those movies there is an umbrella corporation (the government) that has unleashed a virus on the world that turns normal people into zombies. This virus is called the T-virus. At the very end of the fourth Resident Evil movie, the head of the umbrella corporation is sitting in the oval office, as in, the White House for the complete zombies reading this (not you of course). Do you get that the government uses TV as the primary delivery tool for all of their plans?

It took me until the fourth Resident Evil movie to figure out the most obvious point of all of the movies: The T-virus that had been sold to all major world governments as a bio-logical weapon is simply, TV. It took me four entire movies to get the analogy. I suppose that I never figured it out during the first three movies because I was still drinking often, and watching lots of TV. I missed the point of the movies entirely because I was still suffering the zombie-like effects of the T-virus myself. If you choose to adopt the high consciousness diet, this revelation may one day make perfect sense to you.

The other major symbol used in all of the Resident Evil movies was the red corporate logo of the umbrella corporation, a Celtic cross. It was funny because I had just watched a movie with Nazis whom all had the same Celtic crosses on their historically accurate uniforms. We all think of swastikas when we think of Nazis, but upon closer inspection you'll also find Celtic crosses on their uniforms. The same type of crosses can be found in the Roman Catholic Church. My point is, even the most evil of men can use the holiest of symbols to control masses of people.

The Nazi leadership thought that they were doing the world good, right? Do you get that organized efforts of government officials can easily convince huge groups of people on either side of a war, that they are the good guys? Do you get that sometimes the masses get tricked, and perhaps you've underestimated the effects of the T-virus? It must be made crystal clear that there's no way that any human being is going to have a spiritual awakening with one hour of church a week vs. 21 hours a week of T-virus exposure. You'll remain a zombie.

Is the answer to enlightenment no television, and 21 hours a week of mind numbing organized religion? Hell no. A bunch of other zombies inside of our churches that are all hooked on the T-virus won't do a damn thing, except judge you for things that they are guilty of too. Once you've actually unplugged the TV and stopped getting drunk, high, and sedated daily, you may want to try reading a book.

How about trying some material on spirituality, and inspirational books, movies, and music for a change? If you feel like reading an English translated version of the New Testament, then go for it. Whatever spiritual path you choose is up to you. Perhaps you've always been interested in learning about Buddhism, explore! When you're searching for enlightenment, your own truth will resonate with you.

If you're looking for truth on TV, you'll enjoy all of the benefits that those other idiots in the herd are enjoying right now, by following the "norm" diet. You've got to look at the most common activities of the ignorant masses, and then realize that these are the very things that are keeping them spiritually turned off. Millions of people will readily surrender freedom for safety if we're kept fearful enough. What do you think the repetitive TV images of 911 were all about? Did they make you feel more safe and secure, or totally vulnerable? We all know the answer.

Was it really necessary to replay the images of the collapsing Twin Towers over and over again, hundreds of times across the board on TV, eliciting a deep psychological (destroying our logic) and emotional response? It would be as if your own child had been in a deadly car accident, and your captor made you watch the video of them dying over and over again. It wasn't at all necessary to watch that traumatizing image so many times. It was as if the intent of the people who <u>control</u> the media, was to <u>traumatize</u> us all.

If someone trying to control you showed a video of a car smashing into your child, that then got away; you'd likely feel nothing but anger towards that other driver, instead of thinking about if the information being shown to you was accurate or not, right? Do you get that any information given to you after the image of your child being struck by the other car would be clouded by anger? Would you travel to the ends of the earth to get justice?

Do we all make sound and logical decisions when we are angry? How many times have you said or done something terribly hurtful to someone else while you were angry? Did your brain and your critical thinking ability work at all once your emotions had been triggered? Didn't it take until you were calmed down to apologize, and use logical and loving thinking again?

Most of us don't think too well once our emotions have been triggered. Con-men know this, and are masters of triggering your emotions and then taking you for a ride. I am telling you exactly how to get off of their shitty ride. Kill the con-men of our society by killing your TV.

Do you get that your enemy knows that no matter how many times you see the image of your child being struck by a car and dying, that the image is still going to make you angry, and turn off your critical thinking. A traumatizing image is like a computer program that knocks down your brains firewall, and corrupts the logic in your head with the weapon of emotion. Are we better or worse at thinking critically and solving problems when we are filled with rage or terror?

When we are angry or terrified our brains shut down, don't they? It's only when we calm down that we begin to think clearly again and if we can swallow our pride, then we can re-assess the situation and apologize if necessary. How many times have we seen politicians of the other party as our enemies? How many times have their words made us angry?

Any good salesman (con-man) knows that if you want to get the sale, then you've got to tap into the customer's emotions. A customer's logic gets turned off completely, and then they buy whatever the con-man wants them to. Salesmen (Politicians) are experts at getting an emotional response that takes down the customer's (voters) natural defenses using logic and emotion. They then sell the sucker (voter) whatever they want to. Does that sound about right?

Whoever caused the car accident killing our child would then become a great source of anger and fear. We would likely do anything to take down that killer, right? We would have no trouble seeing their whole organization, or even an entire country get attacked to see justice. This is exactly what happened during the con of 911.

Would a corrupt politician show a disturbing image to his people in order to obtain blind obedience from them? After the image was shown a hundred times, we'd do just about anything to avoid it. None of us reading this would do such a thing, but that doesn't mean that Dick Cheney wouldn't do it. Pretending that there are no sharks in the ocean does not stop seals from getting eaten. This would be like making a statement like, "no politicians are lying, cheating con-men".

Would a person with any conscience at all even show such a disturbing video over and over again, unless they had a motive? The emotional trauma caused by the images of the collapsing buildings on 911 was instrumental to close the sale on the Afghanistan and Iraq wars. We were closed. Have I ever been closed by an unethical business man during my adult years? Yep. Have you ever been conned during your adult life?

Without the attack, the people never would have backed the aggressive middle-eastern invasion (not with our troops' lives put at risk. If only The Project For A New American Century did not exist prior to the 911 attacks, but it did. Would a few bad guys hide an entire scam behind a traumatizing image that no parent would even dare to dig up and re-live even five or ten years later? I think that men with so much money that they begin to feel like God would do exactly that. Our human egos are very corruptible and our actual life experience has taught us this.

# Chapter 119- Undoing old programming and calling things for what they really are

Last time I checked, our government is tied in with our money supply, right? Judging by most people's actions, (not words) what do most people spend most of their time and energy pursuing? The moral compass of the ignorant masses, TV, spins a deceptive web of beliefs that has placed money above God. If you can successfully remove the T-virus from your own operating system, then your conscience will turn back on to full power again and money (corrupt bankers) will no longer be your God.

Hopeless beliefs will disappear and once powerful illusions will vanish. Was the Wizard of OZ not shown on a big projection screen making him appear to be bigger and more powerful than he really was? In reality, was the wizard just a rich old white man that had put on a big show to appear to be something that he wasn't?

World bankers are just that, greedy old men that the common man could beat to death in a one on one match. An army of security guards is what protects the little men behind the big screens, not God. God has nothing to do with any of this. These particular men don't believe in God, and don't believe that the rules of cause and effect apply to them. Turn off the big screen and suddenly you'll start to get back what has been taken away from us, our free will.

You must also break the spell of addictive insanity caused by mind-numbing substances. If it's a pill or drink that makes you feel ok amidst your horrible life situation, then it's not going to help you escape from your current mess. The all-powerful wizard wants you to keep his big screen turned on at all times pop "miracle" pills and drink snake oil that does nothing but slow you down.

You now know how to take the governor off of your own brain. Eventually this knowledge will spread to the armed guards that protect our kings (world bankers). Eventually the guards will stand down so that we may face our oppressors one on one, and stop them from bullying us for any longer.

Worldwide poverty is not going to increase so that a tiny ruling class can feel like Gods. They are not our Gods. This is not The Hunger Games and ruling elites on planet earth can piss off. They are simply greedy people that have overstepped the boundaries of reasonable behavior towards the rest of humanity. It's time that this ridiculous behavior comes to an end. We can change this now, and you can fight on behalf of humanity. We all are contributing to make this world what it is. Let's make it a better place.

If there is a loving God that is just, reasonable, and fair, then God will provide protection for those few souls that are brave enough to challenge our oppressors. This ridiculous system cannot be allowed to continue. Our children deserve a less corrupted system to live in. The current system will only continue for as long as the masses fail to challenge it. We all have the power to change this. Fight for good.

It is time to stop waking up in bed with the same set of problems as the day before. The question is, do we all just concede and admit total defeat like 50 million other Americans on food assistance or not? Rich kids with multi-millionaire parents are simply too smart for the rest of us inferior Americans to fight against. They deserve to rule over us for the rest of our lives. After all, they were born smarter and richer than us so they must know what's best for us right? Rubbish, they have cared only about themselves and assigned a lifetime's worth of heavy lifting onto the backs of the American public.

How many Americans have almost no self-control left? How many people are fat, and appear to be absolutely powerless over their weight? If you cannot control how much you eat, then how good do you think that you are at controlling how you treat other people? How many of us drink alcohol every day (not because we want to) but because we have to. Smoke cigarettes that yellow your teeth coat your lungs with brown tar, and give you bad breath?

Smokers, if there's ever been a dead give-away to identify pessimists and assholes, it is cigarette smoking. Non-smokers don't avoid dating smokers because of the bad breath; we avoid serious relationships with them because they are generally more nervous, insecure, pessimistic, and more self-serving than the non-smoking partners that we have dated in the past.

Do you really think the government would allow cigarettes if they didn't produce the most profitable and obedient workforce? Coffee and cigarettes are like liquid and vapor selfishness for a defeated cowardly workforce of self-hating slaves. The big joke is that the rebellious act of smoking is exactly what the billionaire slave owners want. Note that right in the beginning of 1984, Winston smokes his Victory cigarettes, and then rewards his unbearable existence with some Victory gin.

The world elite would prefer for all of the poor people to be completely addicted to anxiety causing substances. Then, these poor wage slaves sedate themselves with nightly brain damage making them even easier to dominate the following day. These are weapons that weaken our will to escape. Thanks smokers for doing exactly what richer assholes want you to do by following the homeless person's diet.

If you want to terrify the elite then address your own emotional damage, drop your chemical crutches. If Americans did this by the millions, the billionaires would be pissing their pants. Without drug and alcohol dependency, we get a hell of a lot faster and smarter. This is not a difficult concept. Disgruntled Americans that are still wrestling with old baggage have even been tricked into labeling themselves.

Lots of tattoos serve as excellent warning labels on emotionally damaged people that tend to act more selfishly than there non-tattoo covered and non-smoking counterparts. Emotionally damaged people tend to dive into the same bars full of other emotionally damaged people for relief. In some pools, the water may not be as clean, but all it takes to become a member is a belief in the same escape that a "magic" drink will provide.

I have certainly used the same emotional crutch of alcohol that millions of us do. I have also been as morally bankrupt as everyone else in the poor people's pool (and rich peoples' pool). I've even learned how to love them with all of their flaws included. Thank you again to the redneck family in Georgia. How else was I ever going to be able to love myself without loving them first for simply being

235

human?  Really, those crazy tattooed drinking rednecks were beautiful people that had been trained to constantly weaken themselves, and then serve the rich.

Just because I'm not marked up with warning labels to illustrate my rebellious nature and a wild past, doesn't mean that I haven't lived it.  Our churches betrayed us all by teaching us about a perfect human that never made mistakes.  If Jesus Christ were here on earth right now, then he sure would do us all a huge favor by letting us know that he made all the same mistakes as the rest of us have (while he was living in a human body).

Boy would that make all of us feel a lot better about ourselves, wouldn't it?  We've all been set up for guilt by an impossible to obtain standard of purity; a standard more likely put into place by the Roman Empire, not by Jesus.  Jesus didn't sell guilt, he sold forgiveness.

The Roman Empire that evolved into the Catholic Church and the Jesuits have had a much larger role in world banking system than the zombie public understands.  They hijacked the name of Jesus for money and control.  It's time for a worldwide comeuppance for unholy people that have badly taken advantage of our group.

For those of you that don't enjoy screwing-over others for money, there's now a key to remove your own mental shackles.  If you'd like to take the governor off of your own brain, you now can.  It's not the tattooed smoking rednecks in America that are the most damaged.  They're not.  In fact, they are actually the strongest and most threatening group to the elites in America.

Our society seems quite retarded in our learning curve regarding well-spoken men with conservative haircuts wearing suits.  What do used car salesmen wear?  What do all of the guys from The Wolf of Wall Street wear?  Who else wears expensive suits and has conservative haircuts?

Aren't most of the momentous lies and screw-overs committed against us in life perpetrated by men lacking tattoos, and wearing suits?  The whole clean-cut and well-spoken image means nothing.  It is and always has been, an illusion of purity.  I'm definitely not perfect and pure, yet I remain tattoo-free and can wear a suit.  Suits and job titles mean nothing. Completely dishonorable people have held positions of power throughout our lives.

I was always clean-cut and well-spoken, but when it comes down to purity, it turns out that I'm a perfectly flawed human just like the rest of you. The biggest gift that we can give to one another is admitting our faults and helping other people to forgive themselves for being human (after a lifetime of impossible to follow rules).

A suit is simply a ceremonial outfit that we have been trained and conditioned to trust and see as respectful. In reality, we should not trust men in suits because they are often wolves in sheep's clothing. Just because someone is dressed classy does not make them a classy human being.

If anything, the American public should abandon the tradition of suits because they make super greedy assholes appear to be self-respecting human beings (when they're not). The body beneath the suit reveals a lot more about a person's level of self-respect and self-control than the clothes that they are wearing. This is probably why many suits are made of wool.

Put all of our governing "officials" in white tee-shirts and shorts, and then see if the public believes that these guys deserve the respect and trust that they expect to receive from us. It's all been a huge con-job and we've been the marks. Do you want to be the victim of con-men for the rest of your life? Without the expensive suits, I'm pretty sure that most of these guys start to look like the same bull-shitters as any other con-man that sells used cars.

The expensive suits and makeup for TV transforms Walmart people into royalty. It is all a bullshit illusion. Our Politicians are nothing more than smart people that are completely full of shit. Our political leaders seem to have lost their ability to tell the truth. They don't serve the God that I believe in, and I wasn't put on earth to serve those that serve criminals.

They have sold us out for money. How many of us know Fat alcoholic guys that can talk a mile a minute, can con anybody, and are totally full of shit? I've met a ton. The only thing missing in this equation is having millionaire parents and wearing expensive suits.

237

All of our politicians might as well be Sawyer from Lost. Once you have sobered up and stopped getting hypnotized by television for three hours per day, their cons become quite obvious and silly.

After sobering myself up, and returning to my home town of Cleveland Ohio, I found myself in a terrible conundrum. I was no longer a practicing member of the poor people's country club, club alcohol and pot. They had allowed me to join before in spite of my polished speech, lack of tattoos, and optimistic attitude. All that was required to become a full-fledged member was a general desire to escape from reality via a drink or two, on a daily basis.

When I returned to the same club refusing to drink, I suddenly found that my popularity had vanished. Without that last common bond of alcoholic escape, my optimistic attitude, clean appearance, lack of tattoos, and non-smoking status made me appear to be another snobby Cleveland rich kid that was born with a silver spoon up my ass. I quickly found that a quick wit, logic, and optimism were not welcome guests while refusing the poor peoples' cure to all of their problems, getting drunk. My smart remarks made me equally as popular as Sawyer from Lost.

There I was back in my hometown, ready to change the world for the better, and on an island I was. The other non-tattoo covered, non-smoking upper class Cleveland kids looked and spoke just like me but, they also belonged to a country club that used alcohol to justify their own superiority and social status (above the poorer Cleveland lower class). The two groups of people did not particularly like one another, and did not get into serious relationships with members of the opposite class.

The whole situation was tremendously frustrating, and made writing a book on how-to free lower-class people very easy. The nightmarish reality suffered by the majority of people there was perpetuated by the daily use of mind-altering substances by both sides. Most of the really smart kids had left town, and the remaining smart kids were constantly drunk or on prescribed pills. Everybody had to justify their own existence as the ruling elite or the pathetic dog-class of a dying rust-belt city.

The wealthier young professionals had lengthier and more expensive educations, nearly always backed by parents that had more wealth than the poor kids that didn't go off to college. Many of the smartest Cleveland upper class kids took their expensive degrees and re-located to larger cities all over the country. The result was, that the less intelligent and less capable rich kids that I had outperformed back in high school, were now running the city in a job market that was completely dominated by nepotism and corruption.

Talent had very little to do with financial security in Cleveland Ohio. There were tons of super-talented and very hard-working people that had been trained to stay in the dog-class of citizens. It was all a God-damned shame to witness. I wasn't about to stay there, nor was I willing to leave that town without recording the way that things were.

If you couldn't buy your way into the rich kids club, then you were carefully kept out of the high paying jobs pool, and prevented from outperforming the less intelligent and lazier rich kids' network (whose parents owned most of the businesses in town). Screw-up rich kids should not be running our country, but I'm pretty sure that our political system has also been managed much like the dying job market of Cleveland Ohio. Multigenerational wealth does not always produce the greatest leaders.

Most Americans agree that screw-up rich kids should not be the leaders of our country. However, when money buys votes, (and we all know, it does) and parents want to see their otherwise screw-up kids succeed; then the possibility of screw-up rich kids becoming our only choice in a declining economy (much like Cleveland) increases with each generation of wealthy kids. We know this has happened.

George W Bush should never have been in the running for President. What about his younger brother Jeb down in Florida? Sure, but not the guy that got elected after losing the popular vote. Do you remember that? How exactly did that turn out for the entire country? Did the U.S. economy get better or worse under Bush?

Had George's family not been extremely wealthy, he never would have stood a chance on the political playing field, due to his lack of speaking skills. His complete absence of job qualifications should have allowed for other more intelligent and well-spoken candidates to outcompete him. However, his father, former President, and former Director of the CIA paved the path for a non-qualified candidate. We all suffered the consequences (except for the 1%).

For decades the American public has been posed with two terrible choices for president, a bought off congress and senate, and some real A-hole Supreme Court justices that make decisions such as: A corporation is equal to a person. The American public has remained too drunk to get off their couches during all of this. We are entirely to blame for remaining completely apathetic while the entire political system has been anally raping us.

Either republican or democrat, it doesn't matter. Both sides have been bought off by one group of elites, not two. That is the huge joke that the zombie public does not seem to get. Believing in the two party systems effectiveness, is like believing in the pull-out method of birth control. Only monkeys that can talk would believe in such a ridiculous notion at this point in the game.

There is a Tri-Lateral Commission and an organization of billionaires that collaborate with each other determining world policy called the Bilderberg Group. They believe that they have the right to determine the policy that governs all citizens on earth, without consulting us. This is the truth. Either way, we're all getting screwed by a bunch of rich guys wearing expensive suits that long ago forgot about the value of our free will.

This group ensures that they control either presidential nominee, because both nominees in every single presidential election belong to the same Tri-Lateral Commission, and The Bilderberg Group. So which mafia guy are you going to vote for this year, the republican, or the democrat? The two "opposing" candidates from the same club have a huge laugh in private, after putting on theatrical performances on television. They are work for the same gang, and make fun of the moronic public, that cannot figure out the trick.

For years of my life, I've watched other salesmen take customers on an emotional ride, dropping their defenses, and then selling them something that they didn't want or need. A skilled salesman using a barrage of logic on a customer is like a computer

240

hacker breaking into your home PC and installing a virus program that takes control of your computer, all, without your knowledge or consent. That is exactly what Politicians are, salesmen for the billionaire owners of this planet.

The politicians work for and fear the billionaire committee, <u>not</u> the public. The politicians that have been running the country are simply front desk workers that are cowardly doing as they are told by the ownership committee of billionaires. They do this for fear of economic loss, or personal injury.

This all takes place, at the expense of billions of people. As citizens, the only way to get any real solutions to our problems is to get past the cashier at the front desk. Walk around them. We need to have a chat with the greedy owner that hides in the back room, behind closed doors that is busy counting his pile of money.

The owners do exist, and I have zero respect for them because they treat most of the public like farm animals. I'd love to have a face to face discussion with them, and debate them using actual logic in front of the rest of the herd. Without their armed guards to hide behind, I'm pretty sure that these individuals that supposedly possess great power would back right down in front of any brave and intelligent US citizen. Armed guards aside, the billionaire elites of planet earth are just a person, having a human experience.

We must speak the truth to their face. There's a huge difference between true bravery, and paid-off security. Many of these heavily-armed security guards have extended families and old friends that are beginning to suffer badly due to their bosses' actions. Surrounding yourself with security guards does not make you a brave person, or a good one.

# Chapter 20 – If divine intervention did show up on earth, would we listen?

If spiritual beings did come down to earth and quietly walked through a Walmart, unseen and unnoticed, what would they say about the shoppers in front of them? Please picture in your head the typical Walmart shoppers and think of the way that they carry themselves. We all want freedom and free will, right? If spiritual beings did show up here on earth and offered us nothing but spoken advice on how to help ourselves, would we follow it?

Please consider that the majority of human beings have spent this lifetime praying to God to help us in this experience. We have prayed our whole lives for the world to become a better place, right? If spiritual beings actually showed up demonstrating pure goodness, but offered only spoken advice (to honor our rights of free will) in a non-interference universe, would we follow their advice?

If your answer is no, then you deserve to be a slave for the rest of this lifetime. Why? Because the bad guys on earth are simply exercising their rights of free will. They will continue to harm the entire group, until brave people decide that they have had enough.

Why would advanced spiritual beings that would like to see humanity learn and grow in a spiritual manner, reward the cowardly behavior of billions of humans? Those of us that act like cowards in our daily behaviors get all of the fruits that cowards deserve. If human beings have such things as spiritual elders; do you really think that rewarding the cowardly actions of billions of people is part of the parenting process?

Good parents that are trying to raise good children do not reward cowardly actions. When somebody acts like a bully towards the rest of the group, then we should hold them accountable. We do not let a few bad eggs continue to bully the rest of us. Does that make sense? Attempt to fight a seemingly undefeatable enemy on behalf of humanity, and you will receive God's help.

We've become a country full of crippled teenagers that got hurt in a drunken driving accident that we caused. We sit on the sidelines on our emotional crutches and ridicule any decent human being that is running on the playing field of life in good health. We hate those who have health, and distrust them in our sick group of sad addicts on the sidelines.

For most Americans, rather than doing the painful rehab process and putting down the drink that caused us to be on these emotional crutches, we continue on the path of least resistance. We have become a big group of crippled victims that are flat out refusing to take the straight forward rehab advice from healthier people. Do you want to be a crippled victim of life when the angels ask you, how you did? I don't. Try some positive inputs, and you might start to become more hopeful. Positive music not found on the radio's top ten can have a vastly uplifting effect on your mood.

Believing in some sort of good intelligence, beyond that of man, is not a bad thing. The alternative is to believe that money is God, and that kissing the asses of wealthy men in order to survive in a corrupted system is the pinnacle of all creation. I know that there is more than this, and I am going to be part of the resistance against evil men on earth. One of my favorite bands is called Muse, and they have a song called "The Resistance".

The big question is for those of us that do supposedly have faith in God; would humanity listen to the directions for obtaining fulfillment and happiness while here on earth? Or, would we cuss-out the very angels that were sent down to earth to free humanity from the greedy few that have gained control of the entire planet? How bad do things in our lives have to get for us to set our egos aside and admit that it's time to make some big changes in our self for the better?

Disasters in our lives aren't a good thing they're a great thing, because they cause pain. Pain then causes us to seek change. When was the last time that the public was all sold hope and change by the T-virus? However, the hope and change never really manifested itself for the middle class now did it?

America is in a lot of pain right now, and that's good, because it lets us know that something is wrong. We are sick, and we need to seek help, not from evil men, but from God. Not at a church, but from within you. You don't need some guy in a fancy outfit to talk to God

243

for you and you don't need to spend money to talk to God either. Help those who need help directly and cut out the middle man.

We've all been throwing food, pills, and alcohol at the symptoms but the relief is only temporary, lasting for only hours at a time. Fantasizing about brief escapes of drunkenness, while spending the majority of your time serving politicians that you don't even respect, is a cowardly way to exist. We're part of a herd of people that is 300 million strong! Unchain yourself by turning off the delivery system of all Billionaires' messages, your TV. Unscrew the cable, and begin tackling the substances that do nothing but knock you out.

Let's use our power for God's sake and help one another. We can easily trample a few wolves that are systematically sedating us, and feeding on us while we sleep. They want to thin the herd, and soon. Let's expose them and watch them panic when they realize that we can see them and are no longer afraid of them. We can do this.

The T-virus is stronger than any of us give it credit for. At this point, most of the U.S. population's logic has been crippled by it. This T-virus (TV) causes people to become fat, dumb, hopeless, submissive, delusional, poor, and gives the victim an overall feeling of hopelessness. Does this not describe those other Walmart people that we all see and make fun of on a weekly basis?

What we don't see is that many of us are slowly becoming them. After all, we have all been exposed to the same virus, haven't we? You can change this right now. You can separate from the herd by abandoning the same daily habits as the rest of them. Obvious choices have been placed in front of you.

There are simple changes that can easily restore the public to strong, smart, and loving human beings. We will see all of the beauty that this life does have to offer. We must cure ourselves first in order to become the good person that will have something that the T-virus zombies will want, brains.

When we follow these stupid simple directions, we will transform ourselves back into the spiritual creatures that many children still are. Don't many little kids possess a sense of innocence and a sense of goodness that most adults wish they still had? I think so. We can all get that feeling back by doing the right thing and helping our group, not just our self.

As you raise your level of consciousness, you will naturally want to help others that need your help. Americans need your help right now, because millions of them are suffering badly. You know this is true, and you're not powerless in this struggle.

To save this beautiful country, we've got to sober ourselves up and get the T-virus eliminated from our systems. Then, we will be able to spread the cure of consciousness as fast as possible to other people that need it. We can only accomplish this by shrinking our own ego first and putting forth the effort to change for the better.

We must have faith that our higher power will help us along the way (through other people) to make these positive changes. Without first surrendering to God and asking for help, the battle is unwinnable. It may sound ridiculous, but it worked for me.

Those whom humor positive human beings that have transformed their lives for the better (and also admitted to us that they too, had surrendered to God first) will be pleasantly surprised for having just a sliver of faith. May you soon see the good side of humanity, and soon see the good in your neighbors. We are infinitely beautiful beings on a learning experience called life, and it's time that we change for the better. It's time that the rules of this game on earth get changed for the better. We can make this happen.

The end

## Special Thanks

Only through the work of pioneers in the field of consciousness have I been able to gain a more thankful perspective for my own life. The work of Alex Jones, David Icke, Bill Hicks, and George Carlin will be forever appreciated by me. These people have stuck their necks out and challenged the status quo. They have absorbed a lifetime of hardships and ridicule because their thoughts were ahead of the crowd.

I thank all of the powerhouses that have refused to conform in order to protect the freedoms of their fellow man, most often at great personal costs. I would also like to thank my parents for being extremely honest, forgiving, and generous to strangers while I was growing up. My parents repeatedly demonstrated unconditional love towards not only their family, but humanity in general. My father has always been uncompromisingly honest and incredibly generous to both family and strangers.

Lastly, I couldn't have finished this book without the support of my true friend Kristin. She has proven to be one of the least materialistic human beings that I've ever met during my 35-year journey on earth. She has been one of those rare friends that stick around when we're facing adversity. While finishing this book, she's been my guardian angel. I couldn't have done it without her.

There is hope for all of us. Things are going to get better, and this world will <u>not</u> be run by evil men forever. Men and woman with good consciences can lead our group. Together, we can create a better world to live both here, now, and in the future. We all are collectively creating the world that we live in. Let's create something good that God would be proud of.

# Suggested Movies to watch

Warm Bodies

The Shawshank Redemption

Joe vs. the Volcano

1984 (remake w John Hurt)

Day Breakers

Rise of The Planet of The Apes

Dawn of The Planet of the Apes

Rise of The Lycans

They Live

Surrogates

Cinderella Man

Loose Change Final Cut (Youtube)

Invisible Empire (Youtube)

The Obama Deception (Youtube)

Made in the USA
Lexington, KY
06 January 2015